A man who, at 89, is in his twilight years with no regrets about the path his life has followed and has the feeling that it has been a full and satisfying life.

To my family and my friends, who encouraged me to write my story but never really believed that I would ever actually write the book.

To, Ginny with
best Wishes
Jim 13/3/20

James Fellows

THE STORY OF JIM

AUSTIN MACAULEY PUBLISHERS™

LONDON • CAMBRIDGE • NEW YORK • SHARJAH

A CIP catalogue record for this title is available from the British Library.

ISBN 9781788487108 (Paperback)
ISBN 9781788487115 (Hardback)
ISBN 9781788487122 (E-Book)

www.austinmacauley.com

First Published (2018)
Austin Macauley Publishers Ltd
25 Canada Square
Canary Wharf
London
E14 5LQ

To family, friends, comrades-in-arms and work associates, who have all influenced in some major or minor way on the tortuous path my life has followed.

Synopsis

The Story of Jim covers my life through childhood under the threat of the commencement of WWII, the early bombing around Birmingham and Coventry, my early teen years when most jobs had been vacated by men on military service.

My military experiences as a soldier and paratrooper, in Northern Ireland, Germany, Hong Kong and Malaya. Life as an engineer and engineering-manager, starting in the UK and then progressing to employment firstly in Canada and then the USA.

I took a two year break from engineering, to join the Falklands Islands Dependencies Expedition, for a two-year trip to Antarctica. FIDS was the former name for the organisation, now known as 'The British Antarctic Survey'.

My life in Canada was interrupted by joining the Arctic Institute of North America's expedition to Devon Island, the largest uninhabited island in the world, but for the expedition's first year only. The Canadian Government later adopted the base we established as their National Arctic Science Research Station.

My working life during a four-year period in Montreal, Canada, amongst the early WWII immigrants. Then followed ten years working in Vermont and Ohio, USA, establishing myself in an engineering career. Like a lot of migrants from UK, I eventually responded to family pressures at a mature age and returned to the UK in the 1970s. This at the time of the three-day working week, a difficult environment for a 45 year old, this brought many changes into my life and a new career.

On becoming a widower, I used my military service to apply for admission to the Royal Hospital Chelsea, a 300-year-old home for old soldiers, conceived by Charles II and designed by Christopher Wren, where I now while away my time, having survived to a mature 87 years of age, with woodcarving, painting, ceramics and writing *The Story of Jim*. The Royal Hospital Chelsea has now become a popular destination for tourists, who constantly ask the same question, "Who are the soldiers who become 'Chelsea Pensioners'?" Every Chelsea Pensioner has his own story to tell. *The Story of Jim* is my story.

Overview of Contents

Chapter One: The lineage of my father's family as well as that of my mother; the effect of the 1929 financial collapse on my early childhood; details of my early childhood; the experience of the bombing; life at a boarding school; early teen years, jobs before compulsory military service; VE street celebrations.

Chapter Two: Army service and initial training in Northern Ireland; posting to the South Staffordshire Regiment, from where I volunteer for the Parachute Regiment and more training. Posted to Hong Kong, Malaya and then Germany before my discharge on to the reserve.

Chapter Three: Out of the army and into a government training scheme to train as a design engineer; with the initial three years training and study complete, I take a break and volunteer to spend two years with an expedition in the Antarctic.

Chapter Four: With the Antarctic trip finished, I settle down to complete my qualification as a design engineer; peace time brings a slowdown in the economy, poor pay and future prospects in doubt; decide against following my employer with a move to Portsmouth; decide to make the break and move to Canada; whilst working in Canada, old Antarctic acquaintances persuade me to sign on with an expedition going to the Canadian Arctic; after an interesting year in the Arctic, I return to Montreal, reality and work.

Chapter Five: Settle back to life in Montreal; get married; consider where best to locate if we want to start a family and decide to move over the border into Northern Vermont.

Chapter Six: A new family life in Vermont and a new rewarding career. But after the birth of my son, problems and personality clashes force me to move to Dayton, Ohio, and pursue a new chapter in my engineering career.

Chapter Seven: My career in Ohio blossoms into an enhanced position for me and looking ahead, I hoped I would hold on until retirement. My daughter is born to complete our family and everything seems just right.

Chapter Eight: My wife starts to have bouts of depression, her mother advises her to come home with the children in England, until she sorts herself out.

Chapter Nine: After Pauline's ultimatum on the advice of her mother, I start to think about how to wind up my affairs in USA and to eventually follow them, to live in the UK.

Chapter Ten: After many false starts with endless hurdles, I eventually establish myself in a new field of endeavour, that of computer aided design. Then just after my retirement from work, my wife dies and I am left to spend the next eight years on my own in a small commuter village. At the age of 82, I apply for entrance to the Royal Hospital Chelsea and am accepted and offered a place there to end my days.

Table of Chapters

Chapter One

Kendrick Fellows was my paternal grandfather, and his ancestry can be traced back to the 17th century, because each generation had a son named Kendrick and each of them was a farm worker who did not marry until the age of 28–30 years of age. Kendrick Fellows married Sarah and together produced four sons and three daughters. These were Frederick (later known as Jack), Margaret, Nellie, Laura, Thomas, James and Albert. Jack married and had two sons and a daughter, Kenneth, Gerald and Teresa. Thomas and James were very much affected by their experiences during World War I and neither married, living on in the family home until they died. Margaret, Laura and Nellie had a series of broken romances, which did not end in marriage, and therefore, they too lived out the remainder of their lives at the family home. After the deaths of Kendrick and Sarah, Margaret, as the oldest, assumed the role of housekeeper and kept house for Thomas, James and Laura, whilst Nellie was living away with a succession of 'lovers' until very late in life, when she eventually returned to take up permanent residence at the family home.

In the meantime, Albert had married Lucy Riley, then working as a housemaid in Tamworth Road; together they had two sons, James and Albert, and a daughter Barbara. Lucy Riley was the daughter of William and Louise Riley and had two brothers Edward and William, plus a sister Gladys. Edward was to die young, at the age of only 21, and this to happen just when Lucy would need all her family support, to hold on to what was left of her life.

William Riley had retired from the army after 22 years of service, which included service on the Northwest Frontier in India and the Boer War in South Africa. After leaving the army, he worked as a 'park keeper' in Sutton Park, whilst his wife Louise worked as a housemaid. He was a man who did not extoll his exploits, holding on to his memories and not sharing them, as far as is known he kept no diaries and yet he was an interesting man about whom more should be known. It was this interest in 'Grandfather Bill' and the lack of any written records that prompted the subject of this book and to ask of his mother, "What was Grandad Riley like"; that question suggested a title for this book. William Junior later married Grace and moved into a cottage near his work on a farm; there were no children from the marriage.

Gladys married Cyril Fletcher and had two sons, Derek and Peter; they all lived at various addresses, and with the advent of World War II, Cyril joined the Royal Air Force. Cyril was eventually discharged from the air force and soon after, his marriage got into difficulties and they separated.

Albert Fellows, by this time married, a 'master painter and decorator', was in business with his two brothers Thomas and James, and things were apparently going well, business-wise that is. He had met my mother Lucy Riley, whilst she was working as a housemaid like her mother before her; eventually they were married and moved into a nice little house in Boldmere. Although all the furnishings were bought on credit, they were comfortable.

In March 1928, a daughter Barbara was born to them and everything seemed to be perfect; to add to this, in August 1929, a son James was born. This was the year of the first stock market collapse that threw the world into a financial crisis. People of all levels of society became worried about their finances and cash flow, all of which had essentially dried up. Albert first felt the crunch when customers were late in paying; eventually in some cases, defaulting completely with a non-payment. On one side he was having customers that were, to say at the least, 'tardy' in paying; on the other, his paint and material suppliers were now allowing little or no credit and instead demanding payment up front. The problem was compounded by the fact that many customers, who had been quoted and contracted for work, now cancelled.

The result was that Albert found himself in a mounting debt situation, but still taking on work where he could find it, without the credit to obtain materials, he was slowly sinking into an abyss of debt. Thomas and James, the men on the job, were only vaguely aware of the problems the business was in and the problems Albert was juggling with. These pressures got to Albert and together with a decline in his health, he seemed unable to cope with his financial problems, choosing to ignore them, as well as his wife and family.

Those around him suspected that he was drinking and were not surprised when he fell ill and died soon afterwards of pneumonia.

His death signalled his creditors' next move, they claimed everything that was not nailed down, including the furnishings; that were only missing two payments to complete. They left Lucy, pregnant with her second son and with two more babies, destitute and about to be forced to vacate her home in Boldmere.

In the meantime, Kendrick Fellows was galvanised into action in an attempt to help his daughter-in-law and grandchildren. He moved them into a rented mid-terraced house in Queen Street, a location close to his home in Lower Queen Street. The house was bare of any furnishings, but by selective visits to 'second-hand shops' and low-end auction houses, he was able to quickly gather together and supply some very basic necessities.

I still think back to those days of my childhood and my life at 44 Queen Street, where I was born. The houses on Queen Street are now a thing of the past, having been replaced by an improvement to traffic flow. But in those days, number 44 was midway down the street, one of a street of terraced houses; the one thing I vividly remember about the tenants of those houses was the time they spent trying to keep them 'spick-and-span' with a minimum of resources. They were proud of their little homes and spent hours scrubbing front steps and cleaning windows, even though some were getting on in years. The Queen Street of my childhood was almost a complete street of terraced houses, on both sides of the street, mostly built between 1850 and 1880. Queen Street ran in a straight line from the Parade down to form a 'T' junction with Lower Queen Street, and it was at this junction, on Lower Queen Street, that 42 was located; the home of my paternal grandparents.

Going back on to Queen Street and looking down it, towards lower Queen Street, on the right-hand side, we had Chamberlains, the greengrocer and fishmongers, next were two hairdressing salons, first a ladies and then the gents. Following on was the cobblers, then 'Pop' Wright's store, which sold groceries, bread and milk, and almost everyone ran up an account with him in the week, to be paid on pay day.

Further down there was a small drapery and haberdashery store, and then the old second-hand furniture store, where most of our furnishings came from. Between these and the other houses, there was the passageway known locally as the 'Gulley', a narrow roadway connecting Queen Street and Newhall Street. This latter provided vehicle access to back of the shops, in that area of the Parade, as well as access to a stone mason's yard, located halfway along the 'Gulley'. After the 'Gulley', there was one of only three detached houses in the street, followed by a string of terraced houses, some with bay windows and others flat-fronted.

Finally came the home of Williams, the property developer and house-builder, alongside the house was his builder's yard, where he matured his building wood-stock and manufactured all the doors and windows he needed for his houses; after which we were on Lower Queen Street.

Now, if we look down Queen Street on the left-hand side, we start with Reeve & Stediford Car Showrooms, flush up against this was an isolated detached house, the home of Mr and Mrs Waigh and their daughter. Further down there was an open space, which was where the stone mason's finished products were displayed for public viewing. After this we had another detached house and then the line of terraced houses, some with bay windows, but in the main they were flat-fronted. It was amongst the latter group of terraced houses that number 44 was located.

Like all rentals at the time, the landlord did little to maintain the state of repair of these properties, particularly with the advent of World War II. I was born August 31st, 1929, and in October of that year came the US stock market crash and its repercussions echoing around the world. My sister Barbara had been born some 18 months before my arrival so that the house at 44 was only just big enough.

The house was typical of terraced houses of that period, two and a half rooms upstairs, with two rooms and a scullery downstairs, no bathroom, no hot water supply and a flush toilet at the bottom of the garden. The downstairs consisted of a 'front room', now we call it the lounge or parlour, and the outer door opened directly on to the street.

The key feature of that room was a large cast iron open fireplace, surrounded by a floor to ceiling mahogany frame, housing a huge mirror over the fireplace. It was a small room with a linoleum-covered wooden floor and was always to be kept tidy for visitors, which means we were seldom allowed in there. The next room was known as the 'kitchen' (not necessarily where any cooking was done), it was primarily where we gathered together and ate together, the family room, you might say.

This room had three doors, the first lead into the front room, the second into the scullery and a third to a cellar under the house. The key features of the room, as I remember them, were four huge cupboards, arranged two on top of two and stretching floor to ceiling.

Next to the cupboards was a six-foot wide cast iron fire-place, with the firebox in the centre, set over a foot off the ground, allowing plenty of room for ashes to fall. On the left side of the firebox was a cast-in holder for hot water (heated from the fire). Below it a brass tap to drain off the water, which was normally used for washing up after meals. On the other side of the fire box was a small oven, which was used to keep food warm after it was cooked, or to slow cook casseroles. Finally, there was a swing-out iron beam that was used to hang a big iron pot, for stewing leftovers and making soup.

The floor of the kitchen was paved with red clay tiles, which my mother covered with her homemade wool and rag rugs. Downstairs it only remains to describe the final room, the scullery; it had two doors, one into the kitchen and one out to the back of the house. On one side, in the corner was 'the copper'; a huge copper tub mounted on brickwork, with a firebox underneath it to heat it. To the left of that was a five-foot long brown-glazed sink, with a single cold water tap over one end.

Next to the 'copper' was a large cast iron gas stove, which was my mother's pride and joy. She black-leaded and polished that stove until it shone like new. She would periodically take out all the loose parts of the oven and boil them to remove any accumulated grease as well as doing the same with all the gas jet components, both those in the oven and on top of it. Every inch of it was kept in pristine condition.

A description would not be complete without a word on the upstairs rooms. The two bedrooms were not over-large but sufficed, with papered walls and linoleum-covered floors and each fitted with a small gas fire for heating the room. The half-room was what later tenants used to convert into a bathroom, once the hardware and know-how became available.

In our case it was used for storage initially. Lest I forget, I must mention that lighting in every room was by gaslight, and it was quite an art to light a gaslight without breaking the fragile mantle, which diffused and spread the light. But I have diverged from my story somewhat in my enthusiasm to describe 44 Queen Street, and it's time to get back on track.

On December 26th, 1930, my father Albert Fellows fell ill and although admitted to hospital, died in hospital of pneumonia, aged 30. His death left my mother with two young children, a girl and a boy, added to this she was heavily pregnant with my brother Albert, who was born February 1st of the following year.

There was a lot was a lot of criticism levelled at my mother by my father's relatives, accusing her of not getting him into hospital soon enough for him to have a chance of surviving. But in my mother's defence, she had been guided by the doctor, who said that it was nothing serious and that a few days' bed rest with aspirin would see him back on his feet. It was several days before he had him moved into hospital. A young mother would naturally be guided by the doctor, who had the knowledge and experience, as opposed to a young inexperienced wife, pregnant and with two other young children to cope with.

The advice that came after the fact might well have had more benefit had it been offered earlier. In later years I had asked my mother what were her thoughts at that time. She told me that she had no thoughts at that time… She just felt numb… She could not think…she just felt numb for days on end, doing everything and looking after us children like a 'zombie'.

My mother and the 'Riley' family were descended from a long line of country folk, where the daughters went into service at the more prosperous houses in the area and the sons either went to the same houses as gardeners, house servants, or as in the case of my maternal grandfather, join the army as a career soldier. My maternal grandmother went into domestic service, as did my mother, and I think their early lives added characteristics that made them effective and efficient survivors throughout the rest their lives.

The Rileys were a close-knit family, father Bill (William), mother Louise, daughters Lucy (my mother), Gladys and sons William and Edward.

On the news of my father's death, they immediately descended en masse, offering advice and support in whatever way they could. In a few weeks the situation was about to get worse, and the effects and the anguish that followed would be with my mother for a long time.

My father's work problems and the onset of his illness had made him neglect or forget some of the side issues. One result of this was in relation to credit purchases made to obtain furnishings after they were married; these financial burdens had not been completely cleared at the time of my father's death. Although my father only owed two payments to complete his credit agreement, his creditors came and took away all the house furnishings, even the new linoleum floor covering from all the bedrooms and the 'front room', and left my mother in an empty house with only the bed she slept in and one chair.

The early days after that incident were hard to imagine; as time went on family members rallied around and found bits and pieces of furnishings to enable my mother to survive with two young children and a newborn baby. Grandfather Kendrick Fellows worked as a porter at an 'auction house' and had always spent his spare time visiting auctions and developing his skills at picking up useful items at rock-bottom prices.

Some of his acquisitions provided the early things given to my mother; he then focussed his abilities on obtaining specific items of furniture that were sorely needed. Also, Grandfather Bill Riley dug into his meagre resources and toured the second-hand stores in the area to obtain basic items of furniture.

As time progressed, some level of stability was restored and whilst Grandfather Kendrick and his family contemplated how they would deal with the family of his dead son, Grandfather Bill and his two sons, William and Edward, immediately set to with direct material help.

Regularly, (every two or three days) they would arrive at 44 Queen Street with bags of coal for heating or carrier bags of essential food items, because the only transport they had were their bicycles. With bags of coal balanced across the frame crossbar, they would not have been able to ride the three miles or so distance from their home, with the carrier bags of food as well.

Somehow my mother survived those early months, I cannot even comprehend how, but she did and seemed to develop an inner strength from the adversity with which she was faced. I came to realise that this was a character of all the Rileys; they all had an inner strength of character and whilst each was individually extremely self-reliant, they all possessed a sense of deep family loyalty.

Kendrick Fellows had two daughters, Margaret and Nora, and two sons, Thomas and James, still living at home. Tom and Jim had come home from the First World War emotionally scarred and haunted by their experiences so that they went about their daily existence in a somewhat robotic mode and always seemed to acquiesce to the opinions of the rest of the family.

So, when it came to the discussions about what their role would be in helping the deceased Albert's family, except for Kendrick's head of the family role, Margaret and Nora's opinions tended to be the ones which prevailed. I should mention at this stage that Kendrick Fellows was nobody's 'pussycat', for it was known locally that he did not 'suffer fools lightly' and, in fact, was known by his neighbours as 'Bull' Fellows.

As in most families, daughters seem to manage to sway father's judgement on any issue, such was the case at 42 Lower Queen Street. The Fellows family were a strong Catholic family, and my mother on her wedding day had pledged to bring up the children as Catholics, even though she herself was not a Catholic.

So, the first thing the family agreed to was that they would ensure that Albert's children would be brought up as Catholics, as would have been his wish. They next addressed the question of how a young mother, with a 3-year-old girl, an 18-month-old boy and a newborn baby, could best be helped by them.

Margaret, supported by her sister Nora, proposed that Barbara, the 3-year-old girl, should come and live with them and be raised by them. They reasoned that with a newborn baby, my mother could not manage more than two children, and it was logical that she should be left with the two boys.

As my Grandmother Riley later explained to me, my mother a very young mother, trying desperately to cope with what at the time must have seemed an impossible situation, and was glad for the offer of help in the short term, without time to consider the terms such help was offered under. It was in an atmosphere of emotional turmoil and fear for the future that she agreed to give up her daughter to be raised by aunts and uncles.

At the time it probably did not appear to be such a drastic decision, because 42 Lower Queen Street was only some 100 -200 yards from 44 Queen Street and at the time it was seen as a temporary measure. From our point of view, my brother and I, it was to have dramatic effects on our relationships with our sister. Because we lived apart from an early age and despite seeing and being together most days, there was never the bonding between brother and sister but rather the relationship between two neighbours' children, or at the most that between distant cousins.

My memories of those early childhood years are vague, just little snapshots of what happened during the years up to eight or nine years old, with big memory gaps in between. I remember a happening around the age of three or four years of age, when we were all sleeping in the same bedroom, my mother, brother and myself. The reason was that my mother's sister Gladys had left her husband with her two sons and had turned to my mother for shelter.

Our two cousins were about the same age as my brother and myself and together with their mother, they occupied the other bedroom. I think it only lasted for a matter of days, and I do not remember how the situation was resolved, but afterwards things settled back to normal from what, I can only guess, must have been total bedlam and chaos.

All memories of those early days are very fragmented and hard to position in sequence; for instance, I remember our mother taking us all by Midland Red Bus to see Grandpa and Grandma Riley regularly on a Sunday when we were quite small, to Worcester Lane, Roughley.

Later when my mother was working full-time, our sister Barbara was given the job of shepherding us, to pay the regular visit to the Riley grandparents. With Barbara, we normally had to walk unless it was raining and then sometimes we would be given bus fares. Those regular visits established, for me at any rate, a strong bond with Grandma Riley, and lacking direct male guidance and advice, it was to Grandma I turned to in later years, including my early teens.

Although I emphasise the regular visits to my mother's parents, do not get the idea that we did not see as much of my father's family; in fact, the opposite is true. Since the Fellows family only lived 100 yards away, we saw more of them in those early years.

Various aunts and uncles used to take us to church on Sundays, and when we were a little older, Uncles Tom and Jim used to take us to Blackroot pool, in Sutton Park, on sunny days; on one particular occasion, they were scolded by our mother, for allowing us to get too much of the sun.

Those first years were hard, with no skills to earn a living, having come from a culture in which the sons would go to work on local farms or enlist in the regular army. The daughters would leave home to become housemaids and servants in the homes of the more affluent. So, my mother, like her mother, became a servant in a large house after leaving school, until her marriage, and it does seem that marriage was the only escape from that way of life.

Now widowed, it was only the skills she had gained as a house-servant that she could now rely on to earn a living, and of these only cleaning and ironing had any potential. She told us, when we were older, that her former employer, a childless widow named Mrs Moore, on learning of my father's death had contacted my mother and suggested that she place her children in an orphanage and return to work for her as her personal maid.

Those early years must have been difficult for my mother, but she was determined to survive and raise her children herself. She canvassed the more affluent areas of the town, going house to house seeking cleaning and ironing work, and eventually built up a group of contacts willing to give her work. The pay was low and in those early days, she had to take both me and my younger brother with her, from job to job.

But despite this difficult start in family life, in the following years, my brother and I enjoyed a stable if somewhat frugal family life even without a father, which in later years I had some regrets over.

My mother was loving, considerate and dedicated to bringing up her two sons as best she knew how; she slaved to clothe us and maintain all the outward signs of a stable family. She hated the idea of ever having to accept any charity, her self-pride was so strong that she rebelled against the idea. But rather than see us lose out, she buried her pride and went to 'Toc H' to ask for help in providing toys for our Christmas.

We did a lot of little things together that strengthened the family bonds; for instance, Mom would show us how to cook simple meals, so that if she was ever late home from work, we would be capable of cooking something for ourselves, such as boiled or fried eggs, beans on toast and fried herrings after first having rolled the latter in flour (we would pop around the corner to the local 'chippy' for a few pence worth of chips).

Again, when she was baking and making cakes, she would let us join in making something of our own, under her guidance. Christmas was always a time when she really involved us; first there was the making of Christmas decorations to decorate the living space. We used the left-over wall paper from her regular house decorating endeavours, and she showed us how to fold up the paper and then cut out a shape so that when we opened it up we had a string of bells and fairies and animals.

The Christmas tree was a traditional routine, because we used the same Christmas tree every year. Mom would go out into the garden and dig up this very healthy Christmas tree and set roots and all into a galvanised bucket, which she decorated with coloured paper. We all had a share in decorating the tree itself, with sweets we had saved, little trinkets that Mom had saved and anything else that we could lay our hands on. After Christmas the process was reversed and off came the decorations and out of the bucket and back into the garden went the tree, to recover ready for next year.

When at about 14 years of age, I had my first pair of long trousers, they needed the legs shortening, so my mother, ever resilient, set to and neatly did the work. But not until she had told me, "Watch very closely whilst I am doing this, because you are short and I suspect every pair of trousers you buy will need shortening; learn now and be able to do it for yourself." I took that advice to heart and throughout my life, I have always shortened my own trousers, which was a skill that proved particularly valuable in the army.

I think both my brother and I grew up confident and self-reliant, attributes for which I am sure we owe our mother. The bombing raids on Birmingham and the surrounding area munition factories became a regular nightly event. Sutton Coldfield did not get too much attention, except that the planes seemed to unload what they had left before they took off for home.

Exactly how, I do not remember, but again the Fellows family at 42 Lower Queen Street became involved in the futures of my brother and myself. A discourse went on between them about the danger from bombing whilst we were on our own, awaiting the return of mother from her work.

The advent of war and the shortage of men to fill jobs was a God-sent opportunity for mother. She was able to quickly learn new skills and after training she settled into full-time employment assembling and refurbishing diesel injectors for the local Midland Red Bus Company. The problem was the long working hours and shift working, its effect on her children's lives was constantly on her mind.

The same original issues of honouring my father's wishes, that we be educated as Catholics, were again discussed, but this time it was an opening gambit, for another life-changing plan for me and my brother. A chance to put forward a plan that would secure our father's wish about religious education. They discussed with our mother the problems they identified as consequences of her long working hours and shift working.

By this time Grandfather and Grandmother Fellows were no longer with us, having departed this life, and by this time Grandfather Riley had also passed on, leaving my mother with only her older brother Bill for male advice, her mother and her sister Gladys for female support.

The Rileys were essentially quiet country folk, very different from the Fellows family, who at that time seemed to think they had all the answers, particularly the daughters Margaret and Laura. They probably inherited their convictions and demeanour from their father, my grandfather Kendrick, who, as already mentioned, was known locally not to 'suffer fools lightly'.

Little wonder then that the 'spinster' sisters-in-law suddenly decided that their nephews could not be properly cared for if my mother had to work long hours and shift work to earn a living, leaving my brother and myself to our own devices after school. In their view, there had to be a better solution, and they obviously set about searching for one that appealed to their sense of values.

Through their church connections, they had found a convent school that was also a boarding school. Because of my mother's limited means, she would only be required to pay a nominal amount, the rest being provided by church charities. We would be allowed home each weekend, and this would fit in well with my mother's work demands.

Now we were all of school age, Sister Barbara, now living permanently at 42, was the oldest and was charged with the responsibility of guiding us all to school. Of course, for the first few days either an aunt, or my mother would take us to school until we had learned the route, since from Queen Street to the Catholic school was quite a step for five to seven year olds. Saint Joseph's as a school was typical of the many small Catholic schools of that era, the infant class was the only class not taught by nuns, the junior class and the senior classes were both taught by nuns and strict discipline was maintained in all classes.

Not having any alternative solution and becoming increasingly anxious over what might happen if an air raid occurred whilst she was out at work, who could she rely upon to look out for me and my brother Albert in the event of such a raid, she reluctantly agreed with the Fellows family. Under considerable emotional arguments and pressure, she agreed with the plan for a boarding school and asked them to go ahead and arrange it all. She had misgivings about her ability to maintain the payments required, despite assurances from Aunt Laura, who seemed to be the main negotiator of the plan.

Then came the day for us to move to St Philips Covent School at Westbourne Road, in Edgbaston, two heart-broken young children and an equally emotional mother. But Mother assured us that we would be safer there during any air raids, with people to look after us, and she would have us at home weekends.

My memories of our time at St Philip's are fragmented and disjointed, the clearest memories are associated with images of activity and routine. St Philip's was located in what must once have been a very large private house, with extensive grounds and gardens, and one of its assets was that it had extensive storage and wine cellars beneath the house, which by then had been utilised as bomb shelters during air raids.

I was by this time aged ten and Albert nine, and never having been away from home, this was a daunting prospect that neither of us was looking forward to. This despite our mother's assurances that everything would be strange, but we would soon get used to the difference from home and that we would be together each weekend. That bus trip across Birmingham to Westbourne Road was a journey that will always be remembered, as something like a trip to the other side of the world. As far as we were concerned, a trip into the unknown.

Our first disappointment was when we were told that it was the normal routine that we would not spend weekends at home for several weeks, to allow time to settle in and accept our new surroundings. I will always remember that first night, I don't think I have ever felt so alone and abandoned.

My younger brother was crying to go home and I remember saying to 'Sister Benedict' "that my brother wanted to go home, I could take him and that I remembered the route on the buses, also that I had money for bus fares." The result of that conversation was a stern reprimand and being forced to hand over the money I claimed to have, which was duly credited to our 'tuck shop' account.

During the period of the regular nightly air raids, it was the normal routine to wrap ourselves up and go down into these cellar tunnels, which were lined with two-tier bunk beds. We could clearly hear the explosions above us, which were a mixture of anti-aircraft fire and bombs.

As we got more used to the routine and having found we were apparently in safe surroundings, unable to sleep, one or two of us would venture away from their bunks and explore the extent of the cellars. We found that they led to what must have been the cellar doors in the courtyard of the house.

This was a glass-covered courtyard, and we had found that on previous days, after an air-raid, pieces of anti-aircraft shell shrapnel and bullets from fighter aircraft guns would crash through the glass panels of the courtyard roof. So, it was only a matter of time before one or two of us became curious enough to peek out through the cellar head doors to watch the flashes of gunfire and the raging flames on the horizon from bomb explosions in other parts of Birmingham.

It seemed that the Edgbaston area of the city was mainly hit by small incendiary bombs, causing fires in the surrounding area, and St Philip's received at least two such bombs, neither of which exploded, lucky for the school. After one such night raid, the air raid wardens searched the gardens for possible unexploded devices and found one. They interviewed all of us boys, asking whether we had found any suspicious devices in the grounds.

Well, the outcome was that an older boy admitted that he had found a small unexploded incendiary bomb and was keeping it to take home as a souvenir. It seemed he had hidden it under his mattress in the dormitory. This caused a minor panic, and the building had to be cleared whilst the 'bomb disposable unit' removed the device.

It seems that many of these small incendiary bombs were damaged on impact with the ground, and although they did not explode, moving them or striking them could have caused them to detonate.

I remember the occasions when we would go home for the weekend by bus, and the Midland Red Bus for Sutton Coldfield had to traverse a route that always had to re-route to avoid the bomb craters from the previous night's bombing.

I clearly remember one trip, where the bus edged around a huge bomb crater near old Lewis's department store, looking down into it from the top of a double decker bus, it looked huge and deep; in the crater there were masses of torn pipes, some obviously for gas and still burning. Also, as the bus drove through Aston, I remember seeing men working on searching the rubble of bombed houses, for victims of the bombing.

The day's routine at St Philips was full and disciplined, washing, cleaning dormitories, breakfast, school, reading and games, supper, bed. Weekends were different, on Saturday, washing, cleaning dormitories (more thoroughly than in the week), breakfast, gymnasium, lunch, games on the pitches, football, cricket and Rugby. On Sunday, as one might expect for a convent school, there was always morning mass in the school chapel and in the evening, vespers, or evening prayers. At the age of 10 or 11, boys were selected to serve on the altar at Sunday mass, and as the service was always in Latin, although we were taught the equivalent in English, we tended to learn the service replies parrot fashion.

Those boys who were successful at the chapel services were coerced into a group that provided altar boys for the services at the Birmingham Oratory, for both weekdays and Sunday services.

The oratory church had a main high altar underneath the dome and then several smaller altars on either side of the main concourse, as well as several chapels in the cloisters of the church. This meant that on any weekday there could be several services being celebrated at the same time and each mass requiring an altar boy. Resulting in the altar boys having a race against time, to get from St Philips to the oratory, to serve mass, back to get breakfast, and then off to school.

It was a race to find cassocks and cotters to wear and there was usually a fight over sizes. This resulted in ripped garments, leaving the last boy faced with having to use numerous pins to hold together his cassock and hoping the cotter would cover all the tears and pins.

The priests varied in how long they took to celebrate mass on weekdays, Father Charles was extremely fast, as was Father Thomas, whereas Father Robert was terribly slow, and the altar boy who was left to serve his mass was almost certain to be late getting to school.

The younger boys attended Oliver Road Boys School and would be marched like a troop of the 'Boys Brigade', chaperoned by a nun from St Philips, along the pavement. This was less any altar boys, who made their own way to school. The older boys attended St Philips Grammar School and made their own way to and from school.

Saint Phillips was what had once been a large country mansion in its own extensive grounds, which had provided space for sports fields, a football and cricket pitch. The interior of the house had been modified to provide the facilities for its new function, and on the lower floor was the dining room and kitchens, a large reading and games room, a large wash-up room for washing before meals, a gymnasium and boot-room and, of course, the mandatory chapel.

The outside rear courtyard was fairly large and glass-covered, which was to its disadvantage, once the German air-raids began.

Under the house were large wine cellars, which had been fitted out with three-tier bunks as an air raid shelter. Of the upper floor a considerable portion of it was closeted off as the nuns' private quarters and was not part of the school accommodation.

The school accommodation was divided into two sections, one for the older boys, under a house-mother known as 'Miss Frain', and the other section for the younger boys, under a house-mother known as 'Miss Margaret'. The overall running and control of the resident children seemed to be under 'Sister Benedict's' control.

All other nuns seemed to have some assigned duties; for instance, a nun was in charge of the kitchen operations and various nuns would sit in and supervise activities in the reading-room and activities in the gymnasium as well as on the sports field. There was a nun in charge of the 'tuck-shop', which was open for a period each evening and on Sunday mornings, and each child could purchase sweets, provided his tuck-shop account was in credit.

On weekdays whenever there was religious observance day and on Sunday mornings, we would have to attend mass in the chapel, and on Sundays we would have to attend vespers in the evening.

Discipline was fairly strict and sometimes seemed unfair; it was said of Miss Frain that her temper tended to get the better of her, and you had better be quick to duck if you upset her. Miss Margaret, on the other hand, was of a very even temper and yet always in control, but fair with any mild punishments she administered.

Sister Benedict, on the other hand, was a cold, hard disciplinarian who permitted few breaches of school rules, with the cane as a likely punishment for minor breaches. It was a certainty that if she caught you using, what in her opinion was, unsuitable language, she would immediately administer a back hander across the face, which for a small child was almost a knockout blow. Looking back, the discipline was reasonably fair and instilled into us a certain self-discipline.

Life settled down into a series of routines, some easy to accept, others a little different from what we were used to, meals, serving at mass, walking to school, the gym, the sports field, weekends at home, the bombing.

The latter had a significant effect for us, because the bus routes through Birmingham to home were never the same after a bomber raid. Because Saint Philip's was a catholic school, religious ritual was very much a part of daily life; as an example, all boys were trained to serve mass in the chapel as well as at the Oratory church on Hagley Road. The latter usually required about six boys for morning masses, because the Oratory had several alters around the church.

Sunday was something different for altar servers, because in the evening there was vespers, which required two candle bearers and one to swing the incense burner. With a fair number of boys of eligible age at Saint Philip's, the duty did not come around too often.

On such days, however, if you got hauled in to the oratory choir, this meant every Sunday, both for practice and the service.

A typical day, without extra-curricular duties, was as follows: up, wash, help tidy the rooms (under the supervision of the respective house-mother), breakfast, off to morning school, back for lunch, afternoon school, back for time in the reading room (and tuck-shop), wash-up and have tea, then time in the gymnasium or out on the sports field, after that it was bath and to bed.

The repeated ritual at the school, with all the other activities that the school involved everyone in, was effective in converting me away from Catholic religion. This by the time I reached my mid-teens (not still at Saint Philips's).

As an example, occasionally, an ex-resident of the school would go on to be ordained as a Catholic priest. If you were unlucky enough to be there at the time and the ordination ceremony was at the Oratory, you all had to attend the ordination ceremony. The whole thing takes best part of a day, and although we did not have to sit through it all, can you imagine how a bunch of 10–13 year olds felt about having to watch most of such an affair?

Another example, if any of the priests at the oratory were to die, then everyone was expected to go to the Oratory, as a group, and troop past the open coffin in one of the side chapels. Again, not a necessary experience for 10–13 year olds and one that I found disturbing.

But in less than two years, the end to our days at Saint Philip's was the order of the day. Unknown to my brother and myself, our mother was finding it extremely difficult to keep up the payments for our board, even though due to her circumstances it was subsidised by Catholic charities.

Finally, Sister Benedict took us on one side and told us to gather up our things and that someone would be coming to take us home and that we would not be returning to the school.

Well, we were not disappointed at leaving, although both of us had left new friends behind, home was home and that was where we wanted to be. Things were strange at first, here we were two little 'altar serving/choir boys' about to enter the local school system again, with about a much 'street cred' as an angel, and I am afraid in those first few weeks it showed.

Being short in stature, I soon found that I had to convince my new friends that 'short' was not an abbreviation for victim and right away started to live up to my nickname of 'Little Bull'. Having no father living and two years of convent upbringing, I was so green, it must have showed, and the only thing I knew about sex was what I overheard the other boys talking about on the sly. But life is a great teacher, and all kids are sponges for soaking up experience and knowledge. In keeping with the wishes of my father's family, after Saint Philips's, we were once again enrolled to attend Sutton Coldfield's St Joseph's Roman Catholic school.

As with all cultural differences, those of religion also set people apart, and this was true with the Sutton Coldfield Catholic and Protestant Schools. The latter was the much larger school and was in the centre of town, whereas the Catholic school was way up the Lichfied Road and a fair step for children. Because it was a small school, classes such as cookery for the girls and carpentry for the boys were joint ones with the Protestant pupils on their premises. Occasionally, religious differences were used to single out a lone Catholic pupil to be bullied, on the assumption that the other side would always be in the majority. But except for the odd incident, we all survived and I think my school days were amongst my happiest.

I won two scholarships, the first to the local art college and the second to a Laurence's College, in Birmingham, having decided along with two of my friends from St Joseph's that accountancy was something with potential.

In the first instance, my mother dismissed the idea of staying on at school to study art out of hand, saying it would contribute nothing to my chances in the job market. The Laurence's College idea she gave serious thought; as to how she might manage to support me whilst I was studying. In the end she said that on her small income she could not manage to clothe and feed me in addition to paying my travel expenses into Birmingham. Her sole income, she said, was not enough, and I would have to resign myself to getting a job and contribute to the family's meagre income. All teenagers of the period under discussion had the expectation that on reaching 18 years of age, they would be called upon to serve in the armed forces for the period dictated by the Conscription Act.

This meant that on the whole, large companies were full up with apprentices who had signed on, in order to defer their military service until after the apprenticeship period had been completed. Those lucky enough to be able to go to university were able to defer their military service for two years.

It was usually a teenager from a working class family whose father steered him towards applying for an apprenticeship with a large company. Often because that was the way they had begun their working lives and with the same company. I had none of that male influence or advice on a working career and the value of an apprenticeship with a large company.

However, my aunts and uncles had always said that going to work in a drawing office was a well-paid job, with a stable and steady future. Advising me that I should sign on to go to technical college, with that goal in mind. So, although I did not quite know what sort of skills I would require for a drawing office, eventually I submitted to being signed up for an ONC in mechanical engineering three evenings a week and, of course, I still had to get a job to help my mother out. At 15, I still had plenty of time before they called me for military service and so it was the job hunt for me.

In those days, because so many men and women were away in the armed forces, jobs for teenagers were plentiful. My first employment was the result of running into a friend, who lived in the next street to Queen Street. He had just started work at a horse riding school as a stable boy, and he said that there was a vacancy for another.

To cut a long story short, I hopped on the Midland Red Bus to Clarence Road, the site of Cutler's Riding School and after being interviewed by Major Cutler (a retired army cavalry man), I was turned over to the 'head honcho', the groom, who instructed me as to my hours of work and my daily duties. The stable had over 30 horses on site, which all had to be fed, groomed and exercised; in addition, of course, 'mucking out' all their stables. Some of the horses were privately owned and normally exercised by their owners. Of the others, for those that were not involved in the daily school activities, it was the responsibility of the stable boys and the groom to take them down into Sutton Park for a good workout.

Many of the horses were used by the local hunt and on such hunt mornings, the stable boys and the groom had to be in early to have the horses ready and saddled by 6 am, with no reduction on finishing times, making such days long and tedious.

In addition to the 'hunts', Major Cutler's two daughters, Beryl and Leila, competed regularly in gymkhanas around the region. This usually meant that one or other of the stable boys would have to accompany them to look after the horses. Which meant that in addition to the long hours in the week, they also lost the occasional Saturday, or Sunday.

It was fun whilst it lasted, but it was hard work for very long hours, at something below the going wage. Come the end of the summer, I decided to move on and as I said before, jobs were plentiful.

My next job was 5 minutes' walk from home in Lower Queen Street, at Lowes Engineering, which was housed in what can only be described as a large backstreet garage. Little workshops were set up all over the place, to machine components for equipment being assembled in the larger main factories. This little workshop specialised in turning, drilling and milling operations on standard components and employed eight people plus the boss.

There was no apprenticeship here, new people were started on simple drilling operations of components, held in drilling jigs. One of the more experienced workers would demonstrate the operation and then watch for a period of time to make certain that the new worker could carry on without supervision. As they became more confident in their mechanical ability, they would be introduced to turning and milling operations.

So that in six months, more or less, I was experienced in turning on both small precision lathes and automatic capstan lathes as well as milling and drilling; machining skill levels that would normally only be acquired after a full engineering apprenticeship. Again, this job was not to last, because the workshop only had room for eight people to work, before anyone else could be taken on someone had to leave. Men were now coming home, looking for their job back. The business owner had promised a former employee that when he returned from the army, his job would be there for him. The boss was so apologetic when he explained the situation to me, but ended up by adding that there was plenty of jobs about and I would not have any difficulty finding a new one.

Opening number three was again a complete change and again five minutes' walking distance from home. I became a 'butcher's boy' working for Walter Smiths at one of their shops on The Parade, next door to Chamberlain's, the green-grocers.

Normally in peacetime, the job would have been errand boy and flunky, cleaning down after the meat cutting and sausage making was finished. But this was wartime, with minimum staff, which at that time was the manager, a cashier, and the butcher's boy, who quickly had to learn how to cut the meat into joints under the watchful eye of the manager.

Their second store had a meat cutter, who failed the physical for the armed forces. In the middle of the week he would turn up, to spend many hours a day teaching me the rudiments of firstly boning out meat joints and then cutting the various meat joints as displayed for sale to customers.

This was followed by many long hours, explaining and demonstrating the techniques for display and presentation of meat. Those first weeks were hard, but I was a willing learner, and I began to enjoy the job and, of course, listened to all the tales the two managers had to tell about the days when they started as butcher boys.

The Lamb Shop, was Walter Smith's other shop and was on the opposite side of The Parade, next door to Macfisheries, the fishmongers. The manager of that shop was the senior of the two managers and as such organised the fundamental operation of both shops.

On Monday morning, he would go to the abattoir in Birmingham and select the cattle to be slaughtered, for delivery to the two shops. Then he would stay there and monitor the whole operation, through to where the carcasses were hung ready for delivery. At this point he would inspect every carcass, before approving it for delivery.

The senior manager also supervised the sausage making, which was from an old recipe handed down through the family, the mix of the meat content, the amount of rusk and the seasoning.

This latter he did personally, and no one else actually ever saw him mix the ingredients of the seasoning. The heads of the slaughtered beasts were not included in the meat ration. The tongues and cheek meat were stripped out; in the case of beef and pork, the tongues were boiled and pressed into blocks to sell as cooked meat; the cheek meat usually ended up in sausages.

Sausages and cooked meat were not part of the meat ration and were normally kept for the shop's regular customers, who were only too pleased to get a welcome supplement to the meagre meat ration.

Butchers' shops were allowed so much meat for trimming waste, when cutting up the joints, or boning out a piece of meat. The shop managers were always careful, to make sure that the waste trimming was minimal, particularly in boning out, and often what should have been trimmed off was sold as part of a ration.

This way the managers accumulated joints of meat for sale to 'special customers' for high prices. Every day customers would come in to see if there were any big marrow bones, that could be boiled up to make soup, and we would saw up the big beef leg bones into small pieces, so they could fit in a saucepan.

Fish was not on the ration so as soon as the fish shops opened, a queue would form, and in a couple of hours the shop had sold out, until the next day's delivery.

At that time there seemed to be queues for everything that was not rationed, fresh fruit, vegetables, bread, cakes; people seemed to join queues without being sure what they were waiting for. Working in a shop during the rationing period was quite an education. My work career was to be interrupted yet again, when after a year, I started to get a rash on the back of my hands and on my lower forearms.

I went to the skin hospital in Birmingham, to see a skin specialist. The diagnosis of the condition was contact dermatitis, it was suggested that the cause was my being allergic to the lanolin in the meat I was handling. The condition gradually grew worse and became more visible to those around me.

In the end the shop manager said that although there was no question of infection, where food was concerned, appearances were very important and seeing me cutting up their meat would not go down well with some customers. I worked my notice and was out looking for a job again.

Within a week I was working at Chambers Ford car agency in South Parade, again only ten minutes' walk from my home. Because I was now getting close to the time for military service, they were not prepared to sign me up for an apprenticeship. I was signed on as an 'improver', which, I eventually learned, simply meant that you learned as you went along.

The dermatitis cleared up it the first few weeks, and I was once again in black oily overalls, another washing burden for my mother. There were no new cars available at that time, so everyone was employed either on repairs, or rebuilding and restoring old ones. My first job was with a bunch of men, restoring an old American Ford Pilot, and as the new boy on the team I got the job of washing and cleaning all the dismantled parts in paraffin, which was about the dirtiest job I have ever had.

The Ford Pilot was completely dismantled, even all the bodywork, everything was cleaned and repainted; over several months the car was reassembled with new interior lining and new upholstery. The car was an eye catcher when it was finished and, I guess, sold for a good price.

Around the time this car was being refurbished, they also had another operation going on. That of converting war surplus airborne jeep trailers, for civilian use and sale. The work involved cutting a flap out of the rear of the trailer with a cutting torch, grinding all the edges on both the flap and trailer square, then finally welding on a pair of strap hinges and flap locks to complete the job.

After that it was into the paint shop, where they received a coat of paint, a polish up and they were ready for the showroom. Another improver was doing this work and was now getting very close to the date when his military service would catch up with him. With the Ford Pilot complete, the garage foreman was looking around for where I could next be fruitfully employed and assigned me to understudy this other improver and learn everything there was to know about modifying these war surplus trailers.

The two of us got on well from the start, and I was soon shown how to adjust the gas mixtures for cutting and welding, as well as the difference between a cutting torch and a welding torch. We were soon working together, either I would do the cutting and he the welding or vice versa, and we both worked on the edge-grinding job, which took more time for each trailer.

He talked about his impending war service and said he was hoping to get into the REME (Royal Electrical & Mechanical Engineers) if he could. He had heard that as conscripts you were likely to be posted to whatever unit suited the army and was considering volunteering for five years to get the unit of his choice. The issue was often raised, the question of volunteering versus conscription, and argued that by the time five years were up, things would be more settled in civilian life.

Listening to him I got the impression he was using me as a sounding board, whilst he convinced himself in favour of volunteering. The day came when I was alone working on the trailers, my workmate had finally gone for military service. Rumour had it that he had volunteered for five years in the end, but this was never confirmed.

The work was monotonous for a teenager, but the routine work meant that I knew what work I had to do and could organise my day. Cutting with a torch is hot and dirty work, overalls covered with metal dust. Soles of shoes and boots ruined, by continually walking over the hot metal globules that fell to the floor from the cutting operation.

Grinding and cleaning up the edges was a welcome break from cutting and welding. The foreman would only appear infrequently to check that my productivity and work quality was up to scratch. Since I was away to one side of the garage, I was left very much to my own devices to get on with my work, only having contact with the others when I needed help in moving new and empty gas cylinders.

Up to now I have only described work life, but what of my home life and social life as a teenager? Well, of course, I had plenty of friends my own age, both from school and those that lived in the adjacent streets to 'Queen Street'. Whilst still at school, we would gather either down at the Holland Road playing fields, or on the strip of wasteland behind the Midland Red Bus garage. Depending on what films we had recently seen at the 'Saturday Morning Cinema', we would be either a safari in Africa hunting wild animals, or Flash Gordon fighting some strange beings from outer space.

We also spent a lot of time in the summer in Sutton Park, either swimming at Keeper's 'open air pool', or on the canoes and rowing boats at Blackroot Pool. As we grew older, we were able to get 'morning paper delivery rounds' or evening jobs delivering groceries etc. on 'delivery bicycles'.

We began to have a little spending money, which was necessary for the Sutton Park activities. This meant a general move from the playing around the streets, or in each other's home gardens, the latter being pretty restrictive and small.

By the time I was 14, or there about, the Catholic Church had started a youth club, which met at the 'Old Guild Hall', on the Lichfield Road. This provided evening games facilities, dancing lessons and Saturday night youth dances. The dancing was an essential social skill in those days and the Youth Club was extremely popular for a while. It was about that time, I started to take note that there were girls in the world, becoming aware that I was rather shorter than the average height and when dancing it was inevitable that my partner was taller than me. There were girls my height and shorter, but I was learning that the shorter girls all seemed attracted to taller boys.

My father had died when I was only 18 months old and later on my world was defined by a mother, or a grandmother, my older sister, three maiden aunts, all women. The only male influence in my life were two uncles, who had been so traumatised by their experiences in World War I that they were always the most unlikely male peers from whom to learn a male attitude to women.

The result was I was always very confused and embarrassed when talking to girls alone, on my own. I really did not have that male influence that would have automatically equipped me for those early male-female encounters. The one time in my life that I felt that not having a father alive to impart the male influence that was essential was a weakness of my early childhood.

All of this, of course, was soon corrected when I joined the army, a somewhat totally male environment. But to get back to the growing-up story and my embarrassed relationship with girls. At the youth club dances, we were there as a crowd and to dance we simply paired off, but when I went to a dance elsewhere, I was on my own and used to be terribly embarrassed when asking a strange girl if she would like to dance. I never stopped to think that most of the girls felt the same way at first.

My mother had always taught me that you had to treat girls with respect, and I think that impaired my approach from the start. Activities for teenage boys and girls was fairly varied in Sutton Coldfield, with at least three dance venues at weekend and two cinemas, the Odeon (at that time a resplendent new one) and the Empress.

Saturday mornings, it was a meet for coffee at Pattisons, or Trow's milk-bar for coffee, and it was at these meetings that we all made dates to go to one or the other dance options. In the evenings, there was Sutton Park and the two main coffee bars, the Rendezvous and The Snackerie.

The latter was owned by a local band leader, who played at many of the local dance venues and for that reason was fairly popular. I guess overall my relationship with girls in my early teens was immature, for I tried to portray someone else other than myself and had trouble expressing my real feelings.

Now I realise that those are problems for most teenagers, who have first to find out who they really are and what in their genetic heritage drives them towards unknown goals and achievements.

Nowadays, teenagers are regularly involved in sex by 15 and some before even that age; it still seems true that girls mature earlier than boys. But in my days as a teenager, although there was some heavy petting, things almost always stopped short of sex.

There was firstly a strong inhibition against sex outside marriage. Girls had it drummed into them, not to dare come home to their parents and tell them they were pregnant. The greatest shame for a family was to admit that they had an unmarried daughter that was pregnant. It did occasionally happen and on such occasions, everyone was told that the girl had gone away to stay with an aunt. When, in fact, she was in some convent that catered for unmarried mothers, the baby to be put for adoption as soon as it was born and the mother return to her parental home. The girls in such situations were carefully controlled and monitored in their activities after returning home and parents were anxious to marry off the offending daughter as soon as possible.

This teenage pregnancy problem became acute after the American army arrived, with plenty of money to spend on anything for a good time. Young teenage working girls could regularly be seen hanging around the gates of the camps, where the soldiers were billeted, and it was not long before the fruits of their labour became apparent.

The US army must have contributed to the increase in the population of Sutton Coldfield considerably. Some were serious relationships, where the girl believed she would get married and go to the USA after the war ended, but most were one-night stands or the result of girls getting drunk on alcohol.

Still, in my late teens, before I joined the army, I shared most of my spare time with a close friend and like others we went around prospecting for girlfriends. He was slightly taller and of a personality that the girls of the day seemed to like. Either at a dance, or the fairground in Sutton Park, he would identify the target pair after first specifying which one he was after and leaving me no choice.

Still, it always seemed to work out okay, although there was never any hint of a serious romance, or ongoing relationship, for most of the girls were just visiting the fair or dance in Sutton Park from elsewhere around the Midlands area. By this time, I had lost contact with all the girls I had met at school and the youth club. My embarrassment at meeting girls had not diminished; in fact, it was worse because I was in open territory and not surrounded by friends and school acquaintances.

Looking back at life and in particular male and female relationships, one thing that stands out for me is that the bulk of the long-lasting marriages and relationships were between couples that had grown up with each other since childhood. They knew each other in every detail and all the 'kinks' in each other's personality.

Other couples try to portray to each other a perceived image of who they think they are, or as they would wish other people could see them. Sooner or later, the real self establishes itself and there is no longer the same basis for a relationship. Teenage years are a search for self-identity without realising the fact. The way they view the world and the way they solve life's problems are a synthesis of the images and solutions passed to them by grandparents and parents. This, in turn, is modified by education and life experience, little of which they have had time for. My mother used to have a saying that fits the bill 'you cannot put old heads on young shoulders'.

I was only 16 years old when the end of the war in Europe was declared and everyone started to prepare for victory celebrations. Every street organised their own street party and in Queen Street they laid out tables the length of the street with food and drink, the like of which I had not seen during the whole of war.

Once begun, the celebrations went on into the small hours of the following morning, with many the worse for too much alcohol. Ronnie Hancox set up his band in front of the Snackerie coffee bar, with a row of barrels full of beer on stands in front of his band platform. He played dance music throughout the day and night, with people dancing right across the width of the road. There was no way a motor vehicle could get through Sutton Coldfield on the main road that night.

Those celebrations were something none of us who were there will ever forget; people had put up with a lot during the war and now suddenly they could forget it all and 'let their hair down'. At least for one night, people just found it hard to believe, that it was really all over.

As a teenager growing up in 'wartime', I guess I never then fully appreciated the full extent of what was going on. Though the radio and the cinema newsreels were a constant reminder, it was always happening somewhere else. The things that really brought it home to me was when neighbours in Lower Queen Street announced that their son, with the Armoured Corp in North Africa, had been killed and a neighbour in Queen Street returned from Dunkirk having lost one leg.

After the end of the war in Europe, people tended to forget about all those who were still fighting in the Far East, or held in Japanese prison camps. Those who served in the Far East war were certainly the forgotten army. The dropping of the atom bombs on Japan, and the capitulation of their government as a result, did not put an end to the fighting. Isolated Japanese army units were still determined to fight on to the finish. It was a long time before every territory that had suffered under the Japanese was once again at peace.

The next 18 months was really a period of waiting, knowing I had to spend my compulsory time in the armed forces, as was the case with most of my close friends. We would spend hours debating whether we would opt for the army, navy or air force, with votes for all three. I had made up my mind it would be the army, mainly because influenced by newsreels of the airborne landings in Europe, I wanted to join the Glider Pilots Regiment. It was this choice that would eventually make me decide to sign-on for five years in the regular army.

Chapter Two

My official call-up date would normally have coincided with my 18th birthday, by the time I had reached the age of 17 and half, I had made up my mind to volunteer, which was legal at that age. I remember, with a great feeling of trepidation, going into Birmingham, to the army recruiting office. Remember my background, convent school, altar boy, some street credibility gained from the teenage friends with whom I had been associating, I was as 'green' as they come. No match for the wiles of an army recruiting sergeant. The recruiting sergeant I faced was no different, maybe a little more persuasive than most, at least I like to think so, but in the end he turned out to be a born liar like the rest.

I learned later 'that you must never believe a single word of what a recruiting sergeant tells you', but I'm afraid that advice came too late. I explained to the recruiting sergeant that having been impressed by newsreels of the performance of the army glider pilots in landing troops at Arnhem and elsewhere, I would like to train as an army glider pilot.

He then put on his best 'let us explain the facts of life to this child' impersonation and proceeded to explain that I could not go directly into the Glider Pilots Regiment (I later found out that it had already been disbanded). First, I would have to enlist in the General Service Corp and after a period of basic training would be assigned to an infantry regiment that was part of airborne operations. After further training was complete, I could then apply for transfer to airborne forces and then apply for training as a glider pilot. Not knowing any better, I swallowed this lot 'hook line and sinker'. I signed on the dotted line and was told I would receive instructions in the mail on where to report to, for basic training.

Well, of course, I was back to tell all my pals that I had done it, and since many had brothers who were doing their time in the army, they offered the advice that, "Oh, for basic training they will send you either to Budbrooke Barracks, Warwick, or Whittington Barracks, Lichfield, and after seven days you get a weekend leave."

Well, my instructions arrived, 'Report to Hollywood Barracks, Belfast for basic training', enclosed was a railway warrant to take me to Stranraer and from there by ferry to Larne in Northern Ireland. There we would be met by army trucks and transported to Hollywood Barracks. Well, I sheepishly conveyed the information to my mother that I wouldn't be training locally and I wasn't sure at all when I would be home on any leave.

My confidence was already on a low ebb for the journey, without having some friendly serving soldiers travelling to our destination to advise me. "No way are you going to become an army glider pilot mate, you are in the infantry. You better get used to the idea," starting with the 28th Training Battalion.

The early details have now slipped from memory, but involved arrival at Hollywood Barracks, medicals, kit issue, assignment to a training platoon, a visit to the camp barber for a regulation 'army haircut'. The initial parade, where the platoon sergeant read the 'riot act' to us, explaining what was going to happen to us during the next few weeks. His dialogue finished with either a threat or promise that he was going to make soldiers of all.

We were then detailed off into sections and assigned to a section corporal, who was to be in control of our lives during the coming weeks of training. The first problem was the fit of the uniforms; it seemed that no one really fits the army's three theoretical sizes, "A bit tight but your training will soon adjust you to fit". "You are lucky you have got a uniform that fits more or less"; then there is "Don't worry you will grow into it eventually", the standard comments of all quartermasters' staff. During the coming weeks, we all man-aged, by swapping amongst each other, to find a reasonable fitting 'best battledress' (there were no dress uniforms in those days) at least.

Everyday working dress was 'denims', which always seemed two sizes too large on anyone. The first evenings were spent getting your kit up to scratch, polishing boots, polishing webbing brasses, putting Blanko on all our webbing equipment. Then squaring it all out with cardboard packing. From day one there were numerous daily inspections, firstly by the corporal, then when he was satisfied the sergeant, and finally, when they were both satisfied the platoon officer. These inspections were a rough ride and designed to demoralise new recruits, who having laboured for hours to produce a perfect kit display, would have it all spread on the floor by a dissatisfied NCO, or officer, then ordered to go over everything again. On those evenings when I had made it through and passed inspection, I would spend some time applying the lesson from my mother, tailoring my own trousers to the right length, not that it really mattered with boots and gaiters.

We were issued with rifles, which would be assigned to us for the period we were stationed at the barracks. Having drawn our rifles from the store, we then had to learn how to clean them. These rifles were drawn from the store each day and cleaned, despite the fact that they had not been fired. I was certain the bore must have been oversize for a 0.303 bullet with all the polishing. The ever helpful corporal assured me that I would never wear it out and made me clean it again just for good measure.

Those early days of physical training were in denim kit with no equipment, five-mile runs, ten-mile marches and regular trips around the assault courses. On the assault course I had a problem with the ditch jump, my short legs making it hard to get the distance needed to clear the ditch. It was soon apparent that others were having a similar problem. In true army innovative style, they solved the problem; they lined the ditch with coils of barbed wire. Guess what, everyone managed to clear the ditch by a reasonable margin.

Slowly, the frequency of runs and marches increased, without any prior warning, and slowly but surely wearing more kit. Finally, the day dawned when it had to be done with rifle and 'full battle order'. This meant the correct items of clothing in your backpack and full webbing. The assault course in full battle order meant invariably you ending up, sooner or later, stretched out in the mud, rifle included. This meant hours of cleaning rifles, boots and webbing equipment, to have it inspected by the platoon sergeant, who invariably made you do it all again before he would say he was satisfied.

Then, of course, there were the days when there was no racing around assault courses, no runs or forced marches. Just a little light relief in the form of 'square bashing', up, down and around the parade ground, hour after hour. Left turn, right turn, about turn, attention, stand at ease, stamping your feet so much you felt that you had driven the heels of your feet up your spine and into the back of your skull.

The parade ground is where the army instils its discipline, with repetitive drills and exercises. To the extent that eventually to obey a command is an automatic reaction to any command. In the end, 80% of all army training, for combat troops at least, has the objective of developing 'team' thinking and 'team' working.

Each man in a section is part of a section team, each section is part of a platoon team, each platoon team is part of a company team, each company team is part of a battalion team and so on up the chain of command.

This emphasis on team spirit also resulted in strong camaraderie and friendships developing, which for some men lasted throughout their army career and for others only until posting to other units split them up. You support each other through the hard times, the fatigue and punishment duties, as well as the social side, when we were allowed out of barracks that is.

As an example, on the assault course, the tall guys would stay on top of the six-foot wall, to help up the shorter guys, who found it not so easy, especially in full equipment. Those that kept getting into trouble on kit inspections would get help, or some inducement, not to let the team down. To a man, you cursed the inspections, the disciplines, the drills, the penalties for failing to match the levels attainment set, the feeling that you were being treated as something less than human. Looking back, you all realise that a trained response was what is it was all about.

Weapon training was something else, this was all the essential skills for combat troops. In any era, this depends on the level of advances in weapons technology at any given time. For us it was the 0.303 rifle, the STEN gun, the BREN gun, the PIAT anti-tank weapon, the hand-grenade and the two-inch mortar. We all had to attain a prescribed level of skills with all these weapons, and some found it easier than others. Marksmanship was competitive, and sections competed against each other to demonstrate individual and team skills.

Social life revolved around the evenings in the NAAFI, drinking and generally seeking relief from the daily routine. Occasionally, there were the Saturday nights downtown in 'Downpatrick', at the local dance, our only chance to meet up with local girls and get some break from an all-male environment.

Through an injury on the assault course, in which I cracked a rib, which in itself was not a real problem, a cyst developed on the site of the injury. A decision was taken to remove it surgically, because it was in such a position that the straps of my equipment rubbed against it.

This meant hospital and afterwards joining a new training section and going through the whole routine again. The second time around, I found it a little easier. This meant that I was in training for some ten months before I got home for any leave.

That first leave was one that I well remember; firstly, the 'fuss' my mother and family made of me and the fact that there were a lot of old friends around. All those that were still not in either the navy, air force, or army, it meant that there were always friends to socialise with. Whereas in almost all subsequent 'leaves', men and women were away in the forces, or working and in the main I was always on my own to fill my day.

After my first leave, I was posted to another training establishment in Oswestry and promoted to lance-corporal. This was a fairly uneventful posting, in that training consisted of field exercises and later assignment to train TA soldiers, billeted in tent camps in North Wales for most of 1948. The only memorable incident was when a fire broke out at the orthopaedic hospital in Gabowen; all the troops in camp were turned out to help move the patients to safety. We all worked throughout the night and some at clearing debris the next day. It was established that more than one of the soldiers had spent the night fraternising with the young trainee nurses from the hospital.

Finally, somewhere around the end of 1948 or early 1949, I was posted to Whittington Barracks, at that time the home of the North and South Staffordshire Regiments. The first battalion of the regiment had been brought back from India, together with the second battalion of the regiment from Germany. Neither battalions were up to strength, so they were amalgamated as the 1st Battalion of the South Staffordshire Regiment. I started off in 'B' company and after a few weeks, volunteered for the sniper/intelligence section and was transferred to 'HQ' company.

In the following weeks, our standard rifles were withdrawn and we were issued with the sniper rifles of the day. These started off as standard Enfield rifles, whose barrels had bench-tested tops for accuracy and were set aside for modification. The main modification was having a telescopic sight mount fitted. In addition, the wooden butt and shoulder pad were fitted by the armourer for the individual user. A long adjustable leather sling was added to complete the personal adjustments. Once the battalion armourer had tailored the weapons to each individual sniper, these rifles were stored in their own individual wooden cases, instead of being stowed in the standard rifle racks when not in use.

Regular training took place in field training, on Whittington heath, to develop stealth and concealment techniques, until they were second nature. Training was also given by the intelligence officer on our duties as members of the intelligence section, whose job was to keep the battalion command post up to date with the latest information on any battle situation. This included basic map making, marking up maps with the enemy and our own situation. In addition, we were responsible for making sand models of the current battle area, for use in the battalion command briefing.

Training dragged on with constant repetition and no end in sight; there were rumours of an overseas assignment, but at the time that was all they were.

So, together with several others in the regiment, I applied for transfer to the Parachute Regiment and parachute training. We were shipped to Aldershot and were subjected to new standards of discipline, where every move around the camp had to be 'at the double', or else. We were then subjected to training that was intended to toughen us up to Parachute Regiment standards.

Starting with 'log' exercises every morning and to illustrate how hard that was, we usually had to change our shirts each lunchtime because those we were wearing were soaking wet with perspiration. In the afternoon, we would be on their 'assault course' and finished the day with another shirt change, again soaking wet with perspiration. Getting so many shirts washed and dried was impossible. The one that came off in the morning was the one that went back on in the evening, hopefully dry by then. For light relief, we had unarmed combat training and a special little event where groups were all put into the ring together. The idea was to fight until you were the last man standing. Before this event, which was designed to develop individual aggression, an old hand had advised me, "Don't play the hero, take an early KO; think yourself lucky and leave the rest to fight on." I don't remember just how things worked out. Whether I acted upon the advice given, I am not sure. I was downed pretty early in the 'punch-up', since nearly everyone had a height and reach advantage over me. We had almost come to the end of the toughening up training at Aldershot, when on a 'full equipment' run around the assault course, I ran at the six-foot high wall, with two comrades atop the wall ready to grab my arms and help me over, but the toes of my boots slipped on the well-worn planks of the wall. My arms were in the firm grip of the men atop the wall. The lower part of my body was simply flung full length by the slip, with the full weight of equipment around my waist, I felt something tear in my stomach muscle area and my legs went dead.

I screamed with pain and the men holding my arms let go, leaving me free to drop to the ground. The training NCO rushed up and shouted, "On your feet man, you are either a stretcher-case, or you are carrying on to the finish, which?" My fellow sufferers all gathered around and encouraged me to carry on. We now only had the run back to camp to finish; somehow half hanging between the shoulders of two helpers, I somehow managed to finish the run.

However, next day it was obvious that I was not going to complete the last two days of training. My stomach muscles and thigh muscles were locked up and I could hardly move. The camp MO ordered bed and rest for the next few days. At the end of the training period, each man went before the training officer for a performance interview. Those that were considered to have failed to meet the standard were offered the option of returning to their original unit or going through the whole of the training again. Except where it was deemed they would not benefit from a re-course.

My interview was short and to the point, "You were doing well up to the point where you failed on the wall. I recommend that you accept the re-course option and go through the training again, almost all get through the training the second time around." I accepted the re-course option and then spent a few days waiting for a new course of trainees to assemble. Of course, there were the usual comments like "Why did you have to do it twice?" In the main, I let them draw their own conclusions; like 'I had failed to meet the standard'.

Second time around, I was fitter than most of the new team, particularly on the assault course, and found it easier to keep up with the rest. From Aldershot we moved to Upper Heyford, for the actual parachute training, under RAF instructors. The day normally started with a five-mile run in PT kit, such a nice change from the full battle-order kitted runs we had become used to. We did not have the starting pace to keep up with our RAF instructor, but our earlier training gave us the staying power at a constant pace for the whole distance. After the first morning, the starting pace had noticeably been reduced.

The early training was in a hanger, jumping off small benches, with our feet turned at 45 degrees to the normal and doing a side roll across our bodies on the floor. Later, the same exercise was repeated, but instead of a bench, it was from the back of a moving 15 cwt army truck. Then came the training in fitting the parachute harness. Hanging there in your harness made you well aware of whether you had adjusted the straps between your crotch. If adjusted firmly around your upper thigh, it would not slip up around your crotch. Those who had failed to heed the advice given on how to adjust the harness were duly seen to hang with a distressed look on their faces. If spoken to, they would reply in a high pitched 'falsetto' voice.

There was then the device to simulate what it would be like bouncing along on the airstream, after you had jumped out of an airplane. This device was simply a slack heavy cable running past a mock-up of a Dakota airplane door. The sudden weight of a jumper on the cable caused it to bounce and shake the jumper in a sinusoidal motion. We would eventually have to complete seven day jumps and one night jump from an airplane, to complete the training course and earn our parachute wings and the extra pay that we would gain. First, they had to introduce us to the parachutes, their care and the people who packed them. I guess they wanted us to have a reasonable level of confidence in our equipment because British Paratroopers, at that time, were not equipped with a reserve-chute. The 'chute' packing sheds were aircraft hangers. On entering, the first sight to greet us was the chutes all hanging from the roof to dry out any moisture they had collected in use. The next step was that each chute, in turn, was stretched full length on a long table. The tables were manned by half a dozen WAAFs, who examined every inch of the silk canopy for any sign of damage, then each rigging lie in turn and finally, the harness itself. After passing this inspection, the chutes were stretched out on individual tables and packed by a WAAF packer. Watching them gave you confidence that they knew what they were doing. Before they would let us loose from airplanes, there was a few more stunts to perform, in order to convince our instructors that we were up to it. In the roof of the training hanger was a tiny little cabin with a narrow steel ladder leading up to it; we had all often wondered what particular torture was carried out up there and now were about to find out. Our instructor explained to us that we would each, in turn, run across the hanger and climb the ladder and get into the cabin. Up top in the cabin would be another instructor, who would show us how to fasten a small belt around our chests and then we were to jump out of the door of the cabin! "Don't we get any parachutes?" everyone asked. "No," said the instructor, and continued, "there is a light steel cable attached to your chest-belt and the drum holding that cable has a 'multi-bladed fan' attached to it. The fan hitting the air will slow down your rate of descent." We were not completely convinced, but by this time we were of a mind to 'have a go' at anything.

One by one we went up to the cabin and jumped, the fan blade was extremely effective in slowing down the rate of descent to the hanger floor, something like 16 feet/sec.

The next piece of apparatus we were subjected to was the 'tower jump', which was a 75-foot-high tower. At the top of tower was a boom, with a steel pulley at its end, around which was wound a steel cable on to a hydraulically-damped drum. The theory, in this instance, was that the drum speed would be damped to one which was within the jumper's safety margin. To add to this, the ground around the landing area was dug up to soften it and then covered with a strong rope net. The ordeal of making your way up endless steel ladders until one reached the platform on the top was such that I think rather than walk back down, most jumpers would have jumped, regardless of the effectiveness of the damping. Once on the platform, the instructor checked that your harness was fitted correctly, then connected it up to the end of the steel cable. The jumper was instructed to move to the edge of the platform. Although the platform had a safety rail around it, with a chain across the gap through which the jumper must pass, standing there with the tower swaying in the wind for those few seconds before being ordered to jump were guaranteed to bring on the odd attack of vertigo. The landing was probably the hardest we had to endure. Most felt as though their hipbones had been driven halfway up into their chest cavity. To amplify the feeling, their boots forced the rope netting several inches into the soft earth.

The day dawned when we were to draw our first parachutes, not to jump from an airplane but to jump from a balloon, tethered on 700 feet of cable, to a winch truck. The balloon had a box-like structure hanging beneath it with an open doorway, clearly visible from the ground. The jumpers, now had their chutes on and were nervously asking their neighbour whether the fitting looked correct. They then loaded themselves, in their turn, into the balloon cage, six at a time. The winch-truck then unwound the cable to get the balloon back to its operating height, with a jump instructor and six jumpers on board. In turn, each jumper was ordered to stand in front of the doorway, which had a safety bar across it at the time and then his static line (the one that will open the jumper's chute) is attached to an overhead rail. The jump instructor then checked the jumper's harness adjustment. After giving some last minute advice about the impending jump, he would utter the commands "Red light on, stand to the door". At this time the safety bar is pulled aside, followed by the command, "Green light on, GO."

That first step is the biggest step one can imagine, it's a straight drop until your parachute opened, and I can only think that it must be the same for free-fall parachutists. The trick of turning your feet off at an angle did seem to make a jumper roll across his body, spreading the impact, which for the first jump was hardly noticed in the excitement. Then if there was any wind, the jumper would go full speed across the airfield on his back, until he rolled on to his stomach and hauled on the rigging lines to collapse his chute. After the jump, each jumper had to roll up their chutes and carry them over to the parachute recovery truck. As each jumper came out of the balloon, a jump supervisor on the ground coached each of them over a 'loud-hailer', correcting their position for landing, or the correct grip of their rigging lines ready for a landing. I do not remember what my instructions were, I was too preoccupied with getting down on terra firma in one piece.

The day dawned for the drops from an airplane and although we all felt trained and ready to jump, there were still mild feelings of apprehension as to what might go wrong, and it was not always related to injury or fatal accidents. The stories of how some men had panicked in the plane doorway, refusing to jump, or simply just frozen in the doorway, unable to move backwards, or forwards, with arms rigidly pressing them away from the door. These stories did not help the mild lack of confidence jumpers felt at this juncture.

I guess we need not have worried, we had been drilled so repetitively to respond to the 'Red light on, stand to the door' and 'Green light on, GO', I think we now responded without any conscious awareness of what we were actually doing. It would probably be the same for plane jumps.

A misty day dawned and 16 jumpers trooped into the old DC3, 8 on either side of the aircraft, and also two RAF jump instructors. They placed themselves at the rear of the aircraft; it was noticeable that they wore 'free-fall' chutes, instead of the same static line chutes we wore. The plane was unlined, uninsulated, with all the ribs showing and the canvas bucket seats hardly built for comfort on long journeys.

The jump instructors briefed us on the jump we were about to make and touched on the subject of jumpers refusing the jump, and claimed that 99.9% of all trainees make their full quota of training jumps. If anyone did refuse a jump, he would be given as many chances as necessary to make the jump before the plane landed.

However, it was spelled out that after the plane had landed, any jumper still on-board would have automatically failed the training course. With everyone standing up, having clipped their static line strapped to a cable running the length of the plane, we started to move towards the door, and the feelings of apprehension had disappeared. Once the first man out had heard that 'Green light ON' and felt the light tap on his shoulder from the jump dispatcher, he was through the doorway and in an instant gone from sight. After that just as fast as each man could step to the doorway and get that light pat on his shoulder, he was gone. It seemed that the moment the doorway cleared, another jumper filled it immediately and then he too was on his way down. Going through that plane doorway each jumper executed what was probably the smartest left turn in his life.

One's body did not seem to fall downwards, instead it was borne in a shallow curve downwards and beyond the rear of the aircraft by the velocity of the plane's slipstream. At the same time, the parachute was opened by the 'static-line' still attached to the airplane. The chute came out stretched, on the rigging lines, ahead of the jumper and the static-line. The outer cover remained attached to the plane.

Then as the canopy passed out of the main force of the slipstream, it would slowly develop and fill; the jumper would swing down under a fully opened parachute. The first part of the downward journey was unreal, one felt detached from space and time, just suspended there. In fact, you were falling at some considerable speed, but without something nearby to gauge any movement against, you were unaware on movement.

Suddenly, you are only 50 feet above the ground, which appears to be rushing up at you at some enormous speed. You try to remember all the instructions on how to manoeuvre your chute down to a soft landing, aiming for somewhere within the drop zone. Usually, the landing was uneventful, particularly when there was little or no ground wind to drag a jumper across the drop zone before he can release himself from the harness. The total time down from 700 feet was something like 36 seconds, and yet most of it seemed like an age.

That was the first paratrooper-style jumps, we had six more in daylight to come and then one night jump, the progress jumpers made became apparent from how far they had to walk from their touchdown point to the parachute recovery truck. The recovery truck was always close to the NAAFI canteen and first jumpers, with no real skills yet in guiding their parachute, had to carry their chute the whole length of the landing field. By the time they got into the NAAFI canteen, it was usually packed out, with no way of getting served in a hurry. By the time jumpers were at least halfway through the course, it was noticeable that their landings were more than halfway towards the recovery truck. One or two jumpers were literally at the tailgate of the truck by the time they were down and had their chute collapsed.

A later jump had to include a 60 lbs of equipment kitbag, strapped to the left leg. The technique, when the time came to jump, was to simply swing the kitbag and your left leg out the plane's doorway. You followed it whether you wanted to or not, inertia was in control and then the slipstream took over. The kitbag was secured to a jumper's leg by two canvas flaps on the side. These were fastened around the jumper's leg by a series of 'eyes' and 'eyelets', with pins securing each one fastened to a pull string for quick release. The kitbag had a 20-foot cord fastened between it and the jumper's harness.

Once the canopy was open and the jumper had stopped swinging wildly beneath his chute, a jumper had to release the pins holding the kitbag, then slowly and steadily lower the kitbag to the full length of the 20 feet of cord. So, there they all were, floating down from the sky, each with a big kitbag hanging 20 feet below them and hopefully, not spinning or swinging wildly.

The theory was that the kitbag hitting the ground just that fraction of a second ahead of the jumper allowed the 'chute' to re-inflate, giving the jumper a softer landing. It seemed to work, providing the kitbag was hanging steady directly below the jumper. If it was swinging, then it could easily hit the jumper when he landed. The night jump was really uneventful, somehow you tended to sense those last 50 feet. The main problem was rolling up your chute and finding the recovery truck in the dark, without any clear idea of how far you had landed from the truck.

There were big celebrations for all those who had passed the course and been presented with their 'parachute wings'. Beer in the NAAFI canteen flowed like water, leaving a few thick heads for next morning. The thing about training courses are that they breed strong camaraderie between the participants, but the strong friendships formed on the course most likely only last the length of the course.

In the case of a parachute training course, we would all be posted back to the same regular battalion and on the same overseas postings. If lucky, those same friendships could endure throughout your army service. Our next move was to a camp at Netheravon, supposedly to await a posting to a battalion. We were to find out that the RAF had to also train pilots to drop paratroopers and guess what we were the 'guinea pigs'. For these jumps you never knew where you would end up, in a pond, in dense undergrowth, or, more often than not, in deep slimy mud.

Eventually, we got back to Aldershot barracks, and the rumour was that we would join a battalion in Palestine. Before that could be confirmed, I was summoned before my company commander for interview. The case he wanted to put to me and several others who had come from the South Staffordshire Regiment was specific. The regiment was one of those the War Department was trying to build up to full strength, to be part of 40,000 man force that the army was sending to Hong Kong, in order to meet a perceived threat from the Chinese Communist army. The latter were massing in Kwantung Province and could attempt to occupy Hong Kong. The government found itself with many regiments massively understrength after the effects of gross post-war demobilisation.

With this new unplanned-for emergency, they had to move men from one regiment to another in order to create enough up-to-strength regiments before they would be able to send two infantry brigades to Hong Kong. This meant that they were grabbing men from where ever they could find them. We were expecting to be posted to Palestine, instead we were posted back to the regiment.

It might be said we had the option, but it was very apparent which direction we were being pushed. There was the parting sweetener that we could always apply for a transfer back to the Parachute Regiment as soon as the emergency was over. In the end, three of us went back to the South Staffordshire Regiment to take embarkation leave and prepare for the long troopship journey to Hong Kong.

My leave before sailing for Hong Kong was something of a non-event, since none of my friends were around during the day. Either they, too, were in the armed services, or they were working. Except for weekends, I was left to my own devices. After all the camaraderie and comradeship that I had just left, leave was just a 'wet squib'. Oh, it was nice to see my mother, but except for weekends, I did not get much time to spend with her.

My days consisted of regular visits to the Snackerie or Rendezvous coffee bars in the hope I would bump into someone I knew. Occasionally, it happened, and I would meet someone to pass away a few hours with. On other days, I would go to the Casino dance hall in Birmingham, which was a regular attraction for men on leave. Girls and women, with nothing better to do, used to frequent the Casino, particularly in the evenings. The billiards hall in Sutton Coldfield was also a daily haunt for a game of snooker with whoever was there. Weekends were a little more exciting, with friends and old girlfriends off from their daily work. All the real activity had to be packed into a couple of weekends, with weekdays reduced to passing the time away.

Back at Whittington Barracks, the place was a hive of activity, with the whole battalion involved in preparing every piece of hardware and equipment we would be taking with us, much of it being trucked down to the docks for loading, in advance of the troops. The ship we were to sail in was the Empire Orwell, a typical troopship of the era, in that the troop accommodation facilities was spartan to say the least. The main troop area was, when empty, like some vast open warehouse. A pattern of tubular pillars spaced about ten feet apart in block patterns, the space between blocks was only slightly wider than ten feet.

These were, obviously, the gangways to move about, when the deck was fully occupied. Each pillar had four strong hooks welded to it, in a pattern, 90 degrees apart.

Each man would have to sling his hammock between a pair of hooks and the space underneath his hammock was where he had to keep his kitbag. All equipment, with the hammock rolled up, had to be stowed neatly, at the end of each night. Near the accommodation deck was a block of washbasins, showers and toilets; all the water was sea water. Everyone had an issue of special soap that would lather with sea water. When that troop-deck was full, you really had the feeling that you were loaded like cattle, the air in a morning lacking oxygen and smelling entirely of unwashed smelly bodies.

Our ship left England with some on deck to see the shoreline disappear from view. Others took advantage of that situation to get their own hammock space sorted and organised, before the main hoard descended to the troop-deck. We were headed for the Bay of

Biscay and some heavy weather. Warnings had been posted, with orders to make sure all our belongings were secure. Nothing should be left loose that could roll about with the motion of the ship in heavy weather. I don't remember much about the 'Bay' weather, a daily routine had been organised for every platoon and section, under their respective NCOs. Starting with on deck physical training, followed by various weapon skill drills, specialised section drills and tasks, such as map reading. In the evening, if we were lucky, they managed the occasional film show.

From the Bay of Biscay, we sailed south and then east into the Mediterranean and on to Port Said in Egypt, to take on water, fuel, fresh fruit and vegetables. The troops were not allowed ashore, the usual number of peddlers were soon alongside in small boats, hoping to sell their wares to the troops on deck, without much success I might add.

We then sailed on through the Suez Canal to Aden, and there we were allowed ashore for a day. A welcome respite from the crowded conditions of the ship. Not that there was much to see in Aden, except the usual traders trying to sell their wares and trinkets, mostly junk. I remember one local rushing up to us and shouting, "Me Scotsman, look me have Scotch skirt!" He had a length of printed tartan pattern cotton wrapped around his waist.

It was at least an opportunity to stretch our legs on land and have a relaxed drink in the local bars, if you could call them that. After that, we were headed out across the Indian Ocean, away from land, giving 'Support' company the chance to fire their guns and mortars from the rear deck of the ship. The six-pounder anti-tank guns were deafening to say the least. Next was the longest stretch of sea between any two ports, Aden to Columbo, on the island of Ceylon. Our arrival at the dockside in Columbo was a day I shall never forget; I could not even conceive the picture of extreme poverty that greeted us as we arrived. The gangs of beggar children all along the dockside, every one of them having to pay part of what they collected to the boss of their respective beggar gang.

These gangs were comprised of young children who had been deliberately disfigured by the binding up of limbs when they were babies, leaving them crippled and disfigured by the time they were ten years old and ready to join a beggar gang. It was both a sickening and pitiful sight and one I shall never forget. We were all glad to get up into town and do a little shopping.

A favourite was sending tea home, for tea was still rationed in England even in 1949. We visited the usual clubs and bars designed to attract troops on leave looking for a little entertainment. Since we were no different, we succumbed to their dubious attractions.

The following morning, we left the Columbo harbour, headed for Singapore and Malaya. We had some troops on-board who were bound for service in Malaya. Whilst on this stretch of the journey, we received information to the effect that a typhoon was building up and heading for Hong Kong. This was to cause us to lay over in Singapore for several days; those few days in Singapore was the 'icing on the cake' for the whole trip.

With plenty of organised activities to fill our day, we were left to our own initiative for night entertainment. A song popular at the time was Frankie Laine's rendition of 'Flower of Malaya'. Looking at all the attractive Malay and Chinese girls, it was easy to see where the inspiration for the song title came from. Days were organised with swimming excursions, film shows, cook-outs. For a few, the odd invitation from the English colonials living in Singapore; in the main for commissioned officers.

Night was something else, dance halls, dancing girls, bars and bargirls. The brilliant lights of the night disguised the 'tatty' look of the old colonial city that had just come through a war, the signs of which were everywhere. Even the famous 'Raffles' Hotel looked tatty on the outside, and I never had the opportunity to examine the inside.

The break in Singapore was thoroughly enjoyed by all, or at least that was the general impression I got talking to everyone as the ship left harbour. There was still a problem with the camp in Hong Kong assigned to the regiment; it seemed that the typhoon had wrecked it. We were to be billeted in a temporary tent camp, near Taipo, in the New Territories on the mainland. On the ship, that prospect did not mean too much to us at the time, but would certainly raise much comment at a later date. It was not realised then that it would require no small amount of ingenuity to cope with conditions that were to come.

It was the monsoon season in the area, and Hong Kong was getting a drenching when we arrived. Because we were moving into a tent camp, there was the question of condition of those tents to be ascertained. An advance party under the quartermaster was sent to survey the condition of the camp and prepare it for the arrival of the main battalion. The advance party found that half the tents had been blown down and those that were standing were flooded out, because no drainage trenches had been dug around them. The quartermaster requested a company to be sent ashore, ready to put up tents and dig drainage ditches around all the tents. It was a couple of days before the main battalion was landed and loaded on trucks for the journey to Taipo. When we arrived at the camp, it was to be greeted by the sight of a muddy morass stretching from the main roadway, down the hillside to the beach. An array of various sized tents was arranged in groups, on level terraces cut from the hillside.

It was raining when we arrived, so between the deep muddy terrain and the weather, it was a problem for each man for find the tent he was assigned to. It did not end there, everyone had to get his kit into his tent without taking in a load of mud. The dress for the day, which was almost over, shorts, boots and gaiters, ideal for rain and mud. By the end of that day we were cold, tired and 'down'. The evening meal, in the big mess tent, was a welcome respite from the confined spaced of the eight-man tents; a 'tot of rum' added to the tea was a real morale booster.

The few weeks we were at Taipo Camp were difficult. Army routines, parades, training exercises still had to be carried out and a smart turnout was expected despite the weather, which had improved. Toilets were long deep pits, on which were erected lines of box style seats. Every few days the line of seats were removed on to a new pit. 'S' company turned its 'flamethrowers' on to the old pit to burn it out, after which it was filled in. We had toilet tents with some fresh water for shaving and the like, but the main wash was down in the sea each evening. By the time we moved, we had solved most of our living problems, even managing to have clean uniforms, not that I am saying we would have liked to have stayed there, but we could have survived there for longer.

However, the move to Queens hill camp was something we had all been looking forward to. It was from there we would operate in our assigned role, in defence of the colony. The camp was still under construction, or reconstruction, after the typhoon. All the large buildings, mess halls, cinema and maintenance garages were of large Nissen style hut design, whilst all the accommodation buildings, although some were unfinished, were of a bungalow design.

With the bungalows, the Chinese labourers and craftsmen first poured a concrete slab as the foundation. They then erected a frame of heavy hardwood pillars as the bungalow frame. Then hollow concrete blocks to fit between the hardwood pillars were cast to makes the walls. Of course, there were provisions for doors and windows. Finally, they put a hardwood roof frame on top and thatched the roof. The result was a bungalow that was attractive, cool in the summer and warm in the cooler season.

There were blocks of these bungalows going up across the breadth of the campsite, which was large. It did mean that because they were not all finished, some people were accommodated in temporary quarters. There were so many Chinese workers employed on the site that it was later to prove a security problem. At that time the number was found to be some 2000. The camp, as usual, had a camp contractor, supplying all of the hair cutting, tailoring, shoe making and shoe repair, soft drinks sweets and fancy goods. Whatever the army wanted the camp contractor could provide, and the Queens Hill contractor was an old hand, having serviced several regiments in India before the British army pulled out. Now they had to look to Africa, Hong Kong and Malaya in order to peddle their services to the army. Slowly but surely, each company got organised and settled down to await the order to move into defensive positions, ready to fight off the Chinese Communist army.

There was a continuous round of military exercises, co-operating with other branches of the army. An example, we were delegated to support any tank attack on the enemy. Which meant that we did a fair amount of getting used to riding around on the back of a tank. That was not the engaging experience it may seem. A tank rolling down a hillside is not luxury travel. Firstly, a tank has all sorts of lumpy pieces all over it. When human shin and bone come into contact with these, the owner has something to remember the contact for quite some time (black and blue). We also had several exercises taking up our assigned defence positions and 'digging in'.

The army established several 'observation posts' along the border of the 'New Territories' to watch and report on activity taking place on the communist side. It was soon apparent that the 'Communist leaders' had no intention of allowing a major communist army to be trapped by the British on one side and the 'Chinese Nationalist army' on the other. We had an observation post near Lok Mau Chow and used to regularly watch the Nationalist aircraft dive and machine gun Communist trucks and supplies at the Lo Wu rail crossing; in fact, missed bullets and empty cases used to rain down on our observation post.

The crossing at Lo Wu had seen a lot of material shipped from the Hong Kong side into China, American trucks that were immediately repainted with a military green coating and the wooden crates in these trucks unloaded. We guessed that these supplies were American aid to the Chinese Nationalist army and this was why the Communist army had pushed so rapidly to the Hong Kong border, not just to capture the supplies but also to cut off a supply route. The Nationalist army attempted to impede that aim by attacking the crossing with American Mustangs that made strafing runs on a daily basis, machine gunning the whole area.

They had problems, if they flew in from the North, then the fire power would strafe the Hong Kong border. If they flew parallel to the border, then there was still the chance that some ammunition could still fall on the British border posts. So, the Chinese Nationalist planes used to loop around over the Hong Kong border and dive on Lo Wu from the Hong Kong side of the border. This must have generated an official complaint at some level. Eventually, a couple of British jet fighters showed up on the border, with the task of blocking the entry of Nationalist fighters into airspace over Hong Kong territory. The attacks eventually ceased, probably because it was obvious by then that the Nationalist army would be defeated on the Chinese mainland. The consequence of this strafing activity was that our observation post had a continuous rainfall of machine-gun cases from the fighters. Including shrapnel from the ground based anti-aircraft fire, a good reason for all of us to keep our heads down. It was all over in a relatively few days.

Alongside this OP was a manually operated boat ferry, where a boatman plied a long oar from the rear of the boat, to move from one side of the river to the other. The cargoes could be people who farmed land on the other side and goods brought up by coolies all the way from Kowloon. It was obvious that the traffic worked both ways and we had no way of knowing who was who. Although occasionally, one of the village children would sidle up to one of us and discretely point to one of the new arrivals, whispering "Corbin, corbin, corbin," meaning that this man was Chinese Communist.

So, it soon became apparent that the Hong Kong police had regular contacts keeping them informed as to what was going on the Communist side. As, no doubt, did the Communist authorities have their contacts, who crossed backwards and forwards to keep them fully informed as to what was going on in Hong Kong.

The OP was manned by an infantry section, who did duties as observers with powerful field glasses, supported by one member of the battalion intelligence section, whose job it was to record and log all the observations. The latter also compiled a daily report, which was telephoned to brigade HQ each day. Since there were many infantry sections in the battalion and only one intelligence section, a weekly change over meant that the eight men of the intelligence section were spread a little thin. In the end, just three of us would do one week on and two off. Life at the OP was camping out, a tent over a hole in the ground with camouflage nets over the whole site, but it was away from the rigours of army discipline, dogma and routine.

After a while, it soon became obvious the other side was well aware of where our OP was located, because we used to watch the change-over of guards at one of their sentry posts. They would always wave and point out our location to each other. We had one visit from the battalion medical officer, who inspected our post and asked whether or not we obtained fruit from the village, and we replied 'yes' and sugar cane. He said that the practice had to stop at once; they did not want dysentery brought back to camp from the OP. One month later, the whole battalion came down with dysentery, and the only people not to get it were the crew manning the OP.

There was always the odd humorous incident involved with the operation of the OP. As an example, because life was pretty cushy most of the time, brigade HQ began to refer to it as 'Butlins Holiday Camp'. It had become the accepted practice when the OP answered the telephone to identify themselves as 'Butlins Holiday Camp'. One day, when the telephone rang, a new National Service recruit answered it and from the look of his face, the conversation was not going well. He said he had answered the call with the usual 'BHC'. There had been a hushed silence from the other end, and then a stern voice had replied, "Then tell Billy Butlin that this is General Evans, and I shall be visiting the OP to inspect it." Of course, we had to defuse the situation and make a complete note of the general's instructions and copy them to battalion HQ.

The visit went off without incident, and no mention was made of the telephone call. As the threat of an invasion by the Chinese Communist army diminished, things began to get refocused and the odd organisational changes were implemented. The old Lok Mau Chau OP was closed down and a new one established with a broader front to observe. The intelligence section members of the team were getting a little fed up with having to pack up every other week and move up to the OP, and at the end of the week reverse the process. Well, Mike Dunn and myself decided that we would not mind doing two or three week duty routines at the OP. This suited us and meant that the section could get on with its other duties and training routines.

Another job that the NCOs of the intelligence section had to do was connected to the vetting of Chinese labour employed in the camp. These labour gangs had a high turnover, and the gang leaders were always requesting the issue of working permits for new workers. The army was the big employer of Chinese labour and anyone entering the colony, legal or otherwise, had to have a work permit before they could seek employment. The easy route around this problem was to work for these labour gangs for a limited period, knowing they would be cheated and exploited by the gang bosses. In the end, they would have a valid permit to work in the colony.

Our part in all this was to run a truck loaded with new applicants on to Hong Kong Island. There a special unit manned by a mix of Hong Kong police and Chinese-speaking NCOs in the Intelligence Corps ran the vetting operation. The police had the job of weeding out illegal immigrants, often with criminal backgrounds. Intelligence Corp NCOs had the job of interrogating applicants for information on what they had observed about Communist army activities north of the border in Kwantung province. They also acted as interpreters for any questions we had to put to them. How they had contacted their respective gang boss? When had they had entered the colony? Our questions arose from a suspicion that many 'gang bosses' had been using workers in their labour gang for long periods of time. This before they put them forward to be vetted for work permits. That they were using this situation to further exploit the workers in their gang. Eventually, those that had been cleared through the vetting procedure were then fingerprinted, photographed and then issued with the highly prized work permit. Of the remainder, many were earmarked for deportation across the border. Others were held for further investigation, and some were arrested for a variety of crimes committed in the colony. We always came back to camp with far fewer Chinese workers in the truck than the number we started out with.

Another job the intelligence section had was to accompany battalion patrols that scoured their area of the New Territories for smugglers. These were taking strategic supplies out of the colony, as well as organising as groups of illegal immigrants smuggled into the colony. These patrols operated at night for the obvious reason that the smuggling activities were best carried out at night. These patrols normally included a Hong Kong police NCO, but not always, so often we would have to turn any captives over to the police at designated police barracks. The strategic materials smuggling mainly consisted of petrol in unmarked sealed tin cans. Each 'coolie' in the team would carry two cans, slung from each end of a carrying pole. I once tested the weight of this load, and I can assure you that I could not have carried the load a hundred yards, let alone the 20 odd miles they had carried it. Admittedly, there is a technique to the way a coolie balances the load and a rhythm to the way they move with the load. The coolies were a mixture of men, women and teenagers; each carried a 20 gallon load of petrol. Some of the coolie gangs were a family group. The police expressed the opinion that these people were not significant in the traffic. They probably could only organise a rare single trip, to make some money for the family. It was the large organised gangs of coolies, that operated on a large scale, that the police were after.

If we caught any petrol smugglers, the policeman in the patrol would make the decision as to what action was to be taken. If an arrest was made, one can of petrol was held as evidence and the remainder destroyed on the spot.

Dealing with illegal immigrant parties was much more difficult. These were led usually by gang members, representing the crime organisation, running the illegal traffic. It was found that these gangs told their clients that if the British soldiers caught them, they would be shot on sight. They should stay with and obey the party leaders, who would protect them. These gangs had a range of strategies for when they had crossed the border.

The commonest one was to take away all their clients' valuables. Then abandon the people, to eventually be found by a British army patrol. Another was the establishment of a holding site, at a house in one of the villages. Whether they got the owner's cooperation by threats of violence or monetary compensation was never certain. The gang members in this case were well armed. Ready to shoot their way out, these were the better organised. In these circumstances, the illegal immigrants were broken up into small parties. Two, three or four people were then transported down into Kowloon by road. Once there, they disappeared into the commerce of the colony. These groups were usually the well-educated and had the financial resources to pay the smuggler gangs. The groups the army mainly came across were those exploited groups who were robbed of their belongings. Abandoned in the hills of the New Territories to find their own way into Kowloon and on to the main island. In the case of these groups, we usually escorted them to the nearest police post and handed them over.

On the social side, when you had leave that is, both Kowloon and Hong Kong island had several 'servicemen's clubs'. On the Kowloon side, there was the 'Nine Dragons Club', where you could get a low-cost meals and dance. The latter was 'taxi dancing', where you purchased tickets and gave one to each partner you danced with. On the Hong Kong side, there was the 'China Fleet Club', which was huge and extremely popular for entertainment and meals. It was, of course, the big 'tombola' game winnings that also influenced its popularity. Servicemen on leave for a weekend, or a week, could rent accommodation in these clubs at very reasonable rates. Because the demand was high, you had to book well in advance. Apart from the servicemen's clubs, there were also scores of little clubs and bars, peddling drinks and taxi dancing, as well as prostitutes. The possibility of being 'mugged' for whatever money you had on you was also was high on the list.

Occasionally, you met English or European families living in Hong Kong and were invited to their homes. One weekend, when Mike Dunn had the same weekend pass as myself, he came up with the suggestion that we try and locate a distant uncle of his, who family members now believed was living in the colony. Well, we used up all the weekend before we finally located his relative living at an address in Repulse Bay on Hong Kong island. We were invited to telephone on the next weekend pass we had, to come and visit them at Repulse Bay, for a meal and a swim. There was quite a time to wait before we both could get a pass on the same weekend. Eventually, we did and made that first of many visits, for a meal and a swim. That first visit was, of course, mainly preoccupied with Mike telling his uncle about the UK side of the family. Mike's uncle then updated him with an outline of his life, since he had left the UK as a much younger man.

Eddy Dunn was a man whose exploits you could have written a top-selling book about. On future visits, over a few drinks, we listened to not only Eddy's exploits but to his other guests. Many of whom had been prisoners of the Japanese, in either Shanghai, or

Hong Kong. All future visits were either Mike or myself, seldom the two of us together. Eddy Dunn was a short stocky man in stature and at 56 years of age, pretty fit, being a golf fanatic who got up at six am most days to play. His wife, 28 years old and of 'white Russian' extraction, he had met in a Japanese prisoner of war camp in Shanghai. Where, as a trained nurse, she had nursed him through some illness. On release from that camp, they had married and eventually moved to Hong Kong. There they had established themselves in a family home, with their two-year-old baby daughter. Eddy's story started with him being the foreign correspondent in Harbin, for a UK News-paper around the mid-1930s. At the time, opinion seemed to be that it was the Telegraph, but that is not confirmed. During those years, Harbin was a hotbed of intrigue between Japan, Russia and China. However, the Russia influence was noticeably the strongest after they had built the railway to Harbin (an extension of the Trans-Siberian Railway).

There was a strong contingent of 'white Russians' settled there after defeat in the Russian civil war. In all, there were 53 nationalities, speaking 45 different languages, represented by some 16 foreign consulates established there. It seemed that this was the environment that Eddy found himself in. In keeping with the thinking of many, he had nursed a desire to move his life to Shanghai. At that time, he did not have the financial resources to make a success of such a move.

It was whilst he was wrestling with the ideas of such a move that he made friends with a young Ukrainian now living in Harbin. We will call him Stan for now, someone who also had the same aspirations about a move to Shanghai as Eddy. Stan was a qualified geologist/mining engineer, who had worked on surveying the route ahead of the actual construction of the railway.

His task was to ascertain the underlying geological structure ahead of the track construction. His father had also been one of the senior engineers with the construction team, who had now settled in Harbin, which meant that Stan had family ties in Harbin. Nevertheless, he confided in Eddy, that he intended to move his life to Shanghai, which was where all the focus and activity seemed to be heading in those days. He further confided his plan to prospect for 'placer gold' in Manchuria as a means to finance the move.

He explained to Eddy that 'placer gold' is the gold that is panned from the inside bends of powerful river flows. That the tiny pieces of gold are flung out of the river flow as it rides around the sharp bend. He said that he had found such a site, where he estimated that in six months they could pan enough gold to finance both their aspirations in Shanghai. Stan had thought the idea through to the smallest detail and said the main risks were from Russian army patrols and Manchurian nomadic bandits. He added that neither of these were likely to pass near to the site he had chosen. Robbery would be the biggest threat they would face, as they got nearer to Harbin on their return journey. He said they would need to equip themselves to be self-sufficient for the whole of the six months. This would mean a fair number of beasts of burden or oxcarts to carry it all, and he listed everything they would need. The one weakness in his plan was that he did not have the 'seed money' to get the idea off the ground.

Eddy spent days mulling over Stan's plan; first, could he muster the money to finance the enterprise? He thought he could just about manage it, but then did he have confidence in Stan? Enough to believe that he actually knew what he was talking about. After all, he had only known the man for a very short time. But to Eddy this seemed like the solution to the problem that he had nurtured for so long. He thought he was a good enough judge of people to be able to say that Stan was a man who gets things done or dies in the attempt.

So, to cut a long story short, they put together their supplies and transport and spread the story that they were going on an academic search for prehistoric fossils. When the enterprise came to a successful end and they had smuggled the gold back into Harbin, they then faced their biggest risk, they had to take others into their confidence. They had to get it melted down into bars in order to smuggle it into Shanghai. Somehow or other, they managed to do all of this. After moving to Shanghai, they had to decide on what sort of business enterprise they would finance with the gold.

Here is where Eddy's experience and knowledge came to the fore. He had long ago identified printing and publishing as a potentially booming industry in the multicultural city that Shanghai was becoming. The publishing enterprise was a success, and they both prospered far beyond anything they could have hoped for, with just the gold itself to rely on. The downturn came when the Japanese invaded China, including Shanghai. Eddy and Stan were interned with the rest of the foreign nationals in a prison camp, until the Japanese were finally defeated. They both had endless stories to tell of their experiences as prisoners. The main incident that effected Eddy was his illness and the attention he received from Maria, a very young and attractive Ukrainian nurse, which culminated, on their release from prison camp, in his asking her to marry him.

Stan and Eddy managed to salvage a lot of the old publishing business and get it going again, so that in a very short time they were stable and thriving. But the storm clouds were still around and they soon realised that having survived the Japanese threat, they were now about to become embroiled in the conflict between the Nationalist and Communist Armies of China. They quietly hatched a plan to maximise the market value of their publishing business and then sell out. The plan was to move themselves and their assets to Hong Kong; after all, Eddy was now married. He was anxious to start a family without the threat of war and conflict at every turn.

The selloff was accomplished and the move to Hong Kong went off without any problems. They moved all their financial assets with them. Before leaving Shanghai, they had recognised that now the war with Japan was over, there were vast shortages of strategic materials and metals. Trading in these was the way ahead for them specifically, with respect to rubber and tin. They bought an existing trading company in Hong Kong. This gave them the right credibility to trade in tin and rubber, through existing connections for trading with Malaya, where the tin and rubber resources existed. We never actually met Stan, Eddy's partner, because after the business was floated in Hong Kong, he moved to Malaya, to organise and monitor the supply of tin and rubber they needed to operate their business successfully. Most of European-run businesses in Hong Kong at that time were run on the 'compradore' system; the compradore mediated between the company and Chinese interests, including labour. Therefore, Eddy's company had a compradore, who held a sort of bourgeois position in the company. So, when we met Eddy Dunn, it was as a man who ran a very successful trading company. A married man with a very young wife (he was 56 at the time), with a two-year-old baby daughter, living in a luxurious house on Repulse Bay, with a houseful of servants and its own private beach. If you never heard his story, you could have been forgiven for seeing him as the typical colonial. One who has made it rich by exploiting the Chinese population, a view that could not have been farther from the truth.

We were to hear many amazing stories from the people he had around him, friends from Shanghai and Harbin. Stories that told of life and death in Japanese prison camps. The married women describing the problems of being pregnant, and then giving birth, in a prison camp, where medical help was non-existent. Where they had to rely on each other for help. They had all survived, and their personalities had been strengthened by the experiences they had endured.

The society that Eddy and his friends moved in was that of the wealthy through their own efforts. Not that of the British colonials, who mainly lived on the 'peak' area and who believed that the higher up the peak you lived, the higher was your position in Hong Kong society. Almost all of Eddy's friends belonged to a mixed marriage society. Europeans married to Chinese, to Eurasians and a general mix of ethnic origins with regard to marriage partners. Europeans married to foreigners was not an acceptable situation in the British colonial society, which inhabited the 'peak'. It was soon apparent that there were at least two different strata in Hong Kong society. I remember meeting an English prison officer who was married to an extremely attractive Eurasian wife, who told me that because of his marriage, they were always exempted from invitations to government official parties, functions and celebrations.

Because Maria was Ukrainian, her menus for Sunday lunch reflected her origins and vodka was always served with lunch. Eddy had some of his own Irish tastes maintained. One example of which was he would always have a big glass jug on the table that was filled with a mix of Guinness and soda water. When available, he would pander to a love of oysters, by getting a few dozen freshly flown in and everyone had to eat them. Eddy's life had been so eventful that you could have written several exciting novels based on the descriptions of his escapades. Eddy, once again, had to make a decision about moving, to safeguard the future of his wife and daughter.

The colony in general believed that the Communist army would eventually occupy Hong Kong. With that in mind, he started to move the operating headquarters for his trading company to Australia. The last we heard of him was that he had moved there with his family to ensure his wife and daughter were safe. After those visits to Eddy Dunn's came to an end, life became very boring. There were no rumours about any new posting to brighten the future. A request for a transfer to the Parachute Regiment ended up in some endless file-tray loop, never to be seen again. Promotion to sergeant seemed a hopeless ambition; it was almost a case of waiting to fill dead man's shoes.

Well, to digress from life in Hong Kong, there were now two new theatres of conflict about to boil over. The USA president had asked United Nations to approve armed intervention in the conflict between North and South Korea. Whilst in Malaya, the Chinese Communist guerrillas were spreading propaganda inciting the core people of Malaya to fight for an end to British colonial rule. For emphasis on their intentions, they started attacking and killing managers and supervisors of rubber plantations and tin mines, including their families, an attempt to disrupt production and deprive the UK of income from these national resources.

In the end, the British colonial government declared a state of emergency in Malaya. The British army's regular strength had been sorely depleted by the mass exodus of World War II soldiers. Without any strategies to rebuild it on the part of MOD, there was now a problem of manpower to deal with any new emergencies. The National Service Act, and the new recruits it brought into the army to rebuild the strength of the infantry regiments, was the government's answer to the situation. These young men, with little more than six weeks' basic training, were expected to replace the thousands of battle-hardened soldiers who had left the army.

These were the men they sent to deal with the new emergency situation that had developed in Malaya. Men without any in-depth training with weapons and none at all in terms of jungle warfare. Against them would be the communist guerrilla fighters, who had honed their jungle fighting techniques against the Japanese soldiers. They were well-armed with captured Japanese weapons as well as those supplied by the UK government, to carry on their guerrilla war against the Japanese army.

It was no doubt this situation that prompted the appearance on noticeboards throughout the British army. In particular, the noticeboards of regiments stationed in Hong Kong, asking for volunteers from regular army NCOs for service in Malaya. In particular, units were asked to recommend regular army NCOs for a 12-week training course at the jungle training school at Kota Tinggi in Malaya.

Nothing seemed to be happening for our battalion and promotion seemed a long ways off. Following the advice of some of the long-serving NCOs, that in a peacetime army you are only going to get promotion by gaining specialist qualifications, 'biting the bullet', I applied for the course. I was immediately summoned before the IO, who questioned my motives in applying, adding that the current intelligence sergeant would soon be moving to one of the rifle companies, to take up a promotion to colour sergeant.

I knew the answer to that because I had already discussed my plans with him. He had told me that he himself would be waiting to fill dead man's shoes for a promotion. In the end, I was recommended for the course and sailed to Singapore in the first half of 1951. I can't remember too much about settling in during those early days of training; I guess that was because they didn't give you much time to settle in. They were obviously in a hurry to get some NCOs through the course and post them to the regiments already serving in Malaya. My companions on the course were from various regiments, some from the Parachute Regiment, Worcestershire Regiment, others from the Welch Regiment.

There were two more South Staffordshire Regiment men, apart from myself, also from Hong Kong. There was a mix of regulars and national servicemen on the training course. The latter were soldiers who had shown strong leadership qualities and would no doubt be given their stripes on successful completion of the course. The course had a fair amount of classroom content. The emphasis was on jungle fieldcraft, survival and stealth when tracking the enemy.

The first few days were spent testing our proficiency with the standard weapons, Le Enfield rifle, Sten gun, Bren gun, PIAT and Browning Revolver. We were also introduced to the shortened version of the Le Enfield rifle, with the thick shoulder pad on the butt. This was introduced for close contact terrain, such as the jungle environment.

I made close friends with a man from the Worcestershire Regiment and another from the Welch Regiment. We were together on most of the training patrols and campouts. The climate was hot and humid. I suddenly found that in that type of moist heat environment, I was very prone to 'prickly heat' all around the back of my neck and shoulders. Out on training, I had to resort to wearing a surgical gauze scarf around my neck to keep my sweaty jungle greens from chaffing the prickly heat.

There was at that time a group of incursion teams under 'Mad Mike' Calvert, comprised of a mix of old Parachute Regiment men, ex-Chindits and some Gurkas. These were dropped into the jungle as small teams to hunt down MCP guerrillas. This operation was deemed to be a failure, due to the lack of discipline in the teams. The Malayan high command was desperately searching for a strategy to outwit the MCP guerrillas, who had honed their fighting and jungle-craft skills fighting against the Japanese.

They now had enough influence, or grip, on the native population to get information about the British army's every move. Add to this that none of the troops sent out from England had any training in jungle fighting. In fact, in the case of the national servicemen, it was said they had very little training of any kind.

Later in the campaign, a special unit was launched to provide well-trained small incursion teams that could go into the jungle. Whose orders were to hunt the small teams of MCP guerrillas, on their own terms. This special force was given the name 'Malayan Scout Regiment'.

After completing our course, everyone was eager to find out which unit they would be posted to. It appeared that everyone was getting their posting confirmed within a few days, except me. The opinion of most of the instructors was that I would almost certainly be posted to the Worcestershire Regiment. In the meantime, I heard that 27th Brigade, consisting of the Argyle and Sutherland Highlanders, the Leicestershire Regiment and the Middlesex Regiment, were the first UK units in Korea. I had just about given up hope of getting the news of my posting when I was summoned to the training adjutant's office.

In a subsequent interview, I was informed that "regiments in Hong Kong scheduled to fight in Korea had first call on all their regular NCOs". Therefore, I and the other two South Staffords would be sailing back to Hong Kong. I said that I did not think that the order applied to us, because the South Staffordshire Regiment had been rated "too under strength to constitute a credible fighting unit, they would not be going to Korea". The adjutant informed me that he understood that the regiment was to be reinforced with men from UK that we must be on the next boat sailing to Hong Kong.

After we reached Hong Kong, I did not see the other two South Staffords, whom it appeared had jobs at 28 Brigade headquarters at Sek Kong. It was a matter of course that I got all the sarcastic cracks about; "Couldn't you take it, too tough for you, was it?"; "Or was it you couldn't stand all the slimy and crawling things in the jungle?" Back with the intelligence section, I soon got updated on the latest rumours and yes, we were to be reinforced with national servicemen from UK to bring us up to full strength. As time went on and more and more reinforcements arrived by ship, it soon became apparent that the majority were being sent elsewhere. Finally, the word came down from the high command that the South Staffordshire Regiment was still understrength. They no longer constituted a fighting unit that could be sent to Korea. The North Staffordshire Regiment would be posted to Hong Kong, to replace them as part of the 28th Brigade when it sailed for Korea.

So, in 1952, the 28th Brigade, less the South Staffordshire Regiment, was posted to Korea. The South Staffordshire Regiment lost some of its new reinforcements to the regiments already in Korea. The remainder were posted first to Northern Ireland, where they were presented with new colours in Lisburn. From there they moved to Elizabeth Barracks in Minden, Germany. 1951–1952 was a time of turmoil and constant change, and the friends I had served with were either finishing their national service and going home or volunteering to serve with other regiments in either Korea or Malaya. The old intelligence section was no longer recognisable as such. Pete Hall, who had been the intelligence section sergeant since we arrived in Hong Kong, had moved back to a rifle company. There he eventually gained promotion, to colour sergeant and later CSM. I was then promoted to intelligence sergeant to take over Pete's old job. Bill Walker came into the Intelligence Section as corporal and took over my job. At least two people in the section, who were on national service engagements, had completed their term.

By the time we boarded the troopship to return to UK, we were a different bunch. Prior to our departure and right up to the time our destination was announced as Northern Ireland, we still believed we were headed for Korea. The troopship we boarded in Hong Kong had picked up a load of wounded Korean veterans from Japanese hospitals for repatriation to UK hospitals. These would travel in a specially prepared section of the ship.

After we were all boarded and equipment stored below decks, the troopship set sail for Singapore. We were due to pick up more wounded and other troops, due for repatriation to UK. The sight of wounded soldiers, some seriously handicapped, took all the shine off the trip home. Some of the stories told of the experiences in Korea made most of us glad we had escaped the posting and were headed to UK instead. From Singapore we next put in at Columbo in Ceylon, to take on fuel and supplies and after that Aden for the same purpose. As we approached the Suez Canal, we received the news of anti-British riots in Cairo, in which at least 20 British nationals were reported killed and Barclays Bank and many other British owned establishments were wrecked.

We were warned to be wary and on the lookout for sabotage attempts as we went through the canal. Our ship was ordered not to go into Port Said for refuelling and supplies. Instead, we were to put into Valletta Harbour on the island of Malta. The passage through the canal was uneventful. We had a few enjoyable hours ashore on the island of Malta. Once the ship reached UK, the first priority was to get the wounded ashore and on their way to hospital. Walking wounded were taken to special trains for their onward journey to hospitals. The remainder put aboard a fleet of army and civilian ambulances, for the trip to whatever hospital they were assigned too. It was well into the afternoon before we were ashore. Memories of the ferry trip to Northern Ireland, and the onward journey to Ballykinler Camp, are now non-existent. I was not that interested in the army at that time, since I was rapidly approaching the date for the end of my service with the army, which was already six months overdue, due to the emergencies in the Far East. Some attempts had been made to persuade me to sign on and extend my service to the full 12 years. I must admit, I seriously considered it for a while; after all, I was enjoying the social life in the sergeants' mess. I can only imagine what sort of life awaited me in civilian life.

Most of our time was now spent on training, ready for the posting to Germany later in the year. Because we had been so grossly under strength, we were now flooded with national service recruits, just out of basic training and needing reshaping to the regiment's needs. There was some specific training for the new soldiers, as well as the usual level of 'bull', drilling and general discipline training. We had to train up an almost new intelligence section from scratch, ready for Germany. The new section was to travel to Germany, in advance of the main body of the regiment. Once there, to take part in a NATO forces exercise, attached to brigade headquarters as the brigade intelligence section.

In the meantime, life in Northern Ireland was a welcome change, the pubs instead of clubs. Dances in the local village halls and the occasional one in the sergeants' mess, instead of 'taxi dancers'. Before Germany we had a spell of leave. During that time, I meant to fully examine my options and make my decision, as to whether or not to quit the army, evaluate what civilian life had to offer; after all, there was that inherent security of life in the army. You did not have to think about it. I talked to men who had come out of the army after 22 years with a pitiful army pension.

The only skills they had were for a job as doorman at a posh hotel in the 'Corp of Commissioners'. Not an enthralling future from my point of view. I realised that I would have to study for some qualification if I was to find a job that measured up to my expectations. That leave was the make or break time, and I had no one in the family who could give me valid advice, other than suggestions as to what sort of occupation I should train for.

The suggestions were bricklayer; Britain was planning a massive house building program. Tool-making was seen as a demand area with the upsurge in manufacturing. Finally, someone suggested 'design draughtsman' as a secure paying career. The latter was a career path I had at the back of my mind for some time, since I seemed to have some inherent drawing skills. I guess that I was sure I could find some success in 'engineering design'. At that time, I had no inkling as to how I would get started.

Back at camp, the intelligence section and an advance party for the main battalion was packing ready for the trip to Minden in Germany, the Channel ferry and then a train to the 'Hook of Holland'. That journey to Germany was uneventful. Our arrival at Elizabeth Barracks simply meant we had to unpack and sort out our field gear, which we needed for the NATO exercise, and await the transport from brigade HQ to take us to the Osnabruck area. Our part of the exercise was to take place near there.

I do not remember that much about the exercise, just those little 'highlights' that made life bearable. One instance I do remember was that we normally worked from an office truck. Every morning we had to drive through this small German village, which had a store that sold fresh bread and some essential groceries. The little corner shop you might say, and like England many food items were still virtually unobtainable. This little shop did not have any coffee, and we had ample supplies of the stuff. Each morning we would go to the shop and ask for fresh bread rolls, ham and butter; the bread was fresh baked and the ham and butter was the local farm produce. We would slice and butter the bread rolls and then stuff them with thick slices of farm ham, one roll for each member of the intelligence section. After which we would barter with the lady, who ran the shop, for how much coffee she wanted. Sometimes she wanted a mix of cigarettes and coffee as payment. These rolls were the height of our day, the rolls were so fresh baked, really crisp, and the butter and fresh ham, so different from the tinned stuff we were used to. I think we would have had a riot on our hands if we had changed the route out.

Another little snippet that sticks in my memory was an occasion when we were away from our comfortable office truck, camped out in a field position with only a couple of canvas sheets from which to erect an improvised office, for our intelligence activities and situation maps. People were not catered for, not even for sleeping, and as we had been having days of torrential rain, everybody was soaked to the skin. Probably without any dry kit left to change into. The troops alongside us were units in support of tanks, and they were all nice, cosy and dry sleeping under the tanks, only having reasons to curse whenever they had to leave the shelter, under the tanks. The morale of our section, on the other hand, was at a very low ebb. To rescue the situation the IO ordered the section out on patrol to update our situation maps with the latest positions of the brigade units. After shivering in the lashing rain, it was a relief to get up and move. The going was tough through deep mud, 'one step forward and two back', almost all the way out and back. We were away just over nine hours and by the time we arrived back, the IO had organised some hot food brought up into the lines, for us. It was noticeable that everyone ate every morsel and afterwards curled up in the pouring rain and with no exceptions went to sleep without a murmur.

It was good to get back to the comfort of Elizabeth Barracks and, of course, by this time the whole battalion was installed and fully functional. Meaning that it was back to the routine 'bull' and discipline of barracks life. As someone who was leaving the army, I was entitled to apply for some form of pre-release training course. The purpose of which would be to enhance my prospects of finding gainful employment on leaving the army. The selection of courses was very limited, but 'accounting' seemed the best available, whilst there were none in line with my employment aspirations. The accounting course also had the advantage that it was located in the centre of Hamburg.

From the reports of all who had already attended the course, the night life in Hamburg seemed to be the biggest attraction. So rather than have no course at all, I signed up for the accountancy course and a hopefully a little 'high life' in downtown Hamburg. The accommodation was at an ex-German Panzer barracks, where all the security guards and camp staff where displaced persons, mainly Poles and Rumanians. The 'Reeperbahn' in the St Pauli district of Hamburg, was where it was all happening. It was where everyone headed, as soon as classes were over and everyone had changed into civilian clothes. A lot of the clubs were 'off-limits' to military personnel and the military police patrols paid regular visits to many of the establishments to enforce the regulations. Which is one of the reasons why everyone changed into civilian clothes.

I had made friends with someone on the course who had married a local German girl. As one would expect, he had become very proficient in speaking the language, even acquiring a local accent. With all this in mind he led us to the clubs where most of the action was. Assuring everyone that with him doing the talking, everyone would assume we were non-military, working for the 'Control Commission'. However, we soon discovered how weak this premise was. When one evening in a particularly notorious night club, a waiter approached our table and announced, "Gentlemen, the military police are in the lobby; the back door is this way." We usually crawled back into barracks in the early hours of the following morning, arriving in class somewhat less than half awake. The course did give one a good grounding in 'basic accounting practice'. How to set up the accounts for a small business enterprise, and certainly, I thought it was worth the effort.

Once back at Elizabeth Barracks in Minden, I was literally 'back pedalling' to kill the time remaining, before I returned to the UK for demob. My final night in Germany ended with a farewell party in the sergeants' mess, and I do not remember much, until I awoke on the train headed for the 'Hook of Holland', that final crossing on the ferry back to UK and the reality of demob. So, I was finished with the regular army, discharged from the Parachute Regiment, transferred to the reserve for a further seven years, which could mean that I could be recalled to active service if there was any 'national emergency'.

It was about this time that reality really began to settle in, the big question was what to do now. It was not just the question of getting a job because there were a fair amount of jobs about. I was seeking some career path that would equip me for my working life. I was no longer the sort of age where I could sign up for an apprenticeship. I did not have any real skills that would transfer over from my army experience. The government of the day had to deal with thousands of men coming out of the forces after World War II.

To cope with this they launched many programmes, designed to aid ex-servicemen to enter a new career. One scheme was funding university degrees in law sciences and medicine to allow ex-service personnel to train for careers in those areas that had been starved of people by the demands of war. They had also organised initiatives in leading manufacturing companies to launch comprehensive training programmes, in-depth programmes to train the people they needed for them to be able to switch to peacetime products. These were companies striving to relaunch the British car industry. Companies in electronics and aircraft industry as well the newly spawned missile and space industry.

One such company was GEC, who had divisions involved in almost all areas of technology. As well as operating a number of research and development establishments for the Ministry of Supply to design and test new weapon systems for our future defence needs. GEC did not have too strong a reputation in the 'good pay' category. However, they had an unrivalled one for the thoroughness of their training and the quality of the technical people they produced from their training programmes. GEC had their basic apprenticeship programmes for technician level skills, which was a five-year programme, with sandwiched studies to ONC or HNC levels. They also had their graduate training programmes for degree-level entry, which entailed a two-year programme with time spent in all departments, both technical and commercial. Now they were going to introduce a third training programme to train people for employment as 'mechanical' and 'electrical' designers. The programme for these people was different from the others. People the programme was designed for may not have any applicable qualifications or industrial experience. They were in an older age group than say apprentices, and they may not have had the in-depth education for any graduate programme.

The scheme was a three-pronged concept where the participants would be given work experience in all the technical departments as well as assigned work later on in the main design office. This work experience was to be sandwiched with a technical college study programme to HNC level.

Well, after many visits to the 'employment office', I was eventually acquainted with the GEC programme. This was associated with their establishment at Brown's Lane Coventry. I had gained a lot of basic machine processes experience in my work prior to joining the army. The opportunity to train as a 'mechanical designer', a job that would have all the credentials, at that time, of stability and a reasonable level of income. Appeared to be a good fit for my needs, being 'mechanically minded' probably had something to do with it. I did think that programme with GEC was a good step in the direction I was attempting to travel. A start on a chosen career path for me.

Of course, I then had to deal with the 'bureaucracy' side of applying. Sending for application forms, filling in the forms, waiting for an interview appointment, waiting for the interview result. Waiting for an assignment on the next training group intake, all of this took many weeks, in fact months. As I had to earn money to live on, I took a job in a small factory as a 'tool-setter', having explained to them that I was waiting for a placement on a government job training programme. They accepted that I would expect to leave giving only one week's notice. The tool-setting job was oily and dirty, which probably explains why there was the vacancy. The company manufactured a range of goods that had 'wire-formed' handles. The raw material for which had to go through a straightening operation and then a series of 'cold-heading' operations, followed by forming and assembly operations. All these operations required a fair amount of lubricant; this resulted in all the materials dripping with oil. Right up to the time they were washed and dried prior to 'plating'. But whatever the drawbacks, it was regular work that gave me the money I needed to live on.

By this time, with very little social life, I used to think back to the social life in the sergeants' mess, the whole camaraderie of army life and even wondered whether I had made a mistake in coming out. I think I did actually consider re-enlisting. The day dawned when I was accepted into the training programme and the following Monday was the big start day. I had been given plenty of warning of the date, so that I could work off my notice with the 'tool-setting' job. The one thing I had not taken into account was the travelling problems, of getting from Sutton Coldfield to Brown's Lane Coventry. This in the end involved catching three different buses and to arrive on time, I had to start early and allow a margin. The first days were organisational ones, touring the site, showing us the activities that were carried out on the site, touring the various departments and filling out more forms. After that we had to sign up at a convenient technical college for the HNC programme in either mechanical or electrical engineering, then inform the personnel office as to which college we were registered with. We would have three evenings of study and one working day. If I registered at the Coventry Technical College, then after a long evening of study, I would still have the long bus journey back to Sutton Coldfield. I opted for Aston Technical College, which was not as far to travel home.

In the early days, we were all assigned to the drawing office. First, to assess our ability in that area and then to assess our general abilities, before sending us for work experience in related departments. My experience of drawing maps meant that I was fairly accomplished on a drawing board. My machining experience gave me the ability to visualise mechanical components, before committing them to the drawing board. Those early days on the 'board' were executing the detailed drawings from a 'senior designer's' layout. All our drawings faced much stronger examination and scrutiny than would be the normal process. Those days were pretty boring, and everyone looked forward to the day when they could be involved in more complex design tasks. The site's primary role was the design and testing of systems and controls for missile systems installed on the latest class of navy cruisers. This involved radar systems, waveguide components, servo-mechanisms, electronic circuitry, printed circuit boards, electronics packaging, control consoles, and cooling systems. Whilst the spell on detail drawing allowed time to do homework, we were to find the work experience departments were more work-intensive and did not allow any spare time. However, most of it had a high interest content. I particularly enjoyed my time in mechanical and environmental testing. It was a time that shaped my outlook and my whole approach to systems design in the future.

The study workload meant that I had very little social life in that first three years. On a wage of a little over eight pounds per week, to cover all my travel expenses, my keep at home. What was left over had to suffice for the odd night out with friends, which was not very often. By the time the three years was nearing its end, almost half the original aspiring designers I had started training with had left of their own accord, or been told that they were not making the grade and should find something else to do.

For my part the pressure of studies and the lack of a social life made me look at what the future held for me and was that what I wanted. When I looked around the drawing office, which was large, there were some 40 draughtsmen, designers and engineers. Plus, almost half that number again of women tracers, all with what at that time were considered to be safe and secure jobs, with a major British company. Despite the pressure, I enjoyed the work and friendship with the people I worked with. What social life I did have was enjoyed with work-related acquaintances, both male and female, since the establishment employed a fair number of women in my age group. Thinking back to those times, I realise that most couples were those who met at work and married each other. The fire at Jaguar in 1957 gave most of the drawing office staff the only chance they would ever have to drive a Jaguar. Unfortunately, I was not there to participate. One Saturday morning, those who were in, working overtime, were all suddenly marshalled over to the Jaguar factory to aid in moving cars. From the factory over into the fields on the opposite side of Brown's Lane. The establishment was next door to the Jaguar factory and, in fact, when GEC vacated the premises to move to Portsmouth, the buildings were absorbed into to an expanded Jaguar factory. So, it was logical that is where Jaguar turned for help, as many people who worked at GEC had family members working at Jaguar.

At that time, I was in my mid-twenties, and as I looked around the office at the senior designers and engineers in their late forties or early fifties, some married to tracers in the office, all having a mortgage, a couple of kids, a car, all the trappings of sedate life. All already talking about their plans when they retired. I thought that that was me in 20 years' time. The prospect of those secure but boring 20 years did not seem very inviting. I wanted some challenge in those 20 years before settling down and planning retirement, so I used to spend my spare time with my nose in the 'Situations Vacant' section of the Daily Telegraph. In particular, the section advertising 'Crown Agents for the Colonies' vacancies, which seemed to all be in exotic-sounding places like Malaya, Fiji, Aden, Palestine, Saudi Arabia and the rest. Offering a variety of work from police posts, oil prospecting to government officers.

I do not really know what I was looking for, what I expected to find, I guess it was my own form of escapism. Then one day an advert did catch my eye and a bell rang in my head. The advert ran 'Wanted General Assistants for Antarctic Expedition. Apply Crown Agents for the Colonies, Box Number 6357'. It went on to give the full details on how and where to apply. The advert struck a responsive chord and after 24 hours thinking it over, I replied to the newspaper advertisement. Realising that I really knew nothing of the Antarctic, other than the story of Scott's expeditions and the 1948 film about the final expedition.

I expected that things had moved on since 1911, but I did not really know in what way, or what conditions and work tasks I was thinking of undertaking. I reasoned that it was a challenge to do something different, and after all, I did not really have a valid idea of what I was getting into when I joined the army; I survived that.

Chapter Three

I plunged in head first and mailed off my letter to the Crown Agents. Then to think about how to first of all break the news to my employers. After all, I would have only just completed my training contract with them. I also had to think about how I would break the news to my mother. She now saw me as settled on a good career path with the potential for a good salary in a secure occupation. I think she wanted to see all her children settled and secure, remembering the struggle she had to endure in her early married life.

My brother at that time was in the air force and stationed in Germany, so he was not around to take sides in the issue. He was more or less on the road to an early marriage, to the girl he had courted for most of his teen years. In a way I was the only 'loose ball' in need of counselling and guidance. My grandmother, who in my early years had always been my font for wisdom and guidance, was of mixed feelings and seemed to understand the need for a new challenge in my life. Ever the realist, she dwelled on the fact that I would again be leaving my mother on her own. Pointing out that over the past few years my mother had not had her children around her.

The first reply to my letter was simply the acknowledgement of receipt of my application. This was followed by another letter stating that I should present myself at a doctor's address in London, for a full physical and at a designated dentist's office for a dental check-up. The second letter further stated that subject to successfully passing these examinations, I would be called at a later date for interview.

Before going ahead with my story, I think I should give you the background information as to how and why the Crown Agents came to be involved with the Antarctic. I knew none of this at the time and, in fact, it was only in later years that I understood the full story. Britain had already issued letters patent in 1908–1909 claiming Antarctic territory within latitude 60 S down to the Pole and within the longitudes 20 W and 80 W, forming a wedge-shaped claim extending to the South Pole. Then in 1937, the British Grahamland Expedition to the Antarctic carried out an exhaustive exploration of what is now known as the Antarctic Peninsula. This they named the Grahamland Peninsula and claimed the area in the name of Great Britain. For administrative convenience, Britain annexed the claimed territory to the nearest Crown colony, which was the Falklands Islands.

Subsequently, these newly claimed territories were titled The Falklands Islands Dependencies. Whilst Britain was involved in World War II, Argentina, probably believing that Britain would be the loser, decided to strengthen her claims in the areas claimed by UK in Antarctica. To this end they established several scientific bases on the Grahamland Peninsula. Since Chile also made the same claims as Argentina and for the same reasons, they also took the opportunity to set up several scientific bases in the same area.

When the war ended, Britain decided that something had to be done to re-assert their presence in the claimed areas of Antarctic. In 1946, the government sent an expedition under the title of 'Operation Tabarin'. To re-establish the earlier British Bases and to extend the survey work The British Grahamland Expedition had completed. After Operation Tabarin, Britain had to make some decision as to how they would maintain a continuity of national presence in the Antarctic.

For some obscure reason, the responsibility for a solution passed on to the Foreign Office, as some sort of colonial problem, hence involvement of the Crown Agents in the recruiting and supply chain. A decision was made to establish and man a chain of scientific stations covering the whole of the Antarctic Peninsula. At the peak, FIDS operated 16 manned and serviced bases. The organisation the government set up at the end of Operation Tabarin became known as The Falklands Islands Dependencies Survey Expedition. Known familiarly as FIDS and as a Foreign Office initiative, it was administered by the Crown Agents for the Colonies. By 1961 the 12 nations that had contributed to the International Geophysical study of Antarctica (1956–1957) signed a treaty designating the whole of Antarctica as an area to be used exclusively for scientific research. Article 4: (states) 'The treaty does not recognise, dispute, nor establish territorial sovereignty claims; no new claims shall be asserted while the treaty is in force'. The treaty clearly spelled out that the countries involved in Antarctic research were in no mood to consider any national territorial claims. Britain, therefore, renamed the Falklands Islands Dependencies Survey to the British Antarctic Survey.

They moved the operational responsibility from the Crown Agents to NERC, The National Science & Research Council. By the year 2000, Britain had reduced the number of bases it maintained to two larger and more sophisticated research stations. The first on Adelaide Island, named Rothera, after the FIDS surveyor who mapped the area. A second station was established on the coast of the Weddell Sea and named Halley Bay, equipped to research many scientific questions about Antarctica that could not be researched from the Rothera Base.

All of the achievements of FIDS slipped into obscurity with the birth of the new name. Even though more than 20 people had died working for their country, without any recognition. Getting back to my story and my application, the big day dawned and a letter arrived calling me forward for an interview. With a great deal of trepidation, I travelled down to London for the interview, not quite having any idea about what an interview at the impressive sounding Crown Agents might be like.

Whatever I expected it did not match the reality. It was soon obvious the FIDS was the 'low man on the totem pole' with respect to facilities allocated. All character references, proof of education, work references and any other documents were checked in the open lobby, by someone who I took to be the doorman. This with people pushing backwards and forwards, as they came into and out of the building, whilst the nearby cage-frame elevator kept cycling up and down. The interview was conducted in a tiny room, which, I found out later, had previously been a stationary storage room. Now it was the total space allocated for the administration of FIDS. This was all the space allocated to Frank Elliot, John Green and Bill Sloman in which to conduct their interviews. From where to run the administration tasks related to FIDS, three people and the place was overcrowded. Frank's desk was strewn with bits and pieces of stores' items he was approving for use on the bases. One item in particular was a string vest, and Frank remarked that his wife was wearing one to make sure they were comfortable.

Frank Elliot had done his time on a FIDS base and was able to give a very detailed description of the sort of things one would be expected to be capable of as well as a description of life on a FIDS base. He said there are two kinds of bases, the 'sledging survey' bases and the offshore island bases. Most people, of course, preferred the former. Except for surveyors, people had their first year on an island base. Then if they were lucky, they would be offered a sledging base for the second year. Of course, they were opening more new bases each year. He read through my résumé and, noting that I had done a certain amount of mapping in the army, asked if I had come with the idea of applying for a surveyor position. Because if that was so, I was in for a disappointment; he emphasised that they had 'surveyor' applicants coming 'out of their ears'. The vacancies they were intent on filling were 'meteorological', 'radio operators' and 'diesel mechanics'. After hearing some details of the various jobs, I opted for 'meteorological assistant'. On the question of how I would get on in confined quarters, with a small number of companions, the question was seen to have been answered by my army service record.

The interview ended with an offer of a position as a meteorological assistant. For which I would be required to attend a six weeks' training course at the Air Ministry training school in Stanmore. I would also be called back to London at some future date for some dental work to insulate all my fillings so that they would still hold in at sub-zero temperatures. I left the interview with the feeling that 'Well, you have done it now' and there is no going back. Now you have to face the problems of telling everyone else and in particular GEC. About that time the press was becoming full with articles about the impending 'International Geophysical Year', which was deeply connected with activities in the Antarctic. There were stories relating to preparations for the Trans-Antarctic crossing expedition to be led by Vivian Fuchs (later Sir Vivian Fuchs) with Sir Edmund Hillary as co-leader. This expedition was to cross via the South Pole from one side of the Antarctic Continent to the other and gave the newspapers a birthday of news to exploit.

So, it was at a time when the newspapers were full of Antarctic stories that I chose to go to the GEC personnel manager and announce that I would be shortly be leaving for an expedition to the Antarctic; that I would be away for slightly over two years. Whether or not he thought that I was going with the TAE, or something to do with the International Geophysical year, I have no way of knowing; instead of a reproach for what I was planning, he enthused about what an exciting opportunity it was for me.

In no time at all it was all around the site and I became a short-term celebrity. On the question of notice there was no problem. Although I would have to re-apply for employment, they saw no reason why I would not be offered a position back in the design office on my return from Antarctica. My mother took a more realistic approach, being concerned with how I would survive all that cold. What if anything happened and no ships could get through the ice? She need not have worried on that count, the ships only visited once a year.

At Stanmore I was installed in a B&B accommodation together with two other FIDS, Cecil Scotland and George Larmour, both from Northern Ireland, all of us destined for the Meteorological Training College at Stanmore. The course was intensive and thorough, concentrating on the practical tasks we were expected to perform, rather than any programme of extensive theory. For us it was basic theory and a lot of practical practice.

After the course was over and I had gotten my teeth fillings attended to, there was still a few weeks before the scheduled sailing for Antarctica. As I was now on the FIDS payroll, it was decided to assign me to the meteorological office at Birmingham Airport, to get some hands on experience. The work there was reading temperatures, pressures and humidity every three hours and filling out weather statistics sheets. My previous army experience with maps and plotting was put to good use, by having me plot out regular temperature and pressure charts for the area that the airport office covered. These charts were used by the weather forecasters and had to be updated on a regular basis. Plotting temperature and pressure isobars was not so different from plotting elevation contours in the army, so I soon settled down to the routine.

The day before the scheduled sailing, I caught the 20 minutes past midnight train to Southampton and was at the dock gates by about eight am the following morning. At the dock gates, I inquired as to how I would identify the John Biscoe and was told, "It's easy, mate; all you got to do is go straight down there. At the quayside look for a ship with a covered in 'Crow's Nest' on the mast." I proceeded as directed and as I looked to the right, along the quayside, I saw this moderate-sized ship with the type of 'Crow's Nest' described. Whilst I was musing over the idea that life could be comfortable on a ship of this size, the voice of the gateman interrupted my thoughts with a cry of, "Not there, mate, around to your left." I moved along the quayside to my left and at first could see no other ship.

Then I noticed a mast just about sticking above the quayside. On closer examination, there was an enclosed Crow's Nest attached to this mast. Walking to the edge of the quayside, I looked over, there below was the John Biscoe. She had been built as a submarine net layer for service on the west coast of Canada. There lay the 'big ship' I was sailing south on, 194 feet in length and 37 feet wide. A wooden-hulled ship that had been designed to drag a heavy anti-submarine net across wide harbour entrances. Not exactly what one would expect for crossing the roaring forties. In fact, I rather felt she would bob about like a cork when in any rough seas.

Instead of the expected gangway up on to the ship's deck, this one had one walking steeply down to the deck level of a ship, whose deck was lying well below the top of the quayside. I went on-board and introduced myself to one of the FIDS who had boarded the day before. He showed me the way down to the bunk area, which lay along the beam of the ship. The area had four tiers of two bunks on either side of a narrow gangway, with very little space to stow personal belongings. After stowing my things on an empty bunk space, I was then lead to what was described as 'the FIDS lounge', equipped with a few padded easy chairs. This lounge also boasted two rows of seats, one on either side of a long mess table, which occupied the majority of the space. It was obviously for dining, and thinking about the number of sleeping bunks, I figured that space in this lounge would be at a premium, except for those sitting at the mess table. That was October 10th, and I then found to my dismay that the ship was not due to sail until the 12th.

After introducing myself to more of the FIDS, who were in the lounge, their opinion seemed to be that the majority of people who had already arrived were either up on deck or had gone ashore to kill time before sailing. The evening was spent getting to know each other, that is, those who had already joined the ship. It seemed there were still several people yet to arrive on board. The following day I joined a group who had decided to spend the day onshore, taking in the sites of Southampton, such as they were in 1955. Then the day for sailing dawned at last; we spent the morning ashore, at least until noon. We had to be back on board, in time to get our briefing from the captain. On that trip down, there were many I would be on base with. These I would get to know extremely well. There were others, which after they landed in the Falkland Islands, I would not see again for years. There were Percy Guyver, John Smith, Colin Johnstone, Len Fox, Pete Bunch, Stan Ward, Joe Axtel, Len Maloney, Gordon Farqhuar, Wally

Herbert, Colin Clements, George Larmour, Cecil Scotland, Eric Broome and a host of others, whose names have passed out of my memory, I am afraid. On deck were all the trappings for a newsworthy sailing, supported by a host of reporters representing both local and national newspapers. It was no surprise to learn that my photograph had appeared in a local newspaper with a report about my departure, to spend two and a half years away from home on an expedition to Antarctica. I am sure the others on board were equally covered, and finally, Lord Munster gave a farewell speech, on behalf of the secretary of state and with that we were ready to sail.

First, we had to be briefed on safety procedures at sea. We were then advised that because we would have so much spare time on our hands, it was planned that we would spend some of our time each day doing ship's chores. Work, such as painting, sharing watches at the 'wheel' with the ship's crew and helping with the preparation of vegetables needed by the galley (peeling potatoes). Cecil Scotland was to be the senior FID and would act as the liaison between the ship's officers and FIDS personnel. It was his job to make up the rosters of people for the daily work-tasks. Daily tasks would be assigned by the bosun to the names on the roster, with the exception of the 'wheel watches', which were listed by name on Cecil's list.

We set sail on the evening tide after a bright but cold sunny day. Afterwards, we retired to the FIDS mess/lounge for our first meal on board, which passed off smoothly even though crowded. I suspect the ship's steward was exhausted by the time he had finished serving that lot. After the meal some retired to a quieter corner in order to write a letter home, to be posted at the first port of call, or sat talking about what was ahead of them all. Some had direct knowledge, others quoted pages from Kevin Walton's book 'Two Years in the Antarctic'. Others went on deck to unwind, since there was no way they could sleep after all the excitement of the departure.

On the 13th we entered the Bay of Biscay and into rough seas, which we had to endure throughout the following day. Only three men took to their bed as sick, and I must admit that at the time, I thought at any moment, I might make a fourth. The next day we sailed into warm and pleasant weather with a calm sea and as might have been expected, the beginning of the on board chores. I was set to 'scaling-off' old loose paint and rust ready for a red-lead paint undercoat, followed by a top coat of grey paint. This work was in the luggage hold. I understood from the regular crew that it had just been repainted in Southampton. Still such chores were to help us pass the time away, and in this instance, it did just that.

The same day the captain invited two FIDS to lunch with him and his officers. He expressed the intention of repeating this arrangement each day, in order to get to know each FID. We were now 585 miles from Madeira, and the meals had increased in volume, as we had a good ship's cook on board. Some evenings in fine weather, we had a film on deck, the only place where there was enough space. On other occasions, two or three FIDS were invited to watch a film in the officers' ward room. Of course, we had to wash our own clothes on a regular basis and were glad of the warm weather for drying.

The meteorological men on board were organised on another work roster to carry out 3-hourly weather observations, on a 24-hour basis. On the 17th, in late afternoon, I was on the ship's bridge to see the island of Madeira. A very picturesque view of spread out villages, rolling hills and vineyards, making it an ideal holiday resort. The following day, it was my turn peeling potatoes, a chore that when prolonged is worse than the boredom it was intended to alleviate. By the 20th the weather had become very hot and oppressive. We were looking forward to our first siting of the Cape Verde Islands, to break the monotony of gazing at endless opens seas. This scenic monotony was sometimes broken by schools of porpoise leaping in and out of the ocean, as they raced alongside and ahead of the bows of the ship.

The first impression of the islands was of a very arid and desolate shoreline, as we approached. Once we had steered into the harbour, we found that appearances had been deceptive. In the harbour entrance we saw three large guns guarding the harbour entrance. Once in the harbour, we could see that Saint Vincent had a modern-looking township and although we never went ashore, most of the houses in sight showed a marked European influence. The island's economy had developed as a coal refuelling and repair station for ships.

But advances in shipping technology and the move to oil as fuel had resulted in the islands being bypassed by the bulk of modern shipping. Even the installation of oil tanks did not improve the situation, only the small short-range ships would put in there for refuelling. There is a marked lack of water so that its vegetables and fruit, of any kind, were all needed to feed the population. Commerce with visiting ships' passengers was restricted to craft goods of clay, wood and coconut shells. In later years, the advent of a healthy tourist trade, fostered by its recognition as an ideal location for the surfing addicts, expanded the island's economy. The official language was Portuguese, but most of the inhabitants spoke a version of 'Creole'.

Once anchored, we were swamped by huge numbers of native vendors selling craft goods for currency. Bartering for unwanted clothes seemed to be another activity, which suggests that they had very little or no import trade. In the evening we set sail again and on the following day the weather was fine, but with a rough sea. To brighten our day, the captain decided to call for a practice 'boat drill', which killed a couple of hours and refocused our minds on the journey. We were now headed for the South American coast, across the South Atlantic in a fairly rough sea, making me feel slightly seasick, but I managed to survive.

On the 26th, we crossed the equator with the usual crossing of the line ceremony. Including 'Father Neptune' welcoming the new initiates across the line with a good hosing down in seawater. On the 2nd of November, we were lucky with the sighting of a school of whales but were unable to identify which species they were. Whatever had attracted the whales also attracted schools of dolphins and porpoise, as well as scores of sailfish. That night we had our first problem with the actual ship; we had trouble with one of its lighting generators. On 3rd the weather was very bad, and the ship had to heave-to, in a heavy gale, for the whole of the day. I think that by the end of that day, everyone was feeling the effects of the storm, with furniture and crockery hurling around the FIDS mess/lounge and no one in a mood for eating.

It now looked as though the recent storm would make us late for arrival in Montevideo, our one opportunity to get the lighting generator reliably repaired. On the 5th, we docked in Montevideo around 2.30 hours in the afternoon, and everyone was impatient to get ashore. I will never forget that first night, with all of us visiting what seemed to be every night club in town and returning to the ship in the early hours of the following morning. The following day was a Sunday, and I slept nearly all day, no surprises there, only to be told on awakening that we were likely to be stuck in Montevideo for several more days. It seems that the ship had a shaft bearing problem and no decision had been made as to the resolution of the problem. In the end, we had to spend a total of 18 days there.

The level of heavy spending ashore had to be financed from salary advances from the ship, using up our salaries before we had even started to earn them. The night life and girls were relatively expensive, compared to our level of earnings. The experience had to last us a long time, and we were determined to make the most of it. Montevideo was a modern city, and weekends there always seemed to have a carnival atmosphere, with richly decorated floats carrying luxurious American cars that were being offered as prizes in daily lotteries.

This city was the right place for us to remember everything we were going to miss. All the 'young senoritas' seemed to be worried as to how we would survive without some sexual outlet. I suppose we drank more than was wise, but we would have plenty of time to fully recover. The food there was excellent and, of course, they served large beef-steaks, something that was not available in the England we had left behind. All the public buildings had soldiers on guard in their traditional dress uniforms. The design appeared to have its roots in the days of glory for the Spanish empire, all very colourful but making them look like life-size toy soldiers. We had been on board ship something little more than two weeks. We all felt like we had been passengers on a cruise liner, having enjoyed a two-week stop-over at a leading tourist destination. It was amazing what that short break onshore did for everybody. So, on the 23rd of November, after many false alarms for sailing, we finally left Montevideo at 2.30 pm, heading out into a calm sea. After the high life in Montevideo, it was hard to settle back to our routine aboard ship. Everyone one was now looking forward to our arrival in Port Stanley, the only township in the Falkland Islands.

The islands were uninhabited when first discovered by Europeans, but there was evidence that parties of Patagonian Indians had reached there in canoes. The British explorer John Davis, in the 'Desire', is credited with landing there in 1592, and the English Commander Richard Hawkins is credited with visiting the islands in 1594. The first settlement in the Falkland Islands was founded by the French Navigator in 1764. In 1775 the British Captain John Byron, unaware of the French presence, explored and claimed land in the western area of the islands and a British settlement was built there in 1776. In 1776 Spain acquired the French settlement and assumed effective control, placing the islands under a governor subordinate to their Buenos Aires colonial administration. Spain then attacked the English settlement, ending the British presence there in 1776. In 1774, due to the economic pressures, Britain withdrew unilaterally from many of its overseas settlements, and in 1776, on leaving the Falkland Islands, left a plaque asserting her claims. Spain maintained a settlement there from 1776 until 1811, at which time they left, leaving a plaque asserting their claims. In 1833, the British returned to the Falkland and announced their intention to assert sovereignty over the islands.

Port Stanley was the nerve centre for all FIDS activities in Antarctica; from a small office there, they administered almost all of the base activities. This involved thousands of items of stores, drums of diesel fuel, bags of coal, cases of food items, compact rations for field parties, sledges, dog harnesses. Plus, radio spares, diesel generators and spares, prefabricated housing, furnishings, kitchen equipment; the list is endless. All these stores had to be ordered from UK and shipped to Port Stanley, with enough time to be sorted and reloaded on the Survey's (little wooden John Biscoe) ship to resupply the various existing bases, as well as to establish new bases. There was a SecFIDS in Stanley as well as in London, and these two people were the coordinating team that linked the two operations. (Frank Elliot and John Green)

The FIDS office in Port Stanley also administered the FIDS personnel, informing London how many people they needed each year, plus the particular work disciplines they had vacancies for. FIDS bases were manned by small teams, of between 6 and 12 men. All teams had a radio operator, one or more meteorological assistants, a diesel mechanic. Then, depending on the particular base's need for work tasks, they could have a geologist, a biologist, or a topographical surveyor. Only the larger bases had doctors on base. Smaller bases had to rely on advice by radio, from a base with a doctor, to handle any health problems.

As a consequence of Britain's territorial claims, all bases had to show evidence of some minimum level of administration. Under international law, there had to be evidence of a system of law and a postal system. The government solved this problem by swearing in each base leader as a British magistrate and issuing each base with sheets of postal stamps and a cancellation punch. Base leaders could be any one of the various disciplines, as an example the base leader of the team I worked with was the diesel mechanic Percy Guyver. He had served in the Royal Navy as a 'stoker'; it all depended on leadership qualities and the way they interacted within any group.

On the 27th November, we arrived at Port Stanley in the Falkland Islands at around 4.30 pm, and only a few people were at the jetty to meet the ship, mostly FIDS office staff. The next few days would be busy ones for the 'John Biscoe' and all the FIDS in Port Stanley, for the ship had to be almost fully unloaded, then reloaded with the stores and supplies for the first bases to be relieved. Each of the bases would have a changeover of some of its personnel, as well as the coming year's supply of food stores and essential spares. Any new bases would mean landing a pre-fabricated accommodation module. The ship's crew and any spare FIDS on board would help to erect the outer shell, and then the wintering team would be left to their own devices to complete the interior. The main problem was that the present John Biscoe had so little cargo space that she would have to make many trips from Port Stanley and back so that all the bases were relieved and resupplied for the coming year. A new ship was due to replace the present John Biscoe, but for then FIDS were stuck with what they had.

On the evening of the 27th November, Colin Johnson and I were told that we would be sailing on a Danish coaster named the Oluf Sven, to Deception Island to help the limited space situation on the John Biscoe. This ship was one chartered by a photographic survey team from Hunting Aerosurveys Ltd, a UK based company that had been contracted for two summer seasons, to carry out aerial photographic mapping of the Antarctic Peninsula from a base on Deception Island. The aerial survey team had adopted the title of FIDASE (Falklands Islands Dependencies Aerial Survey Expedition). Oluf Sven was the ship carrying all the stores and equipment needed to build and equip a base from where they could operate their survey aircraft, which were to follow once the base had been established.

Since the Oluf Sven would be sailing either on the 29th or 30th November, there was not much time to draw all our kit and shop at the Falklands Islands Company store for any extras we needed. I needed a camera and bought a 'Voitlander Vitessa', which seemed a good buy; things were cheap in Port Stanley because there was no duty or taxes added on. I also bought two thick Norwegian sweaters that were made from waterproof wool for whalers and fishermen, which cost me £1 each.

On the 29th November, we were ordered to be aboard ship by midday. On to a ship that was basically a cargo vessel, with the tall superstructure at the stern and series of cargo holds running forward towards the bows. Because all of the installed bunks had been assigned to FIDASE, people already on board, they had to set up some extra camp beds in the mess-hall, rough and ready, but perfectly adequate for us and our kit. The Danish food took a little getting used to; as an example, it's is not the normal English practice to sprinkle sugar all over your fried eggs and bacon. Some of the cheeses that they favoured on board this ship were somewhat strong smelling. The dining table was one single construction, running the whole length of the hold. It was our habit to sit at the opposite end of the table from that which the food and meals were served. This way we could eat up our meal and be clear of the table before the 'foul'-smelling cheese reached anywhere near to us.

The 30th of November, we went back aboard the John Biscoe and spent the night there, returning to the Oluf Sven the following morning; she sailed at 4.00 pm. On this ship everyone took a turn at the wheel, including ourselves. The survey people seemed to be running things and indifferent to the requests of the ship's officers. There is not much to see sailing direct from Port Stanley to Deception Island, just sea and more sea as far as the horizon.

Deception Island is essentially the sunken 'caldera' of a still active volcano; in that the rim of the 'caldera' formed the land visible above sea level. The inner water of the island filled the basin of the 'caldera'. Access to the inner waters of the island, known as Port Foster, was through a narrow break in the rim. Enough room for a single ship to pass through in safety, but not enough for two ships to pass. It is thought that early 'whalers' first found the way into the inner waters of the island, offering a safe anchorage from the sea ice outside the island. This was because the inner waters were kept ice-free for most of the year by the heat from volcanic activity beneath the island.

Eventually, Norwegian whalers established a whale processing plant in one of the sheltered bays formed by the inner waters of the island. They named the bay 'Whalers Bay' and built an extremely strong wooden hut for the wintering parties' home. It was long and wide, and the outer walls were all constructed of 6 cm thick tongue and groove planking, making it an extremely strong construction. They then constructed a rudimentary whale oil processing plant. The centre of which was the planar deck, up which the whale carcasses were pulled by steam-driven winches on to the deck to have the blubber cut away, which was then delivered to the large rendering tanks, where the blubber was boiled to release the oil.

A miniature gauge railway track ran around the operational area so that the tubs carrying the large lumps of blubber could be quickly moved to the rendering tanks. There were all sorts of equipment for filtering the oil to remove the fatty sludge. Huge steam boilers were required to supply the heat necessary to keep the whole process going. Overshadowing the whole complex was a series of oil storage tanks to hold the finished product. Enough storage to hold around two thousand gallons or more.

I have had to guess at the general organisation of the plant, because in 1910 the volcano erupted, sliding most of the factory down into Whalers Bay. Several of the whale catchers anchored in the bay were sunk. A cemetery to the right of the old hut was where the bodies they had found were interred, with a cross marking each grave. This cemetery and a large portion of the accommodation hut was destroyed by a later volcanic eruption in 1968. In the early years of World War II, the navy landed a detachment of marines at Deception Island. Their task was blowing the bottoms out of the whale oil storage tanks, to ensure they could not be used to store fuel oil. They feared that the German Navy's 'Atlantic Raiders' might try to use the tanks, to store reserve fuel supplies.

On the 4th of December, we arrived in the inner waters of Deception Island and anchored offshore in Whalers Bay, at around 1.00 am in the morning. However, it was another 12 hours before we could get ashore. Finally, at 12.30 pm, a transport barge was lowered over the side ready to land cargo and people on the beach and eventually, it was our turn. Once on shore, we quickly headed over to the FIDS hut, (formerly the Norwegian whalers' hut) now named Biscoe House, after a famous whaling captain. The hut was impressive, some 60 feet or more in length by 28–30 feet in width. At that time, it was the most spacious accommodation on FIDS.

On entering the front end of the hut, on the left you had a fairly spacious kitchen and a corner table around which you could seat eight people. Next to that was the wireless room and beyond that a large bunkroom with bunks for eight people. Three bunks down each side of the room and one across each end of the room. Beneath each bunk were a couple of cupboards, where each man could keep his personal clothes and belongings. Beyond the bunkroom was a staircase leading into the roof and beyond that was another outside door. Then right at the end were the toilets and washroom. The toilets were simply a three-'holer' plank beneath which sat three 'soil' buckets. The bathroom, such as it was, had water tanks which had to be filled manually with snow blocks. Facilities were fairly primitive, being simply a bench with three enamel bowls sitting on it and the old galvanised tin bath hanging on the wall. On the other side of the hut starting from the kitchen end, we had an empty room which at a later date was converted to a lounge/sitting room. Next to that we had the 'meteorological office', where all the instruments and records were kept, and next door to that was a tiny darkroom for those who liked to process their own photographs.

The next room was what might be described as the party room, where visitors were entertained to the odd drink, or two; just an ordinary room with a few chairs to sit on. However, the current year's team had used their spare time creatively, transforming the room into stylish cocktail bar with a full-length bar at one end. Behind which was mounted a line of shelves on which the stock of wines and liquors was displayed; the bar was painted a very pale green. One wall was covered with the tie ends of any visitor who ventured inside daring to wear a 'tie'. Obviously, many had made the mistake of wearing a tie; the number of tie-ends pinned to the wall attested to the large number. After the bar was the diesel/generator room and the general base workshop, with two diesel/generator units sitting side by at one end. On a bench nearby was a block of 12volt lead acid batteries, on permanent trickle-charge when the generators were running. These supplied the hut lighting at night, when the generators were off.

The upstairs area was one vast open area the full size of the hut and was where the year's food supplies were stored. Sledges and tents were also stored up there. It was occasionally used as sleeping accommodation for people who were dropped off in any reshuffle on the John Biscoe, because of the ship's limited space, when relieving some of the large bases.

It was good to finally get ashore and know that this would be our home for the coming year. The two of us introduced ourselves to the 1955 team, and they in turn introduced themselves. There was Pidge Palmer, the radio operator and base leader, Ray Cooper was the diesel mechanic. On the meteorological side, we had Dick Clark, Bill McDowell, Brian Gilpin and Paul Phipps. A total of six people. I had to explain to them why we had come down with FIDASE. That the other four men would be landed with the stores, after the John Biscoe had been to Hope Bay and Anvers Island. The main task for Colin and me was to acquaint ourselves with the base routine and the skills needed for the numerous tasks required of us.

Although we were superficially aware of what was happening with the FIDASE team, our focus was all on our own problems. Whilst we were engrossed in our own activities, the FIDASE team were busy unloading everything, and I mean everything, they even had a full-sized tractor-bulldozer to unload. They had plenty of labour to do the work, since the FIDASE team comprised some 32 members, including aircrews. So, there was plenty of activity all along the beach. One of their first major activities was to prepare the beach for parking their aircraft when they arrived. They would be using the Canadian version of the PBY Catalina flying boat, which after conversion in Canada were re-named 'Canso'. They came with a boat hull and stabiliser floats, to take off and land on water. As well as having wheels that would allow them to taxi up the beach on landing. To facilitate all this, they needed to grade an area of beach and stabilise it to carry the weight of the aircraft. To this end, they had brought with them tonnes of 'pierced steel' planking. They covered their area of beach, after grading it, with this pierced steel planking, which all interlocked together, making it a continuous reinforced surface.

In the meantime, they anchored out floating buoys in the bay to serve as floating anchorages for the Canso aircraft, when they arrived. After that they turned one of the old factory storage tanks into a garage/workshop, by cutting a wide doorway with a welding torch. Then make up a pair of hinged doors from the material they had removed. Because the planes would use the full length of the inner waters of Deception Island, it would be necessary to patrol the water to remove any floating objects that might damage the aircraft on take-off and landing. This requirement was further complicated by the fact that the far end of the island was occupied by both an Argentine scientific team and a Chilean scientific team, with individual bases. The planes would taxi out of Whalers Bay and then use the full length of Port Foster for take-off. For the patrol and general support of the aircraft operation, they had brought with them a fairly rugged and fast motorboat.

There were FIDASE stores, still crated, all over the beach area, radio equipment, radio masts, diesel generators, you name it they had it. Sometime later (January 1956), we were to hear from FIDASE that their only helicopter had been caught in a treacherous down draught. It had crashed on Tower Island, one of the peninsula's offshore islands. With the help of HMS Protector's helicopter, they were unable to salvage much of the more valuable items, but because of the lapsed time between the crash and the attempted recovery, the sun had heated the helicopter to the point where it had almost completely melted its way beneath the ice surface.

Finally, FIDASE's prefabricated accommodation hut, with all its internal furnishing, was unloaded. With it erected, they were well on their way towards the complete establishment of their operational base. In the meantime, the John Biscoe had arrived with the FIDS base stores and the rest of our team. We met up with Joe Axtel for the first time, who was designated as our base leader, having been an RAF officer fighter pilot, with most of his service in India. Now that we had a full team, we could get down to organising the change-over of personnel for the coming year. A number of the last year's personnel would be going to a different base for their second year. The remainder would eventually be boarding the John Biscoe for the return trip to UK.

Joe Axtel had taken over as base leader and was also a 'Met' man so he still took his turn at the observations, which had to be done every three hours. The data was sent after each observation in Morse code, which was okay during the day, but at night the observer was on his own. Some were good at Morse and some were not so proficient; the data was all numeric so we only had to learn the 0 to 9 codes and the Port Stanley call sign. However, the problem came when you made a mistake as to how do you correct it without a good command of Morse. We solved most of this by agreeing on a procedure with the Port Stanley operator. We would finish the send with three 'VVV' if we thought it was correct. If we made an error, we would send a long string of dots and then after a pause send the data again, and if it was received okay, then the Port Stanley operator would reply with three 'VVV'. Of course, over time, we would all improve, both at sending Morse as well as reading it.

During the summer season, Deception Island was like a busy port, with ships coming and going to move both stores and people. There was the regular visit of the Royal Navy patrol vessel HMS Protector, which represented Britain's sovereignty in the Antarctic. This meant that people would welcome the opportunity to go and have a drink with those on board any visiting ships. Particularly in the case of the John Biscoe and the people bound for UK. Of course, they in their turn took their last opportunity to drink on base, in the Deception Island's base bar.

It soon became apparent that Joe Axtel had a drink problem, which climaxed with several incidents during which he came ashore from the John Biscoe the worse for wear and started up the generators in the wee small hours of the morning. This did not sit well with those who were so rudely awakened. Finally, he tried the same antic on a night when I was doing the night 'Met' watch, and naturally, I tried to stop him. As one might have expected, he was not going to be put off easily. A fight ensued, and I knocked him to the ground, the fight woke everyone. So, there were plenty of witnesses as to what was going on. Next morning Johnny Green, who was the FIDS secretary in Port Stanley, came ashore to investigate the situation. He mainly wanted to know how we felt about having Joe as base leader, after his behaviour and the recognition that he had a drink problem. So, we were asked who we thought should take over as base leader. Percy Guyver was a popular candidate; I exempted myself on the grounds that I would not feel comfortable taking over after my involvement in the fight.

In the end Percy was voted in. He proved to be an excellent choice, a good leader and a good all-rounder. Joe Axtel was put back aboard the John Biscoe and was assigned to another base. We got a replacement to make up the team of six, who would be based on Deception Island for the coming winter. All of this time the FIDASE team had been working round the clock to finish their accommodation and prepare for the arrival of the aircraft. Ships are still coming into harbour, including Chilean and Argentinian vessels.

The attraction of Deception Island is that it is about the only reliable source of fresh water. The ships regularly stretched out their water hoses to the filter boxes on shore, with pipe connections to the melted water running down off the ice ridge that circumvented most of the island. We had been warned of an impending visit from HRH the Duke of Edinburgh in a year's time. We were asked to list what extra stores (drinks etc.) we would require in order to entertain the royal party.

The royal yacht Britannia would be on her way back from the Olympic Games, in Australia, with the Duke of Edinburgh on board. Probably at his insistence, a visit to the British bases in Antarctica was be included in the ship's itinerary. Because of this impending HRH visit, Lieutenant Angus Erskine was added to the base team for the summer. Angus was a naval hydrographer charged with the task of selecting the ideal sight as an anchorage for the royal yacht, also checking out all the details associated with the safe harbouring of the royal yacht. The ship to shore traffic needs had to be reviewed, where such existed. Their serviceability had to be assured, such as checking that our small floating dock was in good repair. Angus was a natural FID and was immediately accepted by all. He had some previous expedition experience on Greenland in the Arctic.

I remember one particular episode, when Angus and the rest of us were in a party mood ready for any foolish prank. It seemed that Angus had received a special present, from his girlfriend. An old-fashioned long nightshirt, and we all joined forces in getting him to model the nightshirt, which Angus did without too much persuasion. However, once he had paraded around in it a few times, it was decided to 'rag' him and we proceeded to chase him out of the hut bare-assed, in only his nightshirt. Eventually, he took refuge on the top of the small anemometer tower. Perched on the tiny platform at the top of the tower, he fought off any attempts to pull him from his perch. To add to the spectacle, Pidge Palmer, the radio operator from the previous year, danced around the mast, playing his violin to accompany the constant pleas from Angus that he was getting very cold. Eventually, the pranksters lost interest and returned indoors for some warm drinks. In their absence, Angus was able to sneak down from his refuge and into the bunkroom without being noticed. I am sure his girlfriend was duly informed about treatment he had to endure as a result of her choice of presents. Angus left us at the end of the summer with a promise that he would return the following year, in time for the royal visit.

Whilst FIDASE were busy with their work, we had to get on with ours. Whilst we were aware of everything that was going on, our energies and attention were focussed on our work assignments. For instance, the needs of our own base and any improvements we could make before everyone else disappeared and the six of us were left alone to endure our first Antarctic winter. We had spent some time searching in the ruins of the old whaling factory for materials that we could use to improve our living conditions. We found enough materials to implement two major projects. The first was to lay a narrow gauge rail line from the beach up to the base hut, after which we would construct a boat cradle mounted on two rail bogies. We then would have an easy way to launch and retrieve our base dinghy, instead of having to manhandle it up and down the long sloping beach. A winch would be mounted at the top of the rail-track, with which we could let the cradle into and out of deep water. The boat could be floated out and then the reverse procedure of floating the boat into the cradle and then winching it back up to the top of the beach.

Getting clean snow blocks to melt for fresh water was difficult in the summer with people and dogs all over the place. It meant we had to climb farther up the slope as the summer progressed. The solution was to collect the fresh melt water from high on the snow slopes and pipe it down to the base hut. We stripped out enough two-inch diameter pipe from the whaling factory ruins, pipe that had been used to circulate water. Then used it to run a pipeline to collect melt water and feed it down the slope to where we could access it. It was a solution that only worked in the summer, but by the time the summer was over and the melt water stopped flowing, the new snow was back.

We had also used some of the time to visit our Argentine and Chilean neighbours on the island. Pidge Palmer, the outgoing base leader came over on the visit with us, introducing us to our neighbours; they, of course, were also in the process of changing over personnel. The Chilean team were air force men under the command of Capitan Hugo Sage an air force test pilot, his second-in-command was Teniente Arturo Silva. They had about six additional men on base, carrying out the scientific routines. They were a friendly, fun-loving crowd. We were destined to spend many hours over at their base socialising and visiting; they in their turn visited our base.

The Argentine team were under the command of naval officers; I remember that a captain commanded the base. His second-in-command was Teniente Laraldi, with whom I became close friends. They had a civilian geo-physicist with an assistant and two student scientists from the University of Cordoba, the latter collecting meteorological data. They also had a number of rank and file army personnel doing the basic maintenance chores at the base, plus a doctor who was quite a character. This doctor had deserted from the Italian army on landing in North Africa. After many months wandering across Africa, he had finally made it to the West Coast, boarding a ship for Argentina, where he enlisted in the Argentine Navy.

The Argentine base was well-equipped and had a refrigerated storeroom, which allowed it to store frozen meat and food on base. They did not have to rely upon tinned and dried foods, as we did. During that winter the social relationships between all three nationalities strengthened, and the long winter months were brightened by visits to each other's bases, for partying, particularly with the Chilean personnel. I say the latter because with in the case of the Argentine base personnel, there was a marked social division between the naval officers and base scientists and the rank and file army personnel who did the chores around the base. These latter personnel were never allowed off base to socialise at the either the Chilean base or British base. Some close friendships were established that carried over to the next base we were to man in the following year.

The winter eventually ended, and we had fitted out and furnished a new sitting room on the opposite side of the corridor from the kitchen. We had found an old unturned flat-bottomed whaling dory, which we surmised had been used as a shelter for the people who had originally built the hut we were now living in. In the hope of finding artefacts left by these people, we excavated the earth from inside; however, apart from a cast iron heating stove we found next to nothing. On contacting SecFIDS in Port Stanley by radio, we were ordered to re-bury it and leave it 'untouched'. Come the end of December 1956, we awoke one morning to find that there was a lifeboat full of 'whalers' lying out in the mist on the middle of Whalers Bay. We launched the base dingy and went out to see what was going on.

They were amazed to see us and when we told them that we came from a British base only a few hundred yards away in the mist; they then recounted their story to us. Earlier during the previous evening, they had come through the narrows. Because they could see another much larger ship some distance astern of them, the captain had steered a course keeping well to one side in the entrance. This, in case the larger ship should eventually overtake them in the entrance to the island.

However, there is one danger for the unwary when entering Deception Island, off to one side and hidden beneath the surface is a sharp pinnacle of rock, capable of ripping the bottom of a ship open. This whale catcher, later identified as the 'Southern Hunter', had unfortunately found this pinnacle of rock the hard way and became impaled upon it, taking on water that flooded her hull. The crew said they radioed for help and prepared to abandon ship if all else failed; at that moment the ship they had seen astern of them arrived in the entrance. All its decks were fully illuminated and obviously had 'New Year' celebrations underway.

The trapped whale catcher fired distress rockets and turned on their lights in order to attract attention. However, the other ship assumed that the rockets and lights were simply expressions of New Year goodwill and carried on its way towards the Argentine base. It is almost certain that that ship was the Argentinian tourist ship 'Bahia Aquirre' and that everyone on board was the worse for drink. Finally believing that another whale catcher had picked up their distress message, that help was on the way to pick them up, the order was given to abandon ship and take to the lifeboats.

The things that were obvious about that situation was firstly that the ship did not have a chart for the island, otherwise they would have been aware of the 'rock pinnacle' danger. They were unaware of the British and Argentinian bases on the island. Finally, they had not fully assessed their damage situation, otherwise they would have realised that their vessel could not sink completely, since it was securely held by the rock pinnacle. They could have found more shelter in the upper structure of their ship than that offered by an open lifeboat. Even if they had decided it was safe in the lifeboat in case the ship slid off the rock pinnacle, they could have been ashore at the British base, in under half an hour. If they had rowed in the direction taken by the Bahia Aquirre, they would have found shelter aboard that ship, or on the Argentinian base.

As it was, they sat out all night in an open boat in a freezing cold mist, less than a few hundred yards from the warmth and safety of the British base. We listened to their story as the rescuing whale catcher arrived to take the crew on board. It left without any comment or recognition of our presence. The suspicion was that the crew of the wrecked whale catcher were the worse for drink, having been celebrating New Year.

The first ship in after the winter-ice breakup was the navy's HMS Protector. During the year I had carved a small wooden plaque with the FIDS coat-of-arms on it. We had decided it would be awarded to the first ship to bring in mail. Therefore, Percy Guyver, as our base leader, went aboard and duly presented it to the ship's captain. That mail, of course, contained all the letters we were expecting from the Windmill Theatre girls, who had promised to write to us, enclosing a few photographs of them posing in the raw, on stage. The numerous photographs were immediately pinned up around the bunkroom walls, regardless of whom they were addressed to.

My mother had included a cutting, from a national newspaper, showing a photograph of a nice-looking blonde-haired girl, busy writing a letter on the roof of the Windmill Theatre. With the caption beneath it 'Rosemary Phillips writes to James in Antarctica'. There was a second photograph showing me holding one of the huskies, near the anemometer mast on Deception Island. The letter from Rosemary was short and very much like any 'first penfriend' letter. If I remember correctly, it was the only letter I ever did get, even though I did answer it. Then the ships started to arrive; we had the FIDASE crowd back, ready to spend a summer flying aerial photographic cover to map the whole of the Antarctic Peninsula and the offshore islands. They immediately made the place feel crowded. With the Canso aircraft running up and down the full length of Port Foster (the name for the inner waters of the island), Deception Island had become a very busy place.

It was in the middle of this high level of activity that we realised that the impending royal visit was within the next few days, and we needed to check all our preparations. Angus Erskine had arrived back aboard HMS Protector, charged with the task of acting as the official harbour master during the royal visit. Because the volcanic activity at Deception Island made its inner waters ice-free, it was logical that the Britannia be anchored in the safety of the inner waters of the island. Plans were that HRH would, on arrival onshore, be first given a tour of the FIDS base and introduced to the base team. Followed by the similar tour and introduction to the FIDASE team. It was also intended that a lunch of 'seal steak and a penguin egg omelette' would be served to HRH.

We had received information from the base leader of the Argentine base that their naval authorities had issued orders to their ships to stay clear of Deception Island, in order to avoid the possibility of any embarrassing incidents and as a courtesy to a fellow naval officer (HRH). This was a relief to Angus, because he was not quite sure how he would handle the Argentine tourist ship that was prone to show up at regular intervals. Came the day of the visit, and everyone was anxiously waiting to see the first sight of the Britannia making its way through the narrow entrance leading into Whalers Bay. Instead, all that appeared was a small launch carrying the royal party. It transpired that that on arrival in the area, the royal yacht had anchored off Base A Port Lockroy, with HMS Protector close by and keeping a watchful eye on any changing ice conditions that might affect Britannia's safety. The royal party transferred to the FIDS vessel John Biscoe to tour the FIDS bases in that area, and the first call was to Base W, which was a new base established the previous year.

After that he visited Base F, the Argentine Islands, and then Base N, Anvers Island, where a dog-sledge ride had been laid on for HRH. The John Biscoe, having already navigated a passage amongst fairly heavy pack ice, then had to find a route through the ice back to Port Lockroy. Back to the waiting Britannia, where the royal party re-boarded her and made their way towards Deception Island, escorted by HMS Protector. Unknown to us, the weather outside the island had produced conditions where the visibility had reached a low level. It was considered unsafe for the Britannia to attempt negotiating the passage through the narrow entrance into the inner waters of Deception Island.

This assessment was possibly influenced by the knowledge of the presence of a wrecked Norwegian whale catcher that was perched on a pinnacle of rock just inside the entrance. The royal party's launch eventually arrived onshore and tied up at out makeshift floating jetty. They were welcomed ashore by Percy Guyver, the base leader, who was the local magistrate under the requirements international law. HRH had with him Sir Raymond Priestley as his official Antarctic guide, the governor of the Falklands Islands and Dependencies, and his equerry commander Mike Parker.

The royal party were first shown the FIDS accommodation and their sphere of activities and introduced to the team members, as they were encountered. After that the process was repeated for the FIDASE aerial survey team and their accommodation. After touring the area of Whaler's Bay and picking up two whale's vertebrae as souvenirs and the canine teeth from several leopard seal carcasses, the party decided to retire to the base bar, where they were joined by a party of ship's officers from the Britannia. It was soon obvious that some serious drinking was underway. With an imminent lunch appointment planned, the prince was drawn away from the bar festivities with a suggestion of a guided tour of the 'Windmill photographs'. These were in the base bunkroom, and HRH was led there by his equerry, who made sure he did not miss any of the new photographs. So, after another 'Pink Gin' in the bar, the prince, the FI governor and Sir Raymond Priestley, with four members of the base team, sat down to lunch. John Smith, the cook of the day, had been warned that the FI governor would not eat the planned menu. Therefore, a tin of Irish stew was heated up and served for his particular lunch. Everyone tucked into the lunch menu with gusto, leaving no scraps, except on the governor's plate, which was left virtually untouched.

It was later fed to the dogs, who apparently enjoyed it. With lunch over, we all retired to the base bar, where it turned out that one of the officers was celebrating his birthday, with the aid of everyone else, and between them they almost drank the bar dry. In the afternoon, as compensation for our gesture, the admiral commanding the Britannia sent a case of champagne ashore for everyone to drink his officer's health, in celebration of his birthday. About mid-afternoon, the prince's party prepared to return aboard Britannia. But not before he had extended an invitation to the FIDS base team and the leaders of the FIDASE team for dinner that evening aboard Britannia, to be followed by a film show. On his way out of the base hut, HRH put his head into the open kitchen door, to thank John Smith and his helper for a fine lunch, adding that if you ever need a job you know where to come. The drinking in the base bar continued until around six in the evening, at which time the FIDS and FIDASE people 'slid off' to clean up for their invitation aboard Britannia.

The lavishness and grandeur of dining aboard the royal yacht was a real culture shock for simple FIDS. We all revelled in the fine cuisine, amid such luxury and finery. The meal, of course, was absolutely faultless, judged by any standards, and for all of us FIDS it was in sharp contrast to our daily fare, which was all based on tinned staples and dried vegetables. The movie was a new release, as might be expected for such a prestigious vessel, it was 'Seven Brides for Seven Brothers'. Due to the circumstances in which I first saw it, the details are vividly impressed upon my memory.

After the movie we all retired to a large lounge bar, and drinking began again in earnest, with even the most senior of naval officers indulging, and by 11 pm the party was beginning to get somewhat overheated. Being the accomplished diplomat and rather than order the party to be toned down, HRH announced that he was now retiring and wished everybody goodnight. To put this partying level in context, you had to realise that for weeks all these naval officers had to observe strict protocol with respect to every aspect of their behaviour. Now all of a sudden they were free of all those restrictions and free to 'let their hair down' for at least one night.

That partying went on until around 3.00 am, at least that was the time I called it a day. There were many faces absent from the usual island's activities the following morning, except for the FIDS base activities, which had to be completed come hell or high water. Meteorological observations, radio schedules, dog feeds, diesel generator refuelling, kitchen and 'gash hand' duties, all these were essential to the operation of the base.

The next day the royal yacht sailed away and the excitement was all over, and it was back to work for everyone. Not that work routines had really stopped, weather observations and radio schedules had to be done, royal visit or no royal visit. With the royal visit over, our attention was then focussed on our new bases, I say bases because not all of us were going to the same base. Angus Erskine was to be base leader of the new base W, which had been established on Detaille Island; John Smith was also headed for Base W. From there, surveyors hoped to be able to get on to the top of the Antarctic Peninsula, as well as the north side of the Arrowsmith Peninsula. Colin Johnstone would be going to Hope Bay, Base D, and Jack Hill was off back to UK. That left Len Maloney, myself and Percy Guyver headed for Horseshoe Island Base Y. Percy Guyver was to be base leader, and Peter Gibbs, John Rothera, Sandy Imray, George Larmour, Nigel Proctor would join us and with Brin Roberts, our new radio operator, would make up a team of nine.

Waiting for your relief team is probably the most stressful time on base. There was the writing up of reports on all the activities of the team over the previous 12 months, the goodbyes to comrades and companions from the previous 12 months. Then welcoming the new team and helping them get settled in and, of course, helping unload their stores and supplies for the coming year was all part of finishing our stay at Base B, Deception Island.

Finally, we were able to board the New John Biscoe and head across the strait to Base D, Hope Bay on the tip of the Antarctic Peninsula. There we unloaded stores and changed over personnel, some of which would be spending a year with us at Horseshoe Island. Of course, we took on board any outgoing mail. Our next stop was Base N, Anvers Island, and from there on to Base F, Argentine Island, and the routine was more of the same. At each call we would take on board personnel for relocation and, of course, the very important outgoing mail. We had been encountering some heavy going in pack ice up to that time. Now it started to get worse to the point where there was doubt cast as to whether we would be able to get into Base W, or for that matter, Base Y.

But the ship pushed on and eventually reached Detaille Island. The site of the newly established Base W, which had been established the previous year. This was a 'base' which was established to survey the coastal regions and the north side of the Arrowsmith Peninsula. That whole area was not accessible from Marguerite Bay. The amount of ice on the approach close to the base was considerable, but no solid pack ice was encountered. The unloading of stores proceeded, as was the usual routine, as well as the landing of people, including John Smith. He would be spending a year on this island instead of coming to Base Y with rest of us. We had taken to hunting seals on the way down, going out on to any pack ice where there were a number of seals, to land at both Bases W and Y, since we were landing extra dog teams at both.

There was still a lot of work to do on the hut at Base W and that would keep them all busy, whilst the sea ice continued to tighten its grip with firm pack ice. The sea ice showed signs that it would soon be stable enough for sledge travel and for the survey programme to start. By the time the ship moved away from the base, the pack ice was beginning to really close in. The ship found it hard going with the pack ice growing ever thicker. Our ship forced her way westward away from the coast, the plan was to sail offshore along the coast of Adelaide Island. Then into Marguerite Bay. However, the ever-thickening ice was bent on defeating that plan. In fact, there was more than one day when we could not move at all. We took advantage of the situation to go over the side, on to the ice, hunting seals, to add to our seal-meat supply for the dogs at Base Y. The ship's captain tried this way and that in an attempt to find a new route in the direction he wanted to go.

At one time it was discussed as to whether or not the ship should head back to Port Stanley and await changing conditions, before attempting to relieve Base Y in Marguerite Bay. But fate finally played a hand in our favour, and we finally made it out to sea beyond the pack ice and made our way along the coast of Adelaide Island, quite a distance off-shore. Our ship found that the entrance to Marguerite Bay was blocked by heavy pack ice, but she was able to push through it and headed over towards Horseshoe Island, through loose and broken pack ice.

Getting stores onshore took a lot of time, since the landing barge could only make 'slow time' through the ice. Eventually, the task was complete with all stores, the seal meat we had collected, plus the new additional dog teams. The most important thing we brought with us was the mail, letters from home were very essential for the morale of the base team. Introductions between the old and the new teams had to wait until all the mail had been read. A predictable occurrence once the mail had been landed ashore.

With the constant threat of uncertain ice conditions in the bay, the ship's captain wanted to get going with his next assignment. Which was to put up a 'refuge hut' somewhere along the shore of the Arrowsmith Peninsula. This single-skinned wooden hut was to serve as a refuge for both Base Y and W field teams, should the ice and weather conditions turn against them. The ship had now to push its way up the fjord, through broken pack ice, up Bigourdan Fjord to Blaiklock Island, which in those days was connected to the Arrowsmith Peninsula by permanent sea ice. All those still on board would help to unload stores and construct the refuge.

Such as it was, simply a large single-walled garden shed with a tarpaulin roof, held down on the ground by two wire hawsers anchored to cast-concrete blocks. It would protect people from the 100 miles an hour winds, but without much comfort. The small stove inside the hut would not have much effect in the winter's minus temperatures. The stores were stowed in piles around the hut. Unfortunately, no one bothered to map 'what was where' and that caused problems later in the year.

When the ship had finished her work, Pete Gibbs and John Rothera were put ashore to get on with surveying their side of the Arrowsmith Peninsula. When ice conditions permitted, it was presumed that Angus Erskine and Jim Madell would land and start surveying their area of the Arrowsmith as well as their nearby section of the main Antarctic Peninsula. The John Biscoe then made her way back to Base Y, to make her final call and pick up the outgoing mail. We heard via radio that the ship had a hard time calling into bases to pick up outgoing mail, before heading back to Port Stanley and eventually, UK.

Everyone soon settled into their assigned base routines, each taking a week's turn as cook (no exemptions). With Percy Guyver, as base leader, issuing the duty cook with his week's supplies. The food was whatever could be put into tins, with old wartime dried vegetables to add bulk. Tinned vegetables were useless, unless you could prevent them from freezing. The vegetables broke up and separated into a useless 'goo', and since there was no way we could guarantee them not freezing, we had to put up with the dried version, which I might add were nothing like the modern-day product. I remember in particular the dried cabbage, which no matter how you tried to make it juicy and tender, was always tough and chewy, as though you would be better using it for a new sole on leather boots. But beggars cannot be choosers, and if you get hungry enough you will eat anything, as we soon found out. The British bases were fairly basic and unlike the Argentine and Chilean bases, they did not have fridge/freezers, where they could store food under controlled conditions.

Our rations were restricted to tinned meats and dried vegetables, supplemented by the things that the cook could dream up. Using a range of dry goods, they would turn out welcome supplements, such as bread, meat pies, fruit pies and cakes, where rations permitted, with experience and a lot of 'jeering prompts' from the base team diners. Most of the base members developed high-level skills, developing their own 'tasty dishes', for which they received the recognition so richly deserved. Pemmican is the staple of field rations and unwrapped looks very much like a bar of dark-coloured soap; it is comprised mainly of minced beef and fat, with things like vitamins etc. added. I always enjoyed some of the concoctions I used to make with it at Deception Island. Cooked up with pea flour and rice, with the right seasoning added, it was a meal that really 'stuck' to any one's ribs and certainly satisfied the hungry.

On Deception Island there was no need for field travel. The little pemmican that existed was in field ration boxes, which we managed to use in order to supplement our base stores. Horseshoe Island was a field survey base relying on a continuous programme of often lengthy field trips to complete the work programme. Therefore, we could not risk poaching from field rations. I would just have to wait for my turn in the field to enjoy my pemmican concoction. We did, of course, break the monotony of the food with the occasional penguin egg, or seal steak.

These both had their own idiosyncrasies; penguin eggs did not look very appetising. A fried egg yolk is bright gold, and what should have been the white of an egg was instead transparent like clear plastic. Penguin eggs, therefore, were nearly always served up as an omelette. Seal meat, on the other hand, smells and tastes of the sea food it eats. Most of this taste is in the fat on the meat. The answer was to remove all its fat and steep the steak in a nice tasty marinade. But I have spent enough time on the cooking chore, what of the other tasks, for instance the wireless operator Bryn Roberts. He had to maintain a series of tight radio schedules. An example of which was the maintaining of three-hourly Morse, or voice schedules, with Port Stanley, in the Falkland Islands. At such times he would report the work programme intentions, state of health of personnel as well as send the current weather observation data. In addition, he would collect any messages and instructions from SecFIDS, or send out messages to SecFIDS from the base leader.

The diesel mechanic/base leader had to arrange all the refuelling procedures and ensure that everyone understood how to carry out the task. He also had to carry out all regular maintenance and repair tasks that were part of his specific discipline, for which he had been recruited.

The diesel-generators were only run during the day, a bank of 12 volt batteries supplied the lighting at night. The 'meteorological' men (of which there were four on base) had to organise a pattern of day and nightshifts. These had to provide cover for the observations to be taken every three hours. In between times, observers had to compile the data statistics associated with those observations.

The doctor would normally have his own 'physiological study' programme, but in our case we had been assigned an MD whose speciality was gynaecology. He was assigned the job of caring for the dogs. He spent his days up to his ears covered in seal meat and fat, after cutting up the carcasses into feed-size lumps. There were some tasks that had to be completed on both the exterior and interior of the hut. Changes to the bunk-room area and the finishing off of the 'sledge workshop' were priority tasks.

In addition, getting ready for the field work programme meant that all the field equipment had to be checked and, where necessary, repaired. That meant sleeping bags, sleeping mats and tents had to be examined for cracked poles or holes in the tent fabric. Sledges are the biggest job since parts of the type of sledge used were mainly held together with rawhide-thongs, giving the maximum flexibility. The latter property is important when traversing sea ice tide-crack ridges and ice hummocks, frozen into the sea ice as they form. After a season in the field, all the rawhide had stretched to the point where in some cases the sledge was not a rigid structure, in fact just the opposite.

Since the sledges had to carry up to a 1200 lb load, dismantling all of the parts held by rawhide and reassembling with either the original rawhide or in some cases new rawhide is essential. Care had to be taken to stretch the rawhide tight and then carefully secure the ends. The long sledge runners were of wood, with a running surface of 'Tufnol' laminated to it. Tufnol was a fabric-filled plastic composite in wide industrial use at the time. Tests had shown that it had a much longer running life that plain wood, which could be quickly worn away by the abrasive sea ice.

Occasionally, a sledge runner or sledge bridge would be broken attempting the rafted sea-ice hummocks along the tide cracks where the sea ice meets the land; these parts had to be replaced during the rebuild. Dog harnesses were another big job, because after a season of field work, there are not many harnesses that survived fit enough for another season. Since we would have four teams in the field, that meant that we would need something like 50 harnesses, including spares. Dog harnesses are made from wide tubular lamp-wick. This had been found over time, by FIDS, to have both the properties of strength, required for load pulling, and softness, for wearing comfort by each dog. A dog with chafed spots where his harness was rubbing was not going to be a very happy dog. I would think that every FID has spent some evenings learning to cut and sew dog harnesses. It was always considered a good pastime for 'Met' men on the night-observation shift. As well as routine tasks, many people adopted a personal project of their own.

I had built a recording tide gauge at Deception Island, because there did not seem to be any tidal information available. Here at Horseshoe Island I was in a new situation, this made me wonder about the frictional properties of 'Tufnol' on sledge runners, over a range of snow and ice surfaces. These properties would vary with temperature and the nature of the surfaces. I decided to spend any spare time, during my year, measuring these frictional properties.

But it was far from being straightforward. I had no suitable measuring device that I could connect into the dog-lines on a sledge when it was into motion. I devised a compromise approach, using a block-and-tackle, which had to be set up for each measurement. I had to set up the sledge on each new surface area, add that to the fact that conditions varied from thick, heavy wet snow, surfaces to hard, crisp low-temperature surfaces, sometimes with a dusting of tiny snow crystals that had the friction of dry sand particles. For each test run, I would set up a test load using sledge ration boxes, often having to abandon a test mid-cycle because of the onset of extreme weather conditions, requiring that I dig out my test setup.

By the end of May and early June, the sea ice around the island was solid and stable enough to start planning long-distance sledge journeys. The first was a trip to the Emperor Penguin rookery on the Dion Islands, followed by geology trips around the southern end of Pourquoi Pas Island. In the meantime, we received news via the radio that a sledge team from Base W had found itself stranded. It appeared that the sea ice joining the island to the shore broke up, leaving them with no way home. The sledge team was one headed by Angus Erskine, and he had made the decision to make his way across the Arrowsmith Peninsula to the 'refuge hut' on Blaiklock Island.

That refuge hut had originally been conceived for a single or at the most two sledge teams. But with three sledge teams holed up there, space would be stretched to the limit. Due to the lack of real heating, they were to find that it would be more expedient to erect their tents inside the refuge hut. To help out the situation we ran several supply trips up to the refuge, mainly fuel for the hut's stove and alcohol for the stoves in the tents. Since 'midwinters' day was still in the future, it was decided that all the stranded teams would sledge down to Base Y for midwinters dinner celebrations. After which a support team would go back up to the refuge, from where they would organise a combined effort in support of Angus Erskine's attempt to get back on to Detaille Island (Base W). Once the ice conditions were right, almost everyone was out in the field, except for two Met men and a radio operator.

There were occasions when only two men were left on base, these were the occasions when it was Len Maloney's turn to stay on base. This was possible because he was able to operate the radio schedules, which freed Bryn Roberts, the radio operator, to take a turn on a field trip. Finally, Peter Gibbs, a surveyor, sledged back to base with George Larmour, in the company of Angus Erskine and Jim Madell, the stranded Base W sledge party, ready for midwinter festivities. After being one of two on the base for several weeks, it was almost like being taken out of isolation and plunged into an over-populated hotel, with all space stretched to the limit. But it had its compensations, conversation was lively, and everyone had at least one story to tell. Angus Erskine and Jim Madell told of their numerous attempts to get back on to Detaille Island and the various events that had frustrated each effort and held centre stage for most of the time.

Midwinters' day celebrations were special in the Antarctic and for everyone it was their Christmas celebration, which they had missed, because December was a busy month. Because that was the time everyone was on the move, with bases coping with a change-over of personnel, as well as the re-supply of food, fuel and general stores. The June celebration was planned months ahead. Almost everyone on base had brought something special to add to the festive goodies. The better cooks would excel themselves in creating some dish that added the touch of Christmas; cakes, pies, savouries and drinks. It was treated like a formal occasion, and everyone changed into their 'civvy' togs to add to the atmosphere; that midwinters' dinner was special. Although we did not have a turkey, Percy had previously canvassed the base members to get preferences for which it was to be a 'penguin' or a 'cormorant'. The latter was the winner because on the table it would look more like a turkey. Despite the extra guests from Base W, there was plenty of goodies for everyone, probably too much. We managed to hook up over the base radio with other bases, sharing descriptions of each other's celebration dinner. Next day everyone was recovering from too much wine and rich food.

Not much was done around the base except the essentials, feeding the dogs and keeping up the Met observations' schedule. Plus, the three-hourly radio schedules with Port Stanley. Next morning, we loaded up the sledges for the trip up the fjord to the Blaiklock Refuge and the Arrowsmith Peninsula. There was going to be a lot of sledge traffic going in that direction; Angus Erskine and Jim Madell and myself had the Base W teams and loaded the 'pulka' sledge (man-haul sledge) on one of the dog sledges. Sandy Imray and Pete Gibbs had a Base Y dog team the Admirals and had Brin Roberts with them. Brin and I were hitching a ride because we had a hard man-haul task ahead of us. Since everyone was headed for the refuge, as a starting point it posed no problem. Sandy and the Admirals got away first, and it was another half hour before we were ready to leave. The trip to the refuge was 21–22 miles and normally took around 4 hours or a little more with loaded sledges. By the time we got to Ridge Island, we had caught up with Sandy and the Admirals. He had been trying to break-in two new pups into the team, but they had continually caused trouble and were slowing him down. Everyone called at a dog pemmican depot on Blaiklock Island to stock up ready for Sandy, Pete, Angus and Jim Madell's crossing of the Heim Glacier.

When we finally reached the refuge, we found the inside temperature was -15 Fahrenheit, whilst outside it had been -24. Before we could eat we had to go outside and dig amongst the food-stores buried in the snow. Guess what, the only food easy to find buried in the snow was, 'yes', baked beans; these were the only alternative to digging a trench around the refuge whilst searching for a wider selection of tinned foods. To keep warm, we erected the two pyramid tents inside the hut. It was easier to try and keep some heat in the double-walled tent, than in a single-skinned uninsulated wooden shed, held in place against the wind by a couple of stranded wire hawsers.

Next morning the four, Sandy Imray, Pete Gibbs, Angus Erskine and Jim Madell, set out on their respective programme tasks, leaving Brin Roberts and I with the refuge to ourselves, not that it was any great asset. Angus and Jim were crossing the Heim Glacier to get back to their base, if that was possible; whilst Pete and Sandy were tagging along in the hope they could establish a common trig point between bases 'W and Y', if that was possible. Brin Roberts was our base radio operator, and one of the reasons he had made this trip was to attempt a repair of the refuge's radio. A task he was successful with.

This left us free to get our gear sorted for our trip. We ended up with a sledge load of 350–400 lbs and setoff for our objective, which was a headland on the northern tip of Pourquoi Pas Island. The distance was about 8–9 miles, and a good sea-ice surface allowed us to reach a point some quarter of a mile offshore from our target before the failing light was upon us. Instead of risking a search along the shoreline in failing the light for a suitable campsite, we decided to set up camp on the sea ice. The next morning poor visibility and ground level stratus cloud impeded our efforts to move the campsite onshore.

We found that one of our tent poles had snapped clean through during the night, so we had to make a temporary repair (which lasted the rest of the trip). Our new campsite was sheltered in a hollow between two rock outcrops, and it was just as well, because that night we had 80 mile an hour winds, which really tested our temporary tent pole repair. However, all remained secure, and we did not have to venture outside to check on the dogs, since this was a man-haul trip.

The next day, the weather seemed ideal to climb the headland and erect a cairn for the surveyors to use. We found that the approach slope to the headland was deep drift snow, with a choice of two possible routes to the top. Both were very steep, although we only had about 1500 ft to climb. The first route identified was over packed snow and ice and we would need to rope-up and use crampons. Our preference would have been not to use crampons, because we only had canvas mutluks (ex-army) as footwear, not the hard leather footwear that would have been more ideal for crampons. We decided on the second route on a rock scree and ice surface, which we thought might be managed with ice axes and crampons; we roped-up just in case. We had difficulty where some of the rock scree was smoothed over with ice, making a conscious decision not to descend by the same route. On the top, we set about building the cairn and erecting a flag, marking the position as 67 degrees 36 minutes south and 67 degrees 25 minutes west. Barely having time to finish the work before a bank of fog or low cloud closed around us. Our descent was via the ice and snow route, sometimes having to glissade down the steeper parts. That night Brin kept a radio schedule with the base and reported that all was okay. With the task complete, we were glad to get back in the tent for some hot food, which had the desired effect, and we were both soon asleep.

The following morning the weather was not too good, low cloud and poor visibility with snow falling under calm conditions. Such conditions make for a sticky surface, as far as a sledge is concerned; a hard slog when man-hauling. However, we decided to give it a try and broke camp ready to move off just before midday. The snow surface did tend to be deep and sticky, as expected the going proved difficult and slowly got worse with the visibility closing down all the time. Finally, when visibility was down to less than 100 yds, we decided to camp, be it on sea ice, whilst we still had some light. Our plan had been to reach the other side of the bay, a distance of about four and a half miles. Then the following day go around into the 'Narrows' to search for a supplies depot laid the previous year. After that we would take a look at another climb we had to make at the far end of the Narrows on Pourquoi Pas Island. We had only achieved some three miles in over four hours, but eventually we did reach the other side. It was too late to do anything else other than search for a campsite onshore, put our tent up and after a meal settle down to a well-earned night's sleep.

That night we endured gale force winds with heavy drift snow. We were concerned that if our damaged tent pole collapsed on us, the drift snow could bury the tent, but the tent stayed up. When morning came, we took a peep outside to check the weather; it was very apparent that the storm was still raging and in fact did not abate until late in the day. It was another layup day for us, with nothing else to do except lay in your sleeping bag, read, or drink tea, or just try to dose off and get some extra shuteye. The following day, we found that the storm had gone, the sky was clear, the snow surface for travelling on was hard and smooth snow packed by the wind.

The weather we had experienced forced us to take stock of our situation, for both the tent and sleeping bags were badly iced up and we urgently needed to replace the damaged tent pole as soon as possible. The decision was taken to make our way back to the refuge on Blaiklock Island, forget the rest of our journey as planned. To dry out our gear as well as replacing the tent pole. The surface was not as fast as we expected, probably because the temperature had dropped. We arrived at the refuge at about 3.30 pm and found that the temperature was -28 degrees Fahrenheit, with a minimum for the day of -30.4 Fahrenheit, Which explained the slower progress. We stripped the tent and the sleeping bags to scrape all the ice clear and then stretched everything out to dry.

Since we had no tent to put up inside the refuge, we needed some chores to do to keep us warm. We visited some cairns which needed to have their tops dismantled, so that the theodolite could be fitted in position for a baseline extension. The weather turned against us again and became really foul, with winds rising to full gale force at times. We had to spend our days repairing sledging gear and then erecting some racks and shelves in the refuge. Whilst we were doing something, the cold was more bearable. When the weather did abate somewhat, Percy Guyver, John Rothera and Nigel Proctor arrived at about midnight, having made a late start from Nemo Cove, on Pourquoi Pas Island, hampered by deep snow most of the way. Two of their dogs were in a bad way, having come off worst in a dog fight during a two-day layup in a storm. Both 'Taffy' and 'Joseph' had large teeth punctures in the groin; to add to his wounds, Joseph had spent the night trapped in a tide-crack and was still half frozen. On the trip up to the refuge, Taffy ran behind the sledge, but Joseph was in such a sorry state that he had to be carried on the sledge. Both dogs were kept in the refuge for the night to dry out.

The next day was spent reorganising to accommodate the increased 'local population' and trying to assess the state of the two injured dogs. Hopefully, when they are fed and rested, the health picture will be a lot clearer. The following day was mainly a 'sort-out' day for everybody, since we had to prepare for our next task and Percy and Nigel had to tend their injured dogs. The following day Percy and Nigel took their team, less the two injured dogs, back into the Narrows to pick up some stores, which they had off-loaded to make travelling easier in deep snow. John Rothera (surveyor), Bryn Roberts and myself set out on a fairly local trip to set up a baseline for the planned area triangulation.

This was to do the first measurement for the baseline extension. After completing what was a fairly straightforward task, we set off back to the refuge. On arrival finding that Sandy and Pete had returned from their trip over the Heim Glacier, and they informed us that during the trip they had recorded a minimum temperature of minus 44 degrees Fahrenheit (which was our lowest recorded for the year).

The day after, we set out again to make a second measurement of the new baseline, ready for John and Pete (the two surveyors) to go out and extend the baseline. Then tie down one end, by reading the angles to features with previously mapped locations. They would then repeat the process for the other end of the baseline; all this kept them busy for the next couple of days. The following day in fine weather I skied to the mouth of the Reid Glacier, a round trip of about ten miles, to search for a route up on to the glacier. I found what appeared to be a snow ramp that had formed at the western side of the glacier mouth. Satisfied with my find, I returned to the refuge.

Next day weather kept everyone trapped in the refuge and left to their own amusements. Pete and Bryn Roberts (both avid smokers) spent the day scouring the floor of the refuge, picking up cigarette butts, breaking them open and collecting the little remaining unburned tobacco. From these they would make up something resembling a cigarette that they could smoke. It seemed the smokers were out of cigarette supplies until they could find a depot that included cigarettes. Others occupied the time bringing their field notes up to date and playing cards.

The next day brought a let-up in the weather, so Pete Gibbs and John Rothera took the opportunity to read a round of angles from the end of the new baseline to a new survey point. One that they intended to visit shortly to read a series of back angles to the end of the baseline. As might be expected, there had to be at least one day where the 'best laid plans' were thwarted; it was another day to spend trapped in the refuge. The moment the weather pattern changed, Percy Guyver and Nigel Proctor loaded their sledge for a long 'geological trip' around the east coast of Adelaide Island and the Laubeuf Fjord area; they were taking no more chances of getting trapped by weather, in the area of the refuge. With the baseline extension now complete, John Rothera,

Bryn Roberts and I were now free to man-haul our sledge back to base. The surveyors (jointly) had decided on a task for us to complete on route to base. That of climbing each end of Ridge Island to erect cairns the surveyors intended to use, in order to tie the island into their existing triangulation.

On the day we were due to start the trip, Sandy Imray and Pete Gibbs, who had nothing already planned for that day, offered to load our man-haul sledge and gear on to their dog sledge and haul us down to the end of the 'Narrows'. After which they would make a fast run back to the refuge and whatever plans they had for the rest of the day. This meant we would cover the eight miles to Ridge Island in less than half the time of a 'man-haul', leaving us with the maximum window to build the first cairn. As a result, we arrived at the foot of the peak we were proposing to climb by around 12:30 hrs. A plus, so that we could start climbing straightaway; Sandy and Pete offered to set up our camp, an offer we accepted. We immediately put on our crampons and each armed with an ice axe, we set off for the approach to the foot of the glacier. This distance across the glacier was further than we had estimated, and it was an hour before we reached the foot of the peak. The climb that was before us was one relatively short, but a very steep climb, roping up, wearing crampons and using ice axes were all an absolute necessity. We reached the 2000 ft level with visibility closing in rapidly, in view of which we reluctantly decided to descend whilst there was still light.

During the climb we had been able to see Sandy and Pete, well on their way back to the refuge and making very good time by the look of it. Next day the weather was fine and we started to climb the peak for the second time. However, this time we climbed on to the glacier at a point much nearer the foot of the peak and climbed steadily onwards and upwards, and we saw the sun for the first time since it had disappeared in May. This time we reached the top only to face disappointment, in that the site was unsuitable for a survey cairn. It was screened from the points it had to triangulate up to by intervening topographical features. We arrived back at camp in semi-darkness, ate a hot meal of pemmican, pea flour and rice and slept like the dead, one and all.

The weather was still holding, so we broke camp and man-hauled to the southern end of Ridge Island. Our intention was to try and erect a cairn on the peak, at the other end of the island. We started our climb and this time it seemed to be the case of 'one step forward and two backwards' was the order of the day. After only climbing a short distance, the light started to change, still bright with details tending to be lost in a situation of increasing white-out conditions. Ideal conditions for contracting snow-blindness, as I was about to find out. We were still climbing in these bright white-out conditions when all of a sudden, I felt that someone was stabbing my eyeballs with thousands of fine needles. I could no longer see where I was going, I was in agony and I must have fallen, but I am not sure. I next remembered John and Bryn leading me on a rope back down the slope. They got me into the tent and into my sleeping bag and after leaving me with a moistened cloth to hold over my eyes, they climbed back up the ridge, to continue with the task in hand.

I have never before experienced the agony of the endless hours that followed, with the constant feel of those thousands of needles piercing my eyeballs. During those long hours, I would drift off to sleep only to be awakened by the stabbing pains in my eyeballs, which were so sore by this time that I could not bear to open them.

It is assumed that at some time John and Bryn returned to the tent and cooked a meal and offered some to me. But I was not interested in anything except the pain in my eyes. It would appear that I lay in my sleeping bag for nearly two days before I was comfortable enough to open my eyes and engage in normal activities.

A decision was then taken that if I felt up to it, we would break camp and journey back to the base. John and Bryn told me that whilst I was indisposed, they had climbed the peak and built a fairly big cairn, which they considered adequate for the job, having marked it with a flag before descending. My eyes were still sore, but the needle-stabbing pains seemed to have abated. Although I do not seem to remember much, except that I was not much help in breaking camp.

Thrusting against the restraint of the man-haul harness, hour after hour, seemed to take my mind off my eye distress. We started making about four miles an hour, but after an hour that had dropped to three miles per hour, and by the time we reached base we were down to something even less. My two companions were anxious to get all the current news of the field teams, as well as news from elsewhere on FIDS. But for myself, after eating a meal and filling myself up with liquid, I stripped off and got into my bunk and slept the clock around. In a radio contact with Pete Gibbs, John Rothera learned from Pete (the senior surveyor) that the Ridge Island cairn would not now be needed, in a change of plans for the future triangulation from those at discussed. My eyes seemed to be back to normal now.

Just as well, as I was needed back on the meteorological observations schedule, to relieve someone else for a field trip. We were now in August and although survey and geology trips were still being undertaken, the hours of daylight meant that we only had very short working days.

One episode that stands out occurred about this time, but let me first fill in some background details. All of the outside doors have a short vestibule attached, so that there is a heavy door at one end which connects to the outside. Another lighter door gives access into the hut accommodation. It was the 'golden rule' for everyone, DO NOT OPEN THE INNER DOOR UNTIL AFTER YOU HAVE CLOSED THE OUTER DOOR. The reason for this is that high winds rush in with considerable force and do immeasurable damage to the interior structure of the hut. On this occasion, a man came in from the outside to drag a sledge into the sledge repair work-shop; he had the inner door open the same time as the outer, although it may not have been his doing.

We had in the past experienced 100 mph gusts that had only lasted a few minutes, but could regularly occur without warning. Such a gust of at least 100 mph wind suddenly filled the sledge workshop. The workshop window (12 x 4 ft) was immediately torn out of the frame of the hut by its force. The wind carried the window, in one piece, dragging out all the 6-inch nails that held it into the hut structure. Then carried the complete window 30 yds distance, before dumping it on soft snow without breaking a single glass pane. Of course, there was an immediate panic. It was essential to close off the opening before another gust of similar intensity occurred and possibly destroyed the remaining hut structure. This meant finding a large enough sheet of strong canvas, large enough to cover the open window space.

As soon as the wind abated for a few minutes, everyone had to turn out and help hold the canvas over an orifice that had once held a window. At the same time others had to collect wooden batons and nail these along the edge of canvas to hold it to the walls of the hut.

Without that first aid further gusts would had seriously damaged the interior of the hut and, of course, then the hut would have started to fill up with snow. Eventually, in a spell of calm weather, we were able to extract all the 6-inch nails, then remount the window securely back into the wall of the hut, and the incident became just a memory. Those who had now returned from field activities and the refuge took time to straighten out their gear. Then update all of their field notes, ready for the compilation of end-of-year reports.

Eventually, Percy and Nigel returned from their long trip in Laubeuf Fjord. It seemed that the same freak winds that took the window out also wrecked three of their tent poles and, in fact, they nearly lost their tent. George Larmour (now relieved of his meteorological duties) set out with John Rothera, to survey the area of Laubeuf Fjord, where Nigel and Percy had been doing their geology. They would be using a newly formed dog team for the first time. The manner of their start suggested that the team would run well. We had a radio schedule with George and John informing us that they were camping at Cape Laintz on Pourquoi Pas Island and had managed a sixteen and a half mile run.

Our next radio schedule with George informed us that they were camped on the 'Long Ridges' on the Bryand Peninsula and that very good weather had enabled them to progress rapidly with their work programme. Problems always occur in the plural; 'Kim', lead dog of the 'Church-men' team had died suddenly, leaving Percy and Nigel without a full team to finish the geological trip work that was interrupted by weather. Percy planned to move 'Dean' up front as the lead dog and take 'Phi', one of the six-month-old pups to make up the team number. That six-month-old pup seemed to have fitted well into the Churchmen and Dean had settled into his position of lead dog. Percy and Nigel were making their final plans to leave on the continuation of their geological trip and would leave any day now.

I had been doing night-met observations and after a few hours' sleep, I foolishly chose to ski out across Lystad Bay to investigate some strange beacon I thought I had seen; a round trip of about ten miles. By the time I was on the return journey, it was getting quite dark, and I let the shape of the terrain steer my skis. Next day when I looked at my ski trail coming back to the base, I realised how foolish I had been, skiing around the edges of huge snow scoops and bowls. If the edges had broken off, I would have been pitched into any one of these deep snow features, with a minor snow-slide following behind me.

Percy and Nigel have not left on their trip. Instead, Percy loaded a drum of paraffin on to the 'Greenland-type sledge' (it had very heavy solid runners, which wore well on sea ice) to be pulled by the Churchmen. The paraffin and other supplies were needed at the refuge for an early spring start of the field programme. Len Maloney loaded tents and rations on a Nansen sledge, to be pulled by the Spartans, and he followed behind Percy.

During the following days, Sandy Imray returned with Pete from their trip over the Heim Glacier and the western side of Pourquoi Pas Island. Near the end of August, Len and Percy returned from the refuge with their tales of woe. It seems Len Maloney's sledge went over a snow ledge near the refuge, resulting in him losing his boxed sledge compass and the dog driving whip, and he broke a handle off the sledge. That was not all, 'Liz', a bitch with the 'Spartans', broke free from the 'span' overnight. Together with 'Moose', another Spartan, they killed 'Ginger'. She was a bitch who was in 'pup' and whose litter was badly needed to bring the number of dogs up to strength for next year's sledge journeys.

Then to top it all, Percy had a mishap on the way up to the refuge, in which he broke the surface of the sea ice into a layer of unfrozen water beneath it, which instantly froze on his feet as he lifted them clear of the ice. This phenomenon is quite common in sea ice, where under the surface ice (an inch or less) there is a small pocket of unfrozen sea water insulated from the air temperature by the ice above it. These freeze the instant that covering surface is broken. It appears as though Percy had early signs of third degree frostbite, on his heels. This did not seem to bother Percy, because the next day he left base with Nigel to complete the delayed continuation of the geological trip, despite the fact that it was already late September.

That did not stop the exodus from base to the refuge; they were followed by Len and John with the 'Spartans' and by Sandy and Pete with the 'Admirals'. They were planning to spend a week getting an astro-fix completed, combined with a journey across the Heim Glacier. On base we only had George, Bryn and myself, and to our surprise Nun decided to have her pups. But of the eight that were born, only three survived. Surprises were not over, an Argentine team came to visit us that had been based on Deception Island whilst we were there. Some close friendships had been established. They had, it seems, later moved to the Debenham Islands around the time we had moved south. So that once again we were neighbours. Three of them had arrived by dog-sledge, expecting to find our full complement of people home. Instead, they found only three of us, two Met observers and a radio operator and a few dogs. The visitors were Dr Rene Dalinger, geologist/glaciologist, and his assistants, two graduate students from Cordoba University. They came bearing gifts, in the form of fresh meat and a few litres of wine to wash it down with. Though with only three people on base, that would take some time. We welcomed our visitors to our base and cleared some space for them to stow their gear as they would be staying a few days. They were used to a few more home comforts than were available on their base. I guess they counted staying with us as part of the camping out experience. The Argentine teams were supported by their own ice breaker, the General San Martin. A ship that had helped FIDS out of many difficult situations, because FIDS did not own a ship of similar power in ice. Our visitors said that they had heard from their ship's officers that they were expecting difficult pack-ice conditions when the day dawned for them to come south to restock their base.

On the first evening of their visit, we all ate steak, cooked to perfection with loving care and washed down with an ample supply of red wine. We talked all evening about things that had happened between us all and our bases as well as the parties we had enjoyed at each other's bases. They listened in whilst we held our radio schedules with our field teams, with the radio operator relaying messages backwards and forwards. Of course, during their stay, one of us was the night Met-man. He had to spend the final couple of hours hunting and killing a seal to feed the dogs still on base. Since they also had dogs to feed, the two students/assistants readily agreed to help get seals for the dogs. This allowed the night-man free to get his head-down. Their visit was only three days, but it really livened up the pace of life for those of us alone on base. Before the Argentine team left, Emilio extended an invitation to visit them at their Debenham Islands base, which we gladly accepted on behalf of our whole team.

We watched them leave until their sledges were completely out of sight, and then it was back to the same old routines. We were now into December; our weather was foul and we learned from the radio schedule that all the sledge parties were doing a 'lay-up'. Percy and Nigel in their tent on Adelaide Island and Sandy and Pete trapped in the refuge. From a radio schedule with our friends at the Argentine base on the Debenham Islands, we learned that the sledge party which had visited us was now safely back on their base, having managed the 30-mile trip in ten hours. The stormy weather still prevailed, forcing the two field parties into a continued lay-up, unable to get any field work done. News on our round of radio schedules reported that Hope Bay (Base D) was planning a massive sledge journey down the length of the Antarctic Peninsula (around 700 miles). They would be travelling high up at plateau level, which in some places would be extremely narrow.

One of the pups 'Chloe' was ill and the doctor from another base prescribed an enema, followed up with full instructions over the radio. Once the medical procedure had been completed, she appeared to recover. She then had a relapse and her condition did not at first look like it was likely to abate; however, with the passage of time, she fully recovered.

Somehow trouble always followed Chloe around. One morning she decided to crawl under the hut for a 'mooch', only to become entangled in a pile of broken glass. This resulted in a huge deep gash on her nose. So, it was back to the radio for the first available doctor on any base, who after hearing a report of her injuries, said we would have to clean up the wound, remove any foreign objects or glass and then stitch up the wound. This time the doctor stayed on the radio and dictated our actions 'blow by blow', starting with the anaesthetic injections. These Chloe fought against; in the end she had enough to have put the biggest dog to sleep. Cleaning of the wound was fairly straightforward. She did squirm a little, but the moment we started stitching, she screamed with pain, or fear. It was hard to know which; even after all the anaesthetic she had been given, she was still very much aware of what was going on. Eventually, it was all over and we left her to sleep it off. It only remained to say bye to the doctor, then shut down the radio transmitter, after but not before first writing down all the follow-up instructions for Chloe's care.

In the days that followed, she quickly recovered and was soon her old self, and we let her go back to freely roaming the base site. We had first blocked off all the access points where she might crawl under the hut and do herself more harm. I mention Chloe out of all the pups because she would later play a major part in an incident that befell the team that would eventually relieve us at Base Y.

Whilst this last episode with Chloe was going on, Percy Guyver and Nigel Proctor arrived at the base, having crossed the bay from the Dion Islands, covering a distance of 37 miles in one day. They had been away from base with the other teams for a total of 40 days. Having filled in the gaps for the geology of Adelaide Island and sledged a route to the western side of Adelaide, they reported that at the Dion Islands they had seen some 100 adult emperor penguins and between 35 and 40 emperor chicks.

It was now late October and the field work was nearing its end. John Rothera and Len Maloney arrived back at base from the refuge, having had some primus stove problems. Without which they could not prepare any hot food; a real essential item of equipment, on which everyone is dependent. Back at base, the stove was repaired, and three days later they left to finish off their survey work in the Laubeuf Fjord area. Sandy Imray (our base doctor) and Pete Gibbs arrived back at base, for a break from the rigours of living in a tent and to get their kit cleaned up and everything dried out. Then after three or four days on base, Pete Gibbs and Percy left for a compass traverse of the Heim Glacier and part of the Briand Peninsula. They met up with John Rothera and Len Maloney in the Narrows, the latter pair being on their way back to base.

We had planned to visit our Argentine friends on the Debenham Islands but rising temperatures and pools of melt water on top of the sea ice in the southern area of Marguerite Bay made sledge travel difficult, with the possibility of open water leads in the ice south of our base. So, the trip was postponed, and our promise of a return visit at their invitation was one that regrettably we were never to enjoy. In early November we heard that the new FIDS ship RMS Shackleton had struck an iceberg on its maiden voyage as a FIDS ship whilst en route from Powell Island in the South Orkneys to Hope Bay on the Antarctic Peninsula. She was holed in her side below the waterline and first reports said 'she had had it'. But with FIDS and the crew striving to stuff mattresses into the hole in the hull, the latter held in place with timber bulks, she stayed afloat. That is until the arrival of the HMS Protector, with the means to effect temporary repairs, so that the early labour was not in vain. The loss of the ship was to be avoided.

An Argentine ship and a Norwegian whaler all rushed to the Shackleton's aid, all stores and personnel were transferred to other ships. In the end the Shackleton was pulled over to one side to lift the hole clear of the water. Then navy divers went to work fitting a temporary patch over the outside of the hole. After that it was a matter of pumping the water out of the ship. The final work was to construct a wooden retaining cage behind the patch, which was then filled with a mixture of mattresses and concrete. This to support the thin patch against the forces of a wild sea. We heard later that she had managed to limp back first to the whaling station at South Georgia. Then finally the UK for complete repair and structural changes.

Percy and Pete Gibbs had now arrived back on base, having cancelled the idea of a compass traverse and so at last everyone is back on base. It was such a change, having previously only seen two or three other people for months. It was almost like being back in a 'crowded city', such was the contrast. Everyone had now settled down to writing end-of-season reports and final letters home with films to be developed. The thought of and the nearness of Christmas was on all our minds, whilst we patiently waited for news of our relief ship's movements.

We received a message from the expedition office in Port Stanley, which gave rise to feelings of deep unease, as one can imagine. This message asked us to audit all our food stocks and fuel on hand and to be prepared to possibly winter again at Base Y. The ice conditions could force the John Biscoe to head back to the Falklands Islands and abandon any plans to relieve Base Y, until the following summer. That news dulled everybody's spirit, although no one would have really minded another winter. It was just the disappointment of looking forward to mail and the relief ship's visit, all of which was maybe not to happen. After that we hung on every word of news we received by radio, hoping for the news that they had finally broken through the belt of heavy pack ice.

Despite continuing bad news of the ship's progress, life of the base went on as normal. Listing stores and requesting replacement parts for diesel generators, sledges, buildings, met instruments etc. We had 50 miles of solid ice in the bay. We had heard already that the RMS John Biscoe had already made three attempts to relieve Base J before she succeeded and that base was way north of our location. The ship also made it into Base F to have outgoing mail transferred to the RRS Shackleton. The John Biscoe then headed down the Lemare Channel towards Base W and was almost immediately beset by very tight pack ice. When we next heard from her, she had only managed the odd mile or two, and as she moved forward, the heavy pack ice immediately closed behind her. She finally reached Base W, a distance of 60 miles from Base J, after 17 days of fighting her way through heavy pack ice. After several days there, the ship continued her attempt to reach our base. But as she pushed south down the west coast of Adelaide Island, she was faced with what appeared to be 40 to 60 miles of solid pack ice blocking the access to Marguerite Bay and our base.

The captain of the John Biscoe was then faced with a logistical decision, should he spend time continuing in his attempts to relieve Base Y and risk being late to complete the relief of other bases on his schedule, or should he abandon any further attempt to relieve our base and sail northwards to Port Stanley for stores to relieve the still accessible bases.

By this time it was late January, not the time of year to risk getting locked in the pack ice. What has to be remembered is that the Survey did not have ice-reinforced ships that could push their way through pack ice, so they could not take too many risks with the ice conditions. In the final analysis, a decision was made to sail the ship northwards and leave the team at Base Y to stretch their limited supplies and spend a further winter on the base. By February we found that much of the sea ice had broken up inside the bay, and we could see a lot of open water. This meant that the bay ice was moving west and clear of the ice barrier that had blocked the progress of the John Biscoe. In late February, the Argentine ice breaker 'General San Martin' forced her way into Marguerite Bay down to the Debenham Islands to relieve and re-supply their team based there. Since we were in regular communication with our friends there, they were all well aware of our situation due to the ice conditions.

So, it was no surprise when a helicopter arrived from the Argentine icebreaker with an offer to carry all our mail out and transfer it to the John Biscoe, once they encountered it further North. They also brought a present of a few bottles of Argentinian wine. This offer was gladly accepted, since we had all our personal letters as well as films that we had accumulated ready to go to the UK for processing and even more important, the base and surveyor's reports needed for planning the following year's work tasks. There were the two students from Cordoba University on board the helicopter, the two that had visited us by sledge during the past winter. Here this time to say goodbye and meet the rest of our team who had been out in the field during their first visit. It was some time later that we heard the tragic news about the fate of the helicopter. Details were scarce but the helicopter had crashed into the sea on its way back to the Debenham Islands base. Its flotation system having failed, it went straight under. The first report said that the navy crew had been rescued and gave the impression that there had been no lives lost. But to this day, I still wonder about the two students, since their fate was never specifically mentioned. With that helicopter went our precious mail and films. Myself, I lost all my colour films of our activities including sledge journeys, which looking back is somewhat of a disappointment.

In early March, having heard of improving ice conditions in the Lemere Channel and offshore from Adelaide Island, the John Biscoe left Deception Island for one final attempt to reach Base Y in Marguerite Bay. By 12 noon, some two days later, she had reached the southern tip of Adelaide Island. She radioed us to say she was just coming in towards Marguerite Bay. Well, once we were over our elation at the ship's arrival, it was time to set to and unload the new supplies, as well as give a wild welcome for the relieving team, led by John Paisley. The man to take over from Percy Guyver as base-leader. The ship also brought new instructions, to the effect that the four men who were first year men would be landed at the old Base E on Stonington Island. This in the extreme southern end of Marguerite Bay.

The intention was to re-open the Stonington Island base, before others with territorial ambitions could decide to establish a base there. The people from our base were to be Pete Gibbs, Nigel Proctor, Bryn Roberts. They would be joined at Base E by Peter Forster, Alan Hoskins and Henry Wyatt. So, a lot of stores had to be sorted ready for landing at Base E, including some seals and couple of dog teams. The day dawned quickly for the time to wish John Paisley and his team good luck and goodbye, with no sense of the tragedy that was to befall them in a few weeks' time. We sailed south to Base E and arrived there to be frustrated by the fact that the sea was too rough to be able to unload any stores. Before any of the new base people could be landed ashore, everyone would be required onshore to chip and clear the ice that had taken over the base hut. Some rooms had three or four feet of ice accumulated in them.

The seas eventually calmed enough to start unloading stores and people. The dogs were taken ashore and spanned out ready to pull some of the stores from the beach over to the hut site, by sledge. Clearing the ice was particularly hard work, and people alternated between moving stores and clearing ice. The Base E team put up their pyramid tents and camped onshore so as to be on hand to supervise where they wanted their stores and to be responsible for the checking. The ship had stopped periodically on the way down to hunt seals, as a supply of dog food. All these carcasses had to be off loaded onshore. Finally, the time came for the ship to leave, and I personally did not envy any of those moving into the base hut. Although most of the ice was cleared, it would take a long time to dry out enough to warm even the small part of the base they would occupy to start with. I suspected they would spend some considerable time living in their pyramid tents.

They were going to have a tough first few months, and all of us on the ship wished them well with our 'tongue in cheek'. Now the ship was headed back to Port Stanley in the Falklands Islands, only making short stops at one or two bases on route to pick up mail and outgoing personnel. There was still plenty of pack ice around, and the ship's captain had to pick his way through carefully. We did not want any unforeseen holdups now we were on our way out.

I mean, if we ever started to miss the life, we could always sign on for another tour with FIDS. Port Stanley in the 50s was not exactly a thriving metropolis. More like the early western towns in the USA that we used to see on films. There was just the one circular road around the township, with the bars having a sawdust-covered floor. They used to hold pony races down Main Street once a year. The sheep herders would come into town from the sheep camps to take part in the celebrations and races. The population was essentially of Scottish descent, mainly from the offshore islands Orkney, Shetlands and Outer Hebrides. A people who were very much at home in the climate of Falklands Islands and sheep farmers used to managing sheep over difficult terrain.

Later they were joined by a few people of South American descent, either through marriage or as migrants. These people were very much the minority. All commerce, incoming or outgoing, was handled by a trading company granted an exclusive right by the British Government. This was the Falklands Islands Company, which in early years ran the islands affairs. The islands at their peak earned a rich income from 'whaling and sealing taxes', which England enforced with presence of a British warship.

The indigenous population were on the whole fairly heavy drinkers, and the fact that a bottle of whisky incurred the same shipping costs as a bottle of beer meant they were heavy whisky drinkers. This indulgence in 'a glass or two' was further strengthened when any whalers were visiting on their way north. They were not allowed alcohol either on the whaling factory shore stations or aboard the whaling ships. There was just one police sergeant keeping law and order.

The wives, with the cooperation of the bar owners, had their own system for dealing with wayward husbands who habitually came home drunk. They went to each pub or bar and had their husbands' names written up for so many weeks on a publicly displayed slate. For the length of time a name remained on the slate, that person would not be served any drinks. The unfortunate person would turn up at his favourite waterhole only to be told, "Sorry Jock, your missus has put you on the slate."

Crime was not a problem, if one discounted the odd drunken brawl between whalers and locals. Which, in the main, was left to let it sort itself out. So, for the visitor on his way out, there was not too much to occupy his day. Except a little sightseeing and photography, looking at the old hulks of wrecked sailing ships, driven ashore by the stormy weather whilst coming around the tip of South America.

The day dawned when we boarded the RMS John Biscoe for the trip home, and we were due to stop en route at Montevideo in Uruguay to land mail and take on fuel and supplies for the rest of the journey. We would be there for three days, giving us all time to let our hair down. Also re-acquaint ourselves with the female version of the human species. We were able to draw funds (against our meagre salary accounts) from the ship's captain before going ashore to renew our experiences, first enjoyed on the trip south some two and a half years earlier. The less said about our escapades; those we could remember are best left buried without evidence.

That fairly long sea trip back to UK left one with plenty of time to mull over what the Antarctic experience had been to each of us. I felt that the strongest effect that I was immediately aware of was one of inner self-confidence, one that recognised who I was as a person that had evolved in the total real world. Memories of vast empty space, just yourself and a sledging companion to soak up a view that was unique. Or to be standing on some high point and be able gaze to the horizon to see an endless expanse of sea ice. In another direction views of mountains rising to around 6000–7000 feet straight up from sea level. This was real isolation; I think during my time there I seldom thought of UK. Not even family, the feeling was one of detachment and part of a whole experience. The army had given me a sense of self-discipline. A purposeful drive to see through any direction life may take me. The Antarctic gave me the insight into who I really was, the product of genetic history, education. Plus, experience that resulted in one unique individual. Now aware of his limitations, goal-seeking drives and ability to think through problems as they arose and arrive at a solution that my personal psyche could accept.

I will never forget the Antarctic and the superb scenic examples of the creative power of nature. A whole continent that had one time been tropical and was now covered by 3000 metres of thick ice. To have stood there as an individual in isolation, taking in all the colossal mountain scenery of the Antarctic Peninsula. Already it has become something of a tourist destination, but I am thankful that I saw it before all this change. When dog-teams were still the primary mode of travel, a ship the main method of reaching the Antarctic, aircraft being the alternative for a very small select minority. As the ship sailed north towards the British islands, under an un-interrupted blue sky, to see there on the horizon, one isolated layer of cloud, quite small relative to the span of the horizon, everyone knowing that beneath that little patch of cloud was our destination England and Southampton.

One of my close friends, having both worked for GEC and spent a lot of time together, socially with friends and girlfriends, had promised that he would get his father to lend him the family car and drive down to Southampton to pick me up. This would save me the torture of two trains and a bus journey.

As we pulled into Southampton, the quayside was fairly empty except for one or two FIDS officials and a few relatives waiting for someone on the ship. Very different from the crowded quayside when we left, with a band and the press making a big thing out of who was sailing and where we were going. Sure enough, my reliable old friend Colin was there, true to his promise. No car in sight as yet, but no doubt he had parked elsewhere than on the quayside. I quickly gathered my belongings, bid a rapid farewell to my shipmates, people that I probably would not see for a long time, or maybe never again. I hurried down the gangplank with awkward-shaped luggage, which conveniently Colin was able to help me with, in order to reach his parked car.

The car was as I remembered it, in immaculate condition, as his dad always kept it. A Jaguar 'Swallow', just about the first design Jaguar built, after changing their name from Swallow Sidecars. I had always loved that low-slung design of the Swallow. To this day it is still the body design concept that I still think of as the one and only Jaguar design classic. Despite all that has transpired since.

The journey home took quite a few hours, and so we had plenty of time to exchange stories. What had happened in the past two years, girls still around that were not married and, of course, who Colin was currently dating.

Eventually, we reached my home and after quickly dropping me off with a quick greeting to my mother, he dashed off with the parting message that he would pick me up to go for a drink the following evening, since I did not have any transport.

Chapter Four

Now I was back in England, all of a sudden the whole episode seemed to have been some huge anti-climax. There had been such an atmosphere of impending adventure and new experience, as well as all the media publicity, when we left England two and half years ago. We had arrived back virtually unnoticed and, to be honest, that was to be expected, since all the public interest for the 'Trans-Antarctic Expedition had long since waned, and there was no longer a focus point for public interest. There was one call from the (then) ATV television station asking whether or not I would be willing to appear on 'Jean Morton's Rainbow Room' show. This for a short interview about my experiences; an interview that would take place in the informal atmosphere of the Rainbow Room show. I agreed and a few days later turned up at the studios; it was all finished quickly, with the interview lasting about ten minutes.

Those first few days and even weeks were spent re-establishing relationships with old friends and social circles. As well as finding out which of the girls I had known previously where still unmarried. I had also to face the primary issue of what were the opportunities for my career future. I had the fall-back position of re-joining GEC and taking up my employment where I left off before my Antarctic inter-lude. I wanted to consider what other options I had, and two featured prominently in my mind. The first was to sign up for second tour with the Falklands Islands Dependencies Survey. They seemed to have big plans for the coming years.

I started to make enquiries, with the idea of getting taken on as a surveyor and if not as a Met observer. The answer I got was that they had applications for surveyors' positions 'coming out of their ears'. Plus, they had more than a full complement of Met observers. They needed diesel mechanics, radio operators and doctors. The last two were obviously out of my league, and somehow the remaining vacancy, that of diesel mechanic, did not have much appeal to me. So, I said no thank you to a further tour with FIDS. The second option was re-joining the army, and it was an idea that I had wrestled with ever since leaving. In the end I knew that I would be chasing a moving target. Never knowing what career directions in real terms the army would offer. In the end, I fell back on the initial decision, that there was no future for me in the army. I applied for my old job back at GEC, applied electronics division, Coventry and was successful in my application. Very quickly settling in, so much so, that it hardly seemed as though I had ever been away. My life quickly swung into a rhythm, with a good balance between work and social life.

I bought myself a used Morris Minor tourer to get around in. That, in turn, led me to extending my social life to the Rally Club attached to Mallory Park Race track. The draw was being able to go from there into the paddock to watch the car races. From the track we could move up into the club for a dance, or social evening. It was a strong bait when enticing the opposite sex. It was the era of Clive Wormleighton, who owned the park and originally established racing at Mallory Park. Clive used to throw himself wholeheartedly into the success of the Social Club, since it provided the core of his own social life.

The first girl I met after my return from 'down South' was Patricia, a woman a couple of years older than myself, a career woman who was on the rebound from a previous romance. A woman who openly said up front that she wanted a 'no strings' relationship, with all of the benefits. The relationship lasted less than three months, and we both gradually called it a day, with no hard feelings over the split.

Next came Barbara, who in retrospect might have been considered a 'nympho'. One who had more than one boyfriend in tow, who she insisted that she would never go out with more than one boyfriend in any one month. If she ever got pregnant, she wanted to be certain who the father was.

Barbara was a partying girl and the weekends at Mallory Park's socials fitted her lifestyle perfectly. Barbara was around, sometimes in the background, for the next 18 months; she was fun to be with. I thoroughly enjoyed her company immensely; however, I would never have considered marrying her.

Prior to going to the Antarctic, my brother had introduced me to a teenage girl that worked for the same company as himself. With all time taken up with classes and homework, I had very little opportunity to meet any girl. We went out on a couple of dates and when I sailed for the Antarctic, I asked her to write to me. Now back in England I decided to renew my acquaintance with her, although neither of us really knew anything about the other. Patricia (yes, another Patricia) was willing to risk going out on a date. That first date blossomed into a flow of dates and invites to Pat's home to meet her father, mother and sister Gill. The situation was further reinforced when my pal Colin decided to date Pat's sister Gill. From then on we went everywhere as a foursome, for my part the invitations to Pat's home became more and more frequent. It appeared that her mother was convinced the two of us were in a serious relationship.

One night when Pat and I were out having a quiet drink in an isolated country pub, I mentioned to Pat how keen her mother appeared to be. Her mother appeared to have strong ideas about the two of us making a 'go of it', with me as the candidate for a son-in-law.

I had for some time had the idea that Pat had something to tell me. The time had never seemed right to her, now it appeared she would tell all. Whilst I had been in the Antarctic an incident had occurred in Pat's life. One that made her mother focus on moving heaven and earth to get Pat married off. To the first available man who could provide for her. She told me the full details, which have no place in this dialogue. I said that it did not make any difference in the way I felt about her. She was convinced that the day would dawn when I would use it against her. It would then be there, ready to one day destroy our relationship and split us apart. From then on I think we were both trying to grapple with the question of how serious we were about our relationship and find a basis on which to decide our future.

Around that time GEC announced that early in the following year, the establishment at which I was working would be reorganised. The plan was to relocate in the Portsmouth area. That the local council would make council houses available for essential staff to move into. On enquiring I was told that if I moved, I would be allocated one of the available houses. I went home and spoke to Pat. Telling her that if I agreed to move with the company, we could get married and have a house to move into.

Pat's reply was a surprisingly inflexible one; if we married, she would want us to move to New Zealand permanently to live. The implication, which she made obvious, was that the move was non-negotiable. She wanted to leave her one mistake in life behind her. Including the shame her mother appeared to feel she had brought down on the family. There was no way I could accept those conditions 'off the cuff', so we 'called it a day'. We still saw a lot of each other after the breakup and I probably found more to admire in Pat in those final weeks than all the previous times we had spent together. The invites from her mother stopped, so one presumed that Pat had put her mother straight on the marriage situation. Although, it was probably unrelated, her sister Gill stopped dating my pal Colin.

I continued to meet up with Pat for a drink at our favourite watering holes, but the relationship was strictly that of very good friends and a friendship I valued. As one chapter of life closes, so another opens. In this case it all started with a car rally in which another close friend was to compete in his employer's 'Company Car Rally'. Pete was to drive his old Austin Seven (of which he was justifiably proud), with me as navigator. However, he came around to my home early on the day of the rally and informed me that his car had broken down. Would I drive in my Morris Minor with him as navigator?

Well, it was a Sunday all-day rally, typical of what the big companies tended to organise through their company social clubs, in the 1950s, with a lot of navigation stages and timed sections to complete. After the rally was all over, most people headed for the nearest pub for a drink. Amongst the throng were three girls from a car we had followed for at least a third of the rally.

All of the three were known to Pete, because they were employed as secretaries within ICI. As an accountant, Pete had occasionally used their services. We had a few drinks and ribbed each other about humorous incidents that had occurred during the day. I made a date with one of them to meet at the weekend, little knowing the girl would eventually end up as my wife. Pauline was quite different from most other girls I had known; we hit it off right away. Although I still spent a lot of time socialising with my pals, which included Colin and Pete, I did get to see her a lot, and a strong relationship developed.

After the episode with Pat, all ideas of marriage were on a back burner as far as I was concerned. Far from deciding to go to Portsmouth with GEC, I had made up my mind to move to Canada to find work. Though Pauline was now in the picture and blurred the decision process a little. The developing demand in Canada and the USA meant that there were always adverts for design engineers in the UK national newspapers. At that time the adverts were mainly from contract offices. These found the right engineers and contracted them out to defence and aircraft industries at a handsome profit. Contracting was a way of life in Canada and the USA. People with the right experience and qualifications, managers, engineers and designers were offered the promise of a high income.

I finally broke the news of my decision to Pauline and was surprised at her reply. She was also disillusioned at the career prospects that existed in UK at that time. She had actually been thinking of moving to Canada but had been forestalled by the logistics of the idea. A job, place to live and enough funds to survive on until paying employment showed up on the horizon. I pointed out that with my moving there, she could spend the next six months accumulating funds for the journey. I would be there to help her get settled in when she decided to move.

So, in March 1960, I quit my job as a design engineer with GEC and flew to Montreal Canada. There I obtained a position with a contract company and was contracted-out to Canadian Aviation Electronics, to work on the F104 Flight Simulator. Contract working was a way of life for engineers in the USA and Canada. It had that certain amount of flexibility for moving around between jobs and contracts. I was soon to learn engineers spent most of their lives moving between contracts, enjoying the higher salaries and the flexibility of moving between companies. The defence industries liked contracting because they could take on and let go, as the peaks and troughs occurred. Something that was a constant factor in any defence contract. In the USA a corporation could easily lose a contract to a competitor for missing target or progress dates. They needed a flexible workforce to cope with the intricacies of defence development contracts.

Friends who worked in the USA often advised me that contracting was a good way of finding the right job to settle into permanently. They expressed the opinion that if you had good experience gained in the UK, you could expect a good contract pay rate. Because for the higher level of experience, a contracting company can charge a higher rate from clients. I had several friends who had some experience of contract working in Canada; they all said it was a good way to start. When you first get over there, you will have no idea where you want to put down roots. After arriving in Montreal, I had meant to have a short holiday looking around Canada. However, I was destined to meet up with one of the principals of the contract company I would eventually work for.

At breakfast on my first day, he sat down at the hotel table with the opening remark that he had had just arrived back from Scotland, after visiting relatives there. I said I was from England and planned to take a week's holiday looking around Canada, before deciding just where to search for a job. My new Scottish acquaintance, from the contract company, advised me that it would be a better strategy to get into work first and take the vacation later. I could just miss the one opportunity to get taken on with a large company, with a long-term stable contract. It seemed sensible logic.

Although his motivation was that the sooner he had me placed, the sooner he would be taking a percentage on my hourly rate. I asked what sort of hourly rate I could expect. His reply was that it depended on how highly the client company rated my skills or how badly they needed those skills. I agreed, after some lengthy debate, to be driven up to the client's office for an interview with the client company, which turned out to be Canadian Aviation Electronics. They were located at the northern extremity of Montreal, in Dorval near the Montreal Airport. The interviewing committee was, strange to relate, all English; the chief engineer, chief draftsman, two senior designers all of them from English companies such as GEC, Joseph Lucas and Ferranti. All had been working in Canada at least ten years. In addition, there was a Canadian project engineer, on whose project they were looking for contractors with the right skills.

The defence contract that everyone was working on was the flight simulator for the F104 NATO fighter. The atmosphere soon became very relaxed; those from GEC wanted to know the latest 'shuttle-but' about goings on in the company. All with strong convictions that all the English companies faced a precarious future, they were losing all their contracts to USA defence companies. The Canadian project engineer said that he had responsibility for electronics packaging and design of the equipment cabinets. In addition, he was responsible for the design of all the servo systems required for the various system controls. I discussed my experience, which covered most of all of the areas under discussion. With what appeared to a 'put down' attitude, he said, "Yes, I have spoken to some of the English designers who had worked with you on the 'Seaslug Project in Coventry, and they confirm your areas experience." He finally added, "I will take you and introduce you to the people you probably already know." The interview team broke up, I was asked to wait outside the office, whilst they discussed details with my Scottish acquaintance.

After some 15 minutes, he was out with a grin all over his face, saying, "You are in and on a top rate. The chief draftsman Ed Wood wants to talk to you in his office next door."

I said goodbye for now to the grinning Scotsman and went in to face Ed, who introduced himself. He was from Birmingham, another ex-GEC man, and had been working in Canada for over eight years. He owned his own home and had his wife and kids with him. ED was a real Mr Fix-it, he started by asking the question, "Are you in a hotel downtown?" Adding that "We shall have to get you out of there, before you go broke with their prices". He picked up his phone and said to someone on the other end, "Remember you mentioned an apartment or shared house that was vacant?" The voice on the other end said something. Ed continued, "Can you find out if it's still available and what the rent is? Then call me back ASAP, okay?" Ed then turned to me and said one of my Canadian designers mentioned to me that "There was an apartment available out at Point Claire. It's really a half share in a small bungalow, and Point Claire would be an ideal place to get to and from work." He then got me a coffee, and we talked about old times at GEC and his experiences when he moved to Canada. He went on to say that circumstances were different for him because he had his whole family to move across the water. He needed to have secure permanent employment before he could even risk a move.

Contracting meant being available to move, because most contracts were of short duration at that time. Canada was very much living on hand-outs from the USA, with regards to defence work. We went on discussing all the problems of settling in a new country, the tax system, health insurance, having no close friends with whom to build a new social life. The phone rang with the answer, "Yes, the apartment/shared house is still vacant. The landlord, who lives next door, said that if he comes home with me, the whole thing can be fixed up, and he can move in tonight." Ed listened to further details and then put the phone down.

Ed then said he was going to drive me down town to pick up my luggage from the hotel and then to bring me back there. "Then you can wait for Doug, the man who had arranged all this, he will give you a lift to the apartment and introduce you to your new landlord. That is, when he leaves at the end of work today." We rushed down into Montreal and picked up my luggage, and it was obvious that Ed did not want to be away from his office any longer than absolutely necessary. Once we arrived back at CAE, Ed said he would take me to the department where I would be working. The project engineer would assign me to a work team and brief me on the work I would start on next day.

At the end of the day, an easy-going Canadian walked over to me and said, "I'm Doug, your lift to Point Claire." He continued saying that "Three of us share a carpool backwards and forwards to CAE. They have all agreed you can join in, by paying your weekly share of the petrol costs."

The car park was massive, and I had to keep pace with Doug or I would soon have been lost between row upon row of cars. Then finally we drew level with a 1958 Buick, and Doug opened the passenger door and then went around to the other side to get into the driving seat. "Don't worry, we are not in two much of a rush; once we can get out of the car park, the bulk of the traffic will be heading down town and we will be heading in the other direction, towards Pointe Claire."

But as forecast it took us what seemed like ages. It was a problem just to get out of the car park gate on to the dual carriageway and head in the opposite direction to that of all the other traffic. Pointe Claire was very much an old French Canadian settlement, at least in the older part where I would be living, with tree-lined, mostly unpaved side roads. Although there were several established new housing estates to be seen and one or two new houses under construction. The landlord was a typical French Canadian family man who always used the French language at when home with his family, but required good English for everyday life.

The apartment was a half share in a small wooden bungalow. I would have my own bedroom and bathroom but would share the lounge and kitchen with the other tenant. I would be sharing the tenancy with a young Canadian named Spencer, who worked for the YMCA in downtown Montreal and was not yet home. The landlord showed me around and pointed out that there was everything there I could possibly need to get settled in. He concluded with, "We will do the paperwork tomorrow when you have had the time to get your head on straight." Finally, he added, if I needed any help he was right there, in the house next door.

Doug had given instructions that I had to be outside and ready by 7.10 in the morning to be at CAE by 7.30. The others I would be with in the car do not like waiting for sleepy-heads. Well, I had hardly been left on my own for an hour, intending to sort myself out for the morning, when an athletic-looking guy in his 20s walked into the lounge, flopped on the settee and announced, "I'm Spencer. The landlord told me that you would be in here by the time I was home."

He then went on to say that the bedding in my room was his property. He put it in there whilst a friend from the YMCA was staying here. He added, "You are welcome to use it, until you have had time to get to the Dorval shopping centre and get your own." We talked on for a couple of hours, and then Spencer said, "I am going to order in a pizza for supper, do you want me to order the same for you?"

I said, "Sounds okay," and he phoned through the order.

He said, "I don't know whether or not you want to keep your own groceries separate. I have always found it works better if we shop for one lot of groceries and share the expense." I agreed to the option as offered.

That night in my room I lay down realising what a bedlam the day had been for me. I had started the day after breakfast at the hotel, quietly thinking that my first plans would be to see a little of Canada. Yet by the end of the day I was out of the hotel and had found a job, or rather a job had found me. I had found and rented an apartment accommodation and had arranged a car share to get me to and from work. I sat down and unloaded it all in a letter to Pauline and wondered what she would make of it all. It was quite an effort to realise that I had not only left home again, I had left behind the one girl I really cared about.

I always remembered the image of Pauline standing on the railway platform as my train moved off, looking so forlorn. I still have that photograph of her stood alone on the platform, at Birmingham railway station. Hopefully, we would not be apart for too long. The next morning was to be my first day as a Canadian worker and everything that might mean.

I suspected that there were some underlying tensions between the English and Canadian engineers and designers. The English seem to have taken some of the key jobs in engineering. None of the English engineers or designers on contract could be classified as design engineers. Under Canadian law, they had to have at least five years of Canadian engineering practice and have passed the Canadian Registered Chartered Engineers examination. Although some of the English engineers and designers were doing the work and managing much of the design, they could not sign off any of the design as checked and complete. Only a Canadian chartered engineer could perform that function.

Well, my first day was mostly spent being indoctrinated in company procedure, methods of working and the existing 'pecking order', which was to be strictly adhered to. My first day came to a close with only a couple hours on actual design work.

I had to keep a log sheet of hours worked; this was the record sent to the contract office and was the basis on which I would be paid. Of course, it had to be signed by my immediate supervisor, the Canadian project engineer. Next day I was in at the deep end and charged with coming up with a solution to design problems. The project engineer had outlined in sketch form what he wanted in general terms, and my job was to fill in the design detail and calculations and produce some working drawings.

England had a different engineering hierarchy. They required that that a designer had to have an engineering education and experience and the ability to produce his own design and manufacturing drawings. In the USA and Canada this design process was changed to a two-step one, where an engineer would produce a design layout in sketch form together with calculations. Then a draftsman, who in this case would only have a high-school diploma in mechanical drawing, would produce the crisp line drawings. These had to exactly match any detail shown in the engineer's sketch; they were not allowed any design input.

It was not until the English designer/engineer, who produced their own drawings, started to flow into USA and Canada that the procedure come into question, with a preference for the English system. The result was that until the existing culture had died out. No engineers were going to produce their own drawings, their job was design. This attitude showed up in many ways through remarks by Canadian engineers.

As an example, the project engineer over the area of my work, a decent affable guy in every other way, had to always come out with his favourite 'rub'. Amongst English engineers/designers he would say, "Show me any English designer, and I will show you that there is a frustrated engineer buried under the surface."

All in all, CAE was a great place to work. Flight simulators were in their infancy, no computer graphics, only terrain models and a diving, twisting, turning TV camera following a terrain model on a moving belt. Add to that a mass of ingenious devices operated by servo-systems and intricate mechanisms. This was all interesting work, not the kind that can become routine and boring.

That first weekend I accepted an offer from Spencer, of a lift down to the Dorval shopping centre, to get groceries and the bedding I needed. Later, he also gave me a lift to my contract office, to turn in my time sheet and sign papers. Spencer was a boon having a car; we often went out for a beer in the evenings. Then he came along one day and said he had met a girl at some YMCA/YWCA function. He had asked her out for a date, which she accepted, as long as she could bring a friend with whom she worked in a downtown office. The ultimate question was would I come along, to neutralise the presence of her friend, whom she seemed to be bringing as a chaperone.

Well, my answer was yes, and of course, I was mainly thinking of similar situations in England where there would be one 'beauty' and a plain dull companion. You were always told that the 'dull' one was yours, if you came along. The date was to be a Sunday drive out along the lakeshore and a picnic lunch. We were going to bring something for lunch, and when we did get it all together in the car, it looked like enough food for a three-day hike. The girl Spencer had his eye on, Estelle was her name, was slim, tall, Attractive, with a terrific personality, and it was obvious from the word go that Spencer was really smitten. Her companion used the name Helen, but in reality it was the polish name for Helen. It had seemed easier in Canada to use the English name, so Helen it was. Helen was my age, late 20s early 30s, whereas Estelle was about the same age as Spencer, somewhere in the mid-20s.

I was all set for a boring day playing gooseberry to Spencer, whilst he set about wooing Estelle in earnest. I guess I felt guilty going out on a date, whilst thinking of Pauline back in England, but I was fed up with nothing to do. My social life had been the odd trip out for a beer and a fair amount of overtime hours back at CAE. Laying back in the sunshine on the Lakeshore was an environmental goad to relax, enjoy the company and the sunshine. Helen was small petite Polish girl, with a strange sort of attractiveness that was more personality than beauty, although she was attractive to look at when you took a good look. It was obvious that Helen was the 'woman of the world', supporting her working companion on her quest for romance; she had me pegged in a similar role. Helen was a great conversationalist and had many interesting stories. They all centred on her life that had brought her to Montreal.

As an early teenager she had left Poland, being moved from one 'displaced persons' camp after another, from one country to another. At first the camps were well-run and organised and young girls were safe from abuse. As the hordes of displaced persons, people from all sorts of nationalities, moved on towards the French coast, the controls started to break down and teenage girls were freely raped and abused at will. Some of these girls, who were reasonably attractive, found that the only way to survive was to find one man, then give themselves to such a man, in return for his protection from the attention of other men. Although I did not press Helen for details, I knew from the distant look in her eyes that she was recalling many of the experiences and they caused a look of anguish, which had faded with time, but never completely disappeared.

That first date was one I enjoyed, the picnic was a success, and I enjoyed Helen's company. She was obviously a very lonely person and at times looked on with envy at the other two, cuddled in each other's arms, oblivious to the rest of the world. After that we went out on several dates as a foursome, and my relationship with Helen became ever closer and she confided more and more about what had gone before. She had started her journey with a schoolgirl friend, and they had stayed together right until they had reached Montreal. Supporting each other through thick and thin, feast and famine, been the emotional support each needed at one time or another.

However, through the foibles of bureaucracy, which dictated that displaced persons seeking to settle in the USA would be handled on a quota basis for each nationality, Helen and her lifelong friend had been separated, when her friend left Montreal as part of a quota that did not include Helen. She would have to wait for the next quota to be announced. That was several years ago, and she was still waiting. In the meantime, her friend was studying physics at a university in New York and hoped to take up employment as a physicist. Meanwhile, Helen's feelings are that they are drifting farther and farther apart in their search for a new life. She admitted that she had begun to have real doubt whether she will ever be allowed into the USA to join her friend.

Because I had no transport and the bus service to downtown Montreal was pretty infrequent, the foursome dates with Helen, Spencer and Estelle were the highpoints of my social life. However, events were taking place to change all that. A migrant from Scotland name of Bill Borthwick, who had been working contract in Toronto, had now moved to Montreal and was contracting at CAE. For accommodation he had an arrangement to share a flat with a fellow countryman. I happened to mention that I was dissatisfied with my apartment, because it had such poor transport connections with downtown Montreal. Adding that because I did not have my own transport, I was in a no-win situation. Some weeks later, Bill said the man he was sharing with had left. He was stuck with having to pay the whole apartment rent, which was more than he could afford for too long.

His solution was finding a new apartment in downtown Montreal, an apartment in a solid stone building. The stumbling block was finding someone to share the rent with; it would be tolerable for two and even great with three. I had mentioned the problem of my getting downtown, and since we both worked at the same place, getting to CAE would not be a problem. I said goodbye to Spencer and moved house to the apartment on Saint Catherine, in the heart of downtown Montreal.

A little later another acquaintance at CAE mentioned that the he was the secretary of the Town of Mount Royal Rugby Club. As I was unattached, he advised that membership of the rugby club could give me an 'in' to a good social life. At weekends I could train with the two teams and even play in training matches. He went on to say that the big three rugby clubs in Montreal ran the best weekend dances and parties and the overall social life of the club was first class. To cut a long story short, I joined and after that my social life never looked back; girls were attracted to the rugby club dances and socials like flies to the fruit bowl.

One Saturday night out with some of the rugby team after a practice match, I came across Helen quite unexpectedly. She asked how I was settling in to working in Canada and where I was living now that I no longer lived in Pointe Claire. Information she no doubt obtained from Estelle; before parting, she told me that Spencer and Estelle had announced their engagement and planned a wedding for the following spring. I never saw or heard about either Spencer or Helen since that encounter; I guess they only now exist in the store of memories representing my first friends in Canada.

Time had moved on since my arrival, as were the six months that Pauline thought I would need to settle in, before attempting to help her organise a move to settle into a new life in Canada. Joining the Town of Mount Royal Rugby club had been a wise move, so that now, living downtown, my leisure activities and social life took care of themselves. I was glad of the opportunity to train and keep fit with the rugby club, something was needed to balance out the riotous activities that occurred most weekends. Bill Borthwick and I were well settled in our new apartment and with the help of the girl occupants of an apartment on the floor above us, we set about a search for suitable job openings for Pauline to look at.

Our apartment neighbours all worked in different types of employment and ages ranged from 20 to mid-20s. Anna, the oldest, was a 'cooking demonstrator', Carol was a secretary and Connie was a bank clerk. After getting to know them, we were all able make excellent use of their individual work skills. Anna actually cooked real meals in her demonstrations, which were used in promoting the whole range of cooking appliances from cookers to pots and pans. Some of the food she handed over for distribution to the needy and the rest was what the she and the girls lived on. With our arrival on the scene, they suggested that Anna retain more of the dishes, in order to feed the two of us. So, everyone used to eagerly await Anna's arrival home from work to find out what we were having for supper.

Some of her creations were appetising, not always, but we ate it anyways. Then Connie's skills were applied to our well-being; by the time we arrived in downtown Montreal from work, all the banks were shut. It was suggested that we write cheques for Connie to take to the bank and cash, since this was how the girls managed their cash requirements. So, every Friday morning, Connie would collect everyone's cheques; at quitting time Carol would meet her to make her feel a bit more secure, holding everyone's 'nest egg' to get through the week. So, these three girls were on the ball and organised. Who better then to help us with getting some job applications organised for Pauline? They went about the task with a will that would not be swayed.

Each Friday and Saturday, Bill and I would buy all the local and national papers that carried most of the job adverts. We turned them over to the girls upstairs, who would spend the weekend daytime hours collecting likely adverts. We shared one weakness with the girls, that was following Canada's Grey Cup matches. We would gather together in one or the other's apartment to cheer the teams on. I should also state that we were not always rooting for the same team. Of course, the Grey Cup day itself was the pinnacle of the year. We would lay in goodies and plenty of beer ready to watch the big game, usually in the girls' apartment, which had a free access from our apartment via the fire escape.

Pauline planned to travel to Montreal by sea, and at that time there was very little difference in the cost, so it was the matter of preference, and a sea voyage it was to be.

One piece of luggage she planned on bringing with her was her father's old sea trunk. One of those that opens up with a row of drawers on one side and a hanging wardrobe in the other, of a construction that said heavy at a single glance. Having reserved Pauline's initial accommodation at the Montreal YWCA, this until her job location was defined, we planned to store her big trunk in our apartment. The rest of her luggage she could take to the YWCA.

The day dawned for Pauline's arrival, Bill Borthwick had kindly volunteered to supply the transport, as the only one who had yet acquired a car. First, all the luggage had to be gathered in one place so we could load it into the car. There was the hold luggage (including that big trunk), then all the luggage Pauline had with her in the cabin.

The hold luggage was quickly unloaded on to the quayside, separated according to which passenger decks the owners had travelled on. We quickly identified the big trunk amongst Pauline's hold luggage. So, whilst Bill stayed to keep an eye on that item, I went over to the gangway to await Pauline's disembarkation. The same separation organisation that had been followed for hold luggage was applied to cabin luggage. I only hoped that there would be not too much to carry and that it did not turn out to be too far down the quayside. I could see Pauline waving from the deck above me, but there was no sign of any move to disembark. It was only after what seemed an age that I saw Pauline come smiling down the gangway and into my arms.

Pauline lead the way over to her luggage, she had obviously identified its position whilst waiting on deck. There were only two cases, and we were able to manage one each and manhandle them down the quayside, to where we had left Bill Borthwick. After introducing Pauline to Bill and getting through all the excited 'chitchat' that accompanied her arrival, she was excited and we were on a high, realising that all our planning was now nearing fruition, Bill took off to collect his parked car and bring it onto the quayside. He was to bring it as near to the luggage as he could get, leaving the two of us to guard the luggage. We whiled away the time talking about what we had both been doing since we parted in England, many months earlier. Pauline had taken on an evening job as a receptionist at a driving school, to supplement her salary from ICI, and, of course, I had gone straight into a job. Which was not the plan I started with. Of course, I had a couple of accommodation moves with the settling in process.

I told Pauline that we had booked her into a downtown YWCA until she was settled in a job. Since she would have very limited space there, the plan was for her to repack everything she needed for a stay at the YWCA, then to leave the rest stored at mine and Bill's apartment. Bill finally arrived back and appeared to have managed to acquire the loan of a fair-sized luggage trolley on the way over from his car. He had managed to park on the quayside but some distance from where we were standing with the luggage. With difficulty we managed to get all the luggage, including the big trunk, on the trolley that Bill had turned up with.

Then we started to weave our way in an out a miscellany of porters carrying luggage, people pushing luggage trolleys. Plus, cars attempting to weave in and out of this maelstrom of luggage activity. We finally made it to the car. Bills car was a 1957 Buick, plenty of room you might think; well, the small luggage filled the back seat, the trunk just fitted into the boot. The boot lid had to be tied down with a rope tie, and the three of us all road up front on the bench seat. It was quite a lengthy drive up from the docks, because by the time we got away from the docks we were into the busy stream of morning business traffic.

We arrived to find that the girls from the apartment above were down in ours, with hot coffee and doughnuts at the ready. Having put so much effort into finding a right job opening that she might like, plus sending out all the applications as well as lining up appointments, they were as anxious as us to meet the 'lady of the hour'. After all the introductions, the chit chat over, Pauline set to and repacked for the YWCA, with the girls giving all her clothes and shoes the once over, advising her what she would find different in Montreal fashions and what was available in local stores. Meanwhile, Bill and I set to figure out how we could get the big trunk up into our apartment. In the end, it was decided to take it around to the back of the apartment block, then manhandle the trunk up two levels of fire escape steps and into the back door of the apartment.

By the time we were back in the apartment, some time had elapsed, Pauline had finished her repacking and was with the girls talking in the kitchen. All the coffee and doughnuts were finished. Although one of the girls offered to go and buy some 'take-aways', we said we would wait until we had got Pauline settled in the YWCA. The plan was to drop off Pauline at the YWCA, then pick her up in the evening, so all six of us could go out to celebrate at a restaurant. One that came highly recommended from the girls. They added that Pauline would not want to spend many evenings at the YWCA, because it was dead during the evening hours.

She would be well-advised to get the bus and come on over to the apartment in the evenings. At the YWCA, it was pretty straightforward booking in, since the room had been reserved. The one thing we had overlooked was that Pauline would have to be back at the YWCA by 10.00 pm each night (oops). An exception was allowed, by making special arrangements with the night porter. That is if there was going to be some reason for being late. After dropping off Pauline, Bill and I were about bushed, with all the dashing backwards and forwards since early morning. So instead of heading straight back to the apartment, we stopped off at a bar for a nice large cool beer.

When we got back to the apartment, the girls had de-camped and were back in their own pad. Bill and I were left to our own devices, for the first time in the whole day. We took the opportunity to crash out for a couple of hours. Because of this, we were hardly up and about before the girls from above came scrambling down the fire escape. Then in through back door, all dressed in their finery for a night on the town. On the way out, in Bill's car, we collected Pauline, looking very English in the clothes she chose to wear. From then on, the girls took over to guide us to this restaurant, where they claimed we would have a terrific night out.

The meal was good, for the first time Pauline looked relaxed, but perhaps a little tired. The meal over, we all got up on the dance floor. This was not disco stuff and dancing around with Pauline, I realised that it was the first time we had really been alone to talk to each other. Her mother had not been keen on her coming to Canada on her own. The fact was, she repeatedly kept asking if Pauline was sure she was doing the right thing. Had she really thought it through? It was apparent that Pauline felt a little guilty leaving her mother behind. I consoled her by saying that in a couple of years, we should be able to fit in a holiday to England and see everybody. Pauline had already arranged with the night porter to be out until 11.00 pm. But by 9.30 she looked like she needed toothpicks or something to keep her eyes open.

So, we said goodnight to the rest, I got us a taxi to the YWCA, and we were there a little before 10.00 pm. Having wished Pauline goodnight, I arranged that the following day she could either get a taxi, or bus, over to our apartment when she had enough sleep. As it was a Saturday, none of us would be up and around too early. During the next two weeks Pauline was pre-occupied with finding her way around Montreal and attending early job interviews.

Anna, one of the girls from the apartment above, turned out to be a god-send in terms of helping Pauline with shopping and settling in, as well as giving her a more confident attitude towards her job search. Anna was three or four years older than the other two. A realist in every way, she knew Montreal like the back of her hand. Her cooking demonstrations, and the direct contact it had given her with people, developed in her an ability to be a shrewd judge of character. In all she was the ideal person to take Pauline under her wing. Montreal women, like American women, had an overwhelming air of self-confidence. Whereas most new arrival English women tended to be insecure and lacking in self-confidence; Pauline was no exception.

Two of the interviews she had were appointments that involved working for very senior executives as a personal secretary. Knowing that at this level they are expected to literally organise their boss' life, sometimes even handing out minor decisions in his name, made Pauline doubt her own capabilities. Anna got to work and insisted that she had to keep these particular two interviews, because they were the top jobs, with top salaries. Anna reasoned with Pauline, saying that you know you have all the secretarial skills or you would not be applying. Once they hear your English accent, you are half way there, all executives over here want a secretary with an English accent. You have to go to these interviews with the attitude that you are going to get the job, because you are the best candidate.

Anna discussed the other interviews Pauline had already attended and dismissed many of them as hardly worth the trouble. She identified others as a 'shortstop' or temporary job whilst she went on looking for a career opening. I think talking with Anna certainly put Pauline in the right frame of mind, and it probably went some ways towards her success in landing the big job. She had now been in Canada for almost three weeks and had both become close friends with Anna and had made friends with a French-Canadian girl. The latter was living at the YWCA after moving out of her apartment, over some romantic upheaval (no details). The French-Canadian girl named Yvonne was working as a lawyer in downtown Montreal and planned to get another apartment. She also wanted to share an apartment to defray the cost, suggesting that when Pauline's employment situation had been resolved, maybe she might like to consider sharing an apartment.

The day dawned for Pauline's big interview and understandably she was nervous, but still reasonably confident over the coming ordeal. It was not until I was home from the work, out at Dorval, that I heard details of the interview. Her previous boss in England had been a Scotsman with a marked Scottish accent, and she had spent months getting used to his language idiosyncrasies. Imagine her surprise when she found that the man the successful applicant would work for was also a Scot with a strong Scottish accent. This fact gave her confidence level a real boost. She told me that he had asked about her previous work experience and whether or not she would have a problem taking dictation from him with his Scots accent.

Finally, after a lengthy question and answer interview, she was given a typing speed test and a dictation test. The latter she was able to take down in shorthand and translate it back, without a single error. The interview over, they informed her that she would get their decision by mail in two or three days, as there were still other applicants to interview. Those next few days were a trial for Pauline as well as everyone else. Anna and one of the other girls decided to take her shopping and get her mind off the problem.

It was the last working day of the week; then the letter came stating that she was the successful applicant. Would she please telephone the office to let them know what date she would be available to take up employment as 'private secretary to the managing director of Standard Life of Canada'. Pauline immediately telephoned me at the office to tell me the news, it was obviously the news she wanted. Yvonne had suggested that maybe they could share an apartment together to halve the living expenses, and she had already looked at an apartment on Decarie Boulevard, which had a good bus service for Pauline to get to Standard Life offices and the downtown area.

That Saturday morning was fitness training with the rugby club and the evening one of the Montreal Irish's renowned dances and rave-up. A fitting event for celebrating Pauline's good fortune, which we celebrated in style (if my head next morning was anything to go by). After that life settled back into a routine; I split my spare time between the rugby club and Pauline. Pauline split her spare time between me and her new-found social life as an executive secretary in a large company in which some social function or other seemed to be a fact of life for the senior employees. The rugby club dances were almost a Saturday night fixture, except the odd occasion when Pauline was able to take a partner along to one of her company's dinner events. Which, I must admit, was a rare occasion.

Saturday mornings when there was no training, we would go to our favourite little café, order coffee and a big slice of their 'cheesecake', the real kind. A baked cheesecake, this became such a habit that the owner began to look upon us as her cheesecake experts. She would often be waiting for us to try her latest creation and render a verdict. Pauline also started to notice how fashion-conscious the French Canadian women were and started to buy clothes and shoes to compete. I suspect it was the competition in the office among all the other secretaries. Back at CAE, the work on the F104 flight simulator was still our only occupation. Both Bill and myself found the work interesting.

When I had originally discussed my plans with Pauline about moving to work in Canada, I had expressed a wild idea that I might see what work was going in the Arctic before taking any steady job in Montreal. Well, early in the following year, I bumped into one or two ex-FIDS who were headed north up to the Arctic. You can imagine how the trend in conversation soon migrated from what everyone had been doing since leaving FIDS to the subject of what everyone was involved with at that moment in time.

One of them was on his way to join up with The Canadian Polar Continental Shelf exploration. This was a project launched to map all the Arctic territories that were on the Canadian continental shelf. Another FID was off to one of the Arctic 'DEWLINE' stations, as an air dispatcher. The latter obviously after the high money paid for serving on the high arctic stations. However, the one activity that caught my attention was the plans 'Clem' mentioned about the people who were going north with an A.I.N.A. expedition from Montreal to a high-latitude uninhabited arctic island, just below Ellesmere Island. The latter island being the last piece of land before the North Pole, when approaching from Canadian territory. This friend had changed his mind and was instead headed north to join the Canadian Continental Shelf Project. He thought the A.I.N.A. expedition was something I should look into. Although it was organised as a three-year expedition, most of the people involved appeared to have signed on for only the first season's work. A three-man party would be wintering as the camp caretakers and to provide limited capability for some on-going studies.

I started to make excuses, arguing that although I was working as a 'contractor', it was a full-time job and I owed the job some sort of allegiance. Even if I decided to have a go for one year, there was no guarantee that I would get on the team. His reply was to show indifference to my reasoning, saying that in his experience contractors moved around when and where they pleased. The question of getting on the team could be academic. The Montreal office of the A.I.N.A. were handling the admin and logistics side of the expedition and an ex-FID was running the office. The seed had been sewn and although I offered no confirmation one way or the other, it did start me thinking. I now had Pauline to think about, how she would feel left alone in Montreal for best part of a year. That night I talked over the whole idea with Pauline.

I guess she sensed that I wanted to get to the Arctic at least once. She managed to convince me that she had a good settled life in Montreal with a job that looked after her social life as well as her economic needs. She would still have plenty of friends in the rugby club social crowd and was not likely to be faced with problems of loneliness. After rolling the idea around in my mind for almost a week, I decided to talk to the people I worked with. Most thought there would be no problem, because the project was coming to a phase where some contractors would have to be dropped. Although the cuts would not be in my area of work, they could move people around the project team.

So that was it, to cut a long story short, I got in touch with the Montreal office and after an interview with the expedition leader (Spencer Apollonio), I was hired as a meteorological assistant. Because of my engineering background, I would be expected to help with the electrification of the camp once it was set up as well as installing the meteorological equipment. The following week I was packed off to the 'Twin-Cities' to spend as much time as possible at the Onan Diesel plant, in order to familiarise myself with the generator units they were planning to supply the expedition with. Each day, over and over again, I would strip down the unit, have it inspected, re-assemble it and start it up on a test-bench rig and have it inspected again. This cycle I had to repeat for a whole week, until I almost think I could have dismantled and re-assembled the unit in the dark. When I got back to the office in Montreal, it was to be introduced to the other members who had arrived from England, Sweden, Denmark and the USA. Everyone was busy sorting through the supply of clothing and footwear, trying to find an acceptable size before packing their personal kit. I said goodbye to Pauline, feeling very guilty about leaving her on her own, but I had already introduced her to Pat the secretary at the Montreal office with whom we would be in touch with, by mail and radio, when conditions permitted. Pat had promised to make sure that Pauline was kept up to date with everything that was happening. I felt pretty guilty leaving her on her own, without knowing just how much she may have resented my decision to go 'North'.

The A.I.N.A 'Devon Expedition' was in partnership with the Canadian Government, who were interested in taking over all the facilities, after the three years were up, for use as Canada's official Arctic scientific research station.

The expedition strength for that first year was to be 22 persons, although many would only be there for the main summer months. The leader was a young American from Woods Hole Oceanographic Institute, a man who had recently completed a stretch on the T3 ice island. This was very large expanse of sea ice and had a US army team manning it, until the breakup that is. The makeup in terms of skills for the expedition were: one oceanographer and one assistant, two meteorologists and four assistants, one glaciologist and one assistant, two diesel mechanics for snowmobile maintenance, one light airplane pilot, one palaeontologist and one assistant, one geophysicist and an assistant. Then later in the summer, an archaeologist from University of Montreal would arrive with a 'few' assistants. Apart from their designated jobs, everyone would be expected take turns at the household chores, such as cleaning and cooking, this in between their jobs in the field. The skills listed give some idea of the breadth of studies the team intended to cover. We had with us two ex-army snowmobiles (Bren Gun Carriers with wide tracks), two big Massey-Ferguson tractors, plus all the gear to construct six or more 'Jamesway' huts.

The Arctic is very different from the Antarctic, whereas the latter is a giant landmass covered with ice and snow and surrounded all winter by large areas of frozen sea, the Arctic is a frozen sea surrounded on 60% of its boundaries by land, starting with Greenland, followed by the Canadian Arctic territories, then Alaska and on to Soviet Union coastline and that of China. Then you get the open gap near Sweden, Norway and the Svalbard

Islands. Devon Island itself is adjacent and south of Ellesmere Island, which is the last landmass before the North Pole, when travelling that route. Devon Island itself is approx. 900 miles from the North Pole. The Arctic is very different from the Antarctic, whereas the latter is a giant land mass covered with ice, with no vegetation or plant life able to survive there. In the Arctic, once the ice melts, there is a panorama of coarse tussock-grass, lichens and tiny flowers. The summer melt only goes so deep; after that the permafrost level is reached. This is the level beneath which no melting takes place. Eventually, the days dawned when we spent all our time sorting out clothing and stores for the trip and organising ourselves for the journey North. Once all the goodbyes and well-wishes were over, the initial core team travelled from the A.I.N.A. office to Montreal Airport by taxi, where we boarded what can only be described as a half passenger and half cargo aircraft. The front section was filled with about 16 passenger seats and beyond these the space was blocked by heavy cargo nets. These held in place all the stores and equipment for the Arctic scientific research station and other cargo.

This first leg of our journey north was a relatively short flight to Fort Churchill, which in the 1960s was literally still mainly an Inuit village alongside a large army base. We would be staying there at the army base for a few days to await the arrival and departure of our own chartered aircraft. This would take us the rest of the way to Devon Island. Bad weather was destined to make our stay at Fort Churchill a longer one than that which we had budgeted for, both in terms of time and finance.

When I first saw the chartered aircraft, I wondered at the choice, but the Bristol Freighter, with its clamshell nose, had the advantage of short take-off distance and maximum cargo space for its size. There were no passenger comforts, just an unlined, uninsulated fuselage. Leaving us travellers to make ourselves comfortable as best we could, just sitting on the cargo, or on one or two net seats along the walls of the aircraft, with an outside temperature of -50F in flight. Our route would take us from Fort Churchill to an Inuit settlement at Baker Lake. There we would manually refuel the aircraft. From there we would be flying to another refuelling stop at Fox Main, a Dewline station. Then on to our final destination, Devon Island.

Our stop at Bakers Lake was uneventful, but weather again took a hand and grounded our plane, forcing us to buy accommodation at Fox Main. We decided to take advantage of our forced stay on the ground and contact the Canadian Air Force based on Cornwallis Island. We asked if they could fly over Devon Island and give us a report about the weather and landing conditions. The report was that the weather was reasonable and that there was deep soft unpacked snow on our intended campsite and the adjoining space for an airstrip. They went on to warn us that only an airplane equipped with skis could make the landing. A wheels landing was out of the question.

That really started our problems, as if we had not had enough already with weather delays. Now we discovered that the Bristol Freighter was probably the only plane flying in the Arctic that could not be fitted with ski-landing gear. We then had to consider our alternatives, or find some solution that would allow us to continue north. In the end, we decide to fly to the Canadian Air Force base on Cornwallis Island to find out what help we could charter to get ourselves and our stores on to Devon Island.

The flight to Cornwallis Island was in bright sunshine and clear flying weather for a change. The terrain we had flown over since leaving Montreal was a mix of barren rock and sparsely covered snow surfaces. This gradually gave way to snow-covered forests. These extended right up to a line beyond which trees could not grow. The snow-covered ground beyond that line looked so flat. One had the impression that one could roll a ball smoothly across the surface from East to West. Below us was now sea ice, and we began to be on the lookout for Cornwallis Island. On landing, accommodation was arranged for us, as well a welcome meal. After which, the question of what planes where there available for charter had to be answered.

In the end, it was down to a single choice, an old de Havilland Beaver; the old workhorse of the Arctic. This plane, although sturdy and reliable, did not have a large enough space to load one or two of the larger pieces of cargo. For instance, the diesel generators and anemometer masts. In the final analysis, we hoped to persuade the Canadian Air Force to fly the big items to our final destination.

We had just about settled into our lodgings on Cornwallis Island when Ross Carswell, our pilot, showed up in his Super Cub high-wing monoplane. Which, although small, would be a welcome addition to our transport resources. The time taken in unloading the cargo from the Bristol Freighter and watching it depart gave us time to conceive a rudimentary plan of action for moving everything to Devon Island. Firstly, the Beaver would fly four people to the base campsite, to handle the unloading of cargo and stores. The Canadian Air Force had agreed to fly one trip to the island for us and carry the largest, most bulky of loads, defined as those which could not be easily broken down into lighter load. So, a DC3 fitted with ski-landing gear was made available to us to make one trip to the island, carrying the diesel-generators and the long anemometer mast assembly kits plus, one or two bulky or extra heavy items. The remainder of the stores we broke down into loads small enough to fit into the Beaver.

From then on, the Beaver pilot was flying around the clock, transporting all the reduced-size loads. In parallel to all this, Ross ran a single passenger service, moving people between the two islands.

We were forced to abandon some stores temporarily into the care of the Canadian Air Force until such time as we had the means to transport them to Devon Island. On the island things were a bit chaotic, 'shambles' to say the least. So, under the direction of the expedition leader, we organised ourselves into work parties, for specific tasks. The previous year a small party that had landed by ship placed some stores on shore. Consisting of a large supply of fuel, together with the vehicles, beds and sleeping bags, extra Jamesway hut kits and an assortment of tools. They had also erected two Jamesway Huts in which to house all loose stores, those most needing protection from the weather. The remainder was left to be buried under the winter's snow.

The first order of the day was to erect another four Jamesway huts. These huts look a little like the British Nissen hut, but only in shape. The floor is made up of wooden box sections fastened together. On these are mounted a line of wooden half-round beams, looking similar to the ribs of some giant creature. On each pair of beams are stretched roof-mats, these looked like big canvas mattresses filled with insulation material. Once all the roof-mats were in position, it only remained to lace up all the edge flaps to create a weatherproof roof. To complete a hut, prefabricated wooden end panels, complete with hinged door and windows, were fitted to seal each end of the hut assembly. It did not take too long to get four huts up and shipshape. One of these huts would house two of the diesel-generators units. The setting up of which was a shared task, including stringing the supply cables running between the various huts.

As I already mentioned, one hut was assigned as the generator hut. Yet another as the sleeping hut and additional ones as the dining, kitchen hut and general living accommodation. Another was assigned as the laboratory hut for oceanography, meteorology and glaciology activities. The final two huts were for all the stores we had accumulated in terms of food, clothing and scientific gear. Fuel drums then had to be dug out of the snow and placed at an accessible location, for use by the vehicles.

Finally, the vehicles themselves had to be brought back to life, after a winter under a covering of snow and ice. Luckily, the snow had almost cleared away. The Massey Ferguson tractors only needed a little coaxing, by playing a welding torch on the engine sump to warm up the oil. After a couple of false starts, those big batteries brought the engines back to life. The snowmobiles were not so cooperative. They took quite a bit of coaxing, with booster batteries and starting cartridges, before they came back to life.

With the camp more or less shipshape and because none of the field parties were ready yet to leave base for work in the field, things were a little crowded. During this period one or two additional people arrived, so that in the end we had a strength of 22 persons. Made up of Americans, English, Swedish, Danish, Canadian and Swiss. This made it an international effort, even if it was not a planned ingredient. We had Spencer Apollonio of the Woods Hole Oceanographic Institute leading the oceanographic programme, Stig Eckman of Denmark leading the glaciological programme, and Bjorn Holmgren and Lars Dalgrin from Sweden leading the meteorological programme.

We had Kurt Vogtlich of Switzerland leading an attempt at an ice cap thickness measurement, using a new method he had perfected. This geo-electric resistance method had been used to map the various rock layers across the whole of Libya, to speed up the oil prospecting process. Kurt had modified the theory to be able to map ice layers; we hoped to a depth in excess of 1000 metres. Then there was John Cowie from Bristol University, who would lead the palaeontology programme. Finally, we had Gordon Lowther from University of Montreal, who would lead a brief archaeology programme. For the rest of us, we were all specialist assistants in one of the programmes. One or two were just general assistants, for overall support of the expedition's logistic functions.

The generators were installed and connected to all huts, with a simple system of suspended cabling running around the campsite. The 40-foot anemometer-mast was erected and fitted out with ventilated thermo-couples, for a micro-climate study. Only then was the base camp ready to function. Time now to look towards the icecap and the resources and facilities to be transported for erection on its top. Plans were to establish a weather station on the top of the 2000-foot ice cap. This to be manned by one meteorologist and an assistant. Their accommodation would consist of a Jamesway hut, fitted-out for two men to operate independently of the base camp. An anemometer mast and the necessary meteorological instrumentation to carry out a programme of weather data gathering completed the ice cap station.

A team of three men, consisting of a glaciologist, his assistant and a driver/mechanic for the snowmobile would be left behind, camping on the ice cap. Their task would be to carry out and support a glaciology study programme. Roy Koerner (ex-FID) was later to be one of the team of four, led by Sir Walter Herbert on the polar journey from Point Barrow Alaska across the pole to the Swalbard Islands). Roy was selected as Stig's assistant and in later life became a renowned glaciologist. Geoff Stewart (ex-FID) was their driver/mechanic. The meteorologist chosen for the ice cap station was Bjorn Holmgren. Alan Gill (ex-FID), also a member of Sir Wally Herbert's team for his polar journey, was his assistant. The ice cap base would be serviced, for all renewable essential supplies and mail, by Ross Carswell and his light aircraft.

The third field team was Kurt Vogtlich with John Greenhouse as his assistant, for the early phase of the ice cap depth measurement. Kurt was an employee of the Swiss Postal Service and, as a senior systems engineer, was only on a short term loan. He would train John Greenhouse, graduate geophysicist, in his method. John would then take over the expert role and have an assistant assigned to him for the rest of the project.

Life for Bjorn and Alan was going to be an isolated and lonely one. The only other people they were likely to see would be the small field parties working on the ice cap. The latter may or may not visit the ice cap station en route to a new worksite, on the adjacent glaciers. Once the ice cap station erection had been completed and its two man crew installed, there only remained the task of helping the field team to the site of their initial work areas, where they had more supplies than they could carry on their own vehicle.

When all this had been completed, the rest of us climbed aboard the snowmobiles, with the now empty trailers, for a cold, windswept and totally uncomfortable journey back to basecamp. The trip back was hampered by a snowstorm that made the going very difficult, to say the least. My impressions, after that round trip in the snowmobiles, was that 3/8 inch steel plate structure (the main body structure) of these ex-army vehicles was not the best material to maintain a warm 'rear end'. I made a mental note that on future trips, being towed along on skis would be a much more tolerable experience. In the end, we made base camp, tired, hungry and all ready for some well-earned sleep.

With so many people still at the base camp ready to 'pitch in' and help, a meal was soon on the table. Everything was getting more organised as the weeks passed by. The base camp Met team were busy building a desk for their people to work from, with the continuous daily observations. In addition, there were still some special observation equipment to set up, as soon as ideal sites had been identified. John Cowie and his assistant made one or two day trips out from the base to their work areas and lived most of the time in their tent. Gordon Lowther made daily trips to his main archaeological site, with whoever was available on any particular day as his work team. Spencer Apollonio (the expedition leader), together with his assistant, was always fully engrossed with the details of his study to measure the annual nutrient in the waters of Jones Sound, which at that time had over six feet of ice cover.

The two of them would, on a daily basis, take several ice cores from the sea ice and scrape away the small, thin layer of green chlorophyll created by the sun's energy which had penetrated the sea ice cover. In addition, they would take many water samples from the same cored holes. These were analysed for their nutrient content. Ross Carswell (the pilot) was always busy flying mail and stores to the ice cap station and field parties. The incoming and outgoing mail he organised to fit in with his scheduled visits to the Canadian Air Force station on Cornwallis Island.

The Weasels (Snowmobiles) were, it seems, always in need of maintenance, either blocked fuel lines or broken tracks. Danny Welch was the kingpin for all that work, aided by anyone he could coerce into helping him in fair and foul weather. Everyone took their turn as cook, there was no escaping that task. Although in the early days some people, who shall be nameless, took some time to develop any flair or skill for the task, in time everyone was up to speed, turning out good meals, bread and occasionally cakes. Taking into account that all this cooking had to be achieved on a standard two-burner camping stove, the standard was good.

Baking bread and pies was accomplished with a homemade oven, constructed from a large empty flour tin. The kitchen was a corner of the main living hut, which was heated by a Colman convection heater. The dining table, such as it was, occupied most of the floor space. So, with space indoors being so restricted, non-work activities were restricted to table games. Monopoly, cards, dominoes etc., listening to music records, or some quiet reading. Whoever was on weather data observations would have to break off whatever they were doing and read the weather instruments every three hours.

If we had any snow, someone had to go out, take a sample and measure the density and depth of new snow. When people were indoors, there was also a lot of data to sort and record before settling down for any relaxation. Life became a routine, with everyone settling in to their specified work assignments during the day and then gathering together to socialise at the end of the day. There were little episodes which broke up the tedium of unchanging routine.

One example was when a member of the Canadian Mounties arrived with an Inuit driver and sledge team, supposedly to take a census of the population. I should explain that in these high arctic settlements within Canadian jurisdiction, a Mountie posted there represents the total authority of Canadian law. He would have to be policeman, judge and jury. The representative of the Canadian Government, with the responsibility for administering the law, in whatever capacity was necessary. They were more than just the law. They organised the setting up of Co-ops, and the administration of them.

They helped the Inuit market their crafts and products back in Mainland Canada. They also led and supervise the settlements' annual walrus hunt, ensuring quotas were not exceeded; at that time the walrus was the basis for most Inuit settlement's economy. Inuit were also allowed to hunt polar bears for their skins, as well as the occasional caribou, when such an opportunity arose. When the ice on the fresh water lakes melted, they would also fish for Arctic char. This was marketed in Canada, through their Coop.

Getting back to the story about our Mountie, yes he had truly come to include us in a government ordered census check. He also had another purpose for his visit, some English conversation and a few social beers. Having travelled some 250 miles by dog-sledge, he, his driver and the team of dogs, all needed a well-earned rest.

After pitching his tent on the sea ice, our Mountie came up to the base hut for the head count. There were 22 of us in total, the whole population of Devon Island, at that time the largest uninhabited island in the world. With the official business complete, we all got down to socialising and a little serious drinking. After spending a night camped offshore from the island, our Mountie and his Inuit driver reloaded their sledge and started on their long return journey, back to the settlement on Ellesmere Island.

The Geological Survey of Canada were working across our area. Part of the government's program to map the topography and resources of Canada's continental shelf. This in order to substantiate its claims to territories and resources in the Arctic. These teams worked from helicopters, which meant they found it necessary to establish frequent fuel and food depots along their flight route. The helicopter crews often put down near our base for a chat and news update.

It was during one of these visits we found out that as they moved forward along their flight path, they had to abandon whatever stores and supplies they were not able to carry away. This often included tea, coffee, fuel and other miscellaneous supplies. Ross Carswell hatched a plan to use his light-airplane, which he figured he could land at most of the helicopter's depot sights, then backtrack along their flight path to pick up the worthwhile supplies they had left behind. Top of the list, of course, was fuel for his plane, with that we got plenty of tea and coffee. Along with a variety of odd luxury food items.

All this time the field teams and ice cap team were isolated from any such encounters. Although they did report seeing the odd helicopter pass overhead. Back at base camp, the warmer weather was bringing a thaw. This was melting the deep ice and snow, exposing the rocky terrain, becoming a vista of red-brown tussock grass and numerous fresh water lakes. This thawing was in the active layer, which lies on top of a deep down perma-frost layer, below which nothing melts. The melting exposed a predicament that we had not foreseen. Our base site had been chosen before the summer melt, whilst the thick cover of ice and snow was still on the ground. A site had been chosen with a long flat space in front. The belief was that there would be room to land a fairly heavy aircraft. Early experience of the site made it seem ideal. This was the original site chosen, on the shores of Bear Bay, by the 1960 crew. They were the team that came by ship, with the bulk stores.

When the melt started, we soon realised that our nice flat landing strip was in fact an ice-covered freshwater lake. Throughout the high Arctic islands there are numerous large and

164

small lakes that melt out each year. These lakes are an abundant source of freshwater fish and in this case they were 'Arctic char', something between a salmon and a trout. It was soon very obvious that we would have to move camp and quickly. To move anything, we only had sledges and for them to operate, we needed snow. The big Massey Ferguson tractors were well-matched to the job of continually dragging cargo sledges. These we loaded with dismantled huts, machinery, instruments, personal belongings and data records. It seemed to be a never-ending stream of sledge loads to be moved to the new campsite. All this time, the snow was rapidly disappearing, making it ever harder for the tractors to haul the sledges. In fact, the conditions got so bad that by the time we had finished, the only parts left intact from the two heavy cargo sledges were the tow bars.

Despite all the hardships, the camp was eventually moved completely and at this new site, we again actually had a huge freshwater lake near us. This to provide a source of fresh fish, not a landing strip. The surrounding vista, although at the moment one of broken red-rock terrain, continued to expand with the advance of summer and would transform the whole picture. To one of rolling tussock grass, interspersed with rocky outcrops, covered with tiny arctic flowers and fauna. In the following weeks, there were the incidents that tend to act as memory prompts, to remind us of what the Arctic was all about.

One example was an encounter with a caribou that started near the base camp. Our part of Devon Island had only a few lone caribou that had strayed across the sea ice from elsewhere. On this occasion I had gotten out of my sleeping bag fairly early, after being on all-night meteorological observations. It was a bright sunny afternoon; I wandered a couple of miles away from base and spotted this lone caribou standing looking towards me. It would make an excellent subject for some photographs, or so I thought. I needed to get much closer to get really worthwhile photographs; with this in mind, I slowly moved towards the animal. The beast let me approach so far, then it would turn away and move off. After moving a short distance, it would then stand looking at me and again I moved in closer for a better camera shot, only to have the caribou turn away and trot off.

This cycle of me closing on the caribou and then it turning and moving away, repeated itself several times. The animal was obviously as curious about me as I was about it. After trailing it for well over an hour, hoping to get a good photograph, I finally gave up and headed back to base. After having done a night's meteorological observations, I wanted to get some sleep. Having just woken up from that sleep, I heard several of my base companions, talking about a lone caribou that had suddenly appeared in the basecamp area. It had come close enough for everybody to get some really good photographs.

I realised that they were talking about the same caribou I had followed earlier in the day. Such was its curiosity that it had followed me back to camp and was there for everyone to photograph. Except me, who was, of course, in bed, asleep. However, night observations did have its compensations, because a lot of the animal life on the island tended out to be nocturnal. It was whilst doing a 'long stint' of night observations from choice that we agreed to these sort of arrangements, so that 'Met' men could get a break, working with the field parties.

During one of these 'stints' I had this night encounter with a lone arctic wolf. This whilst I was doing the 3.00am observation. Of course, at this time of year the sun was still above the horizon. I noticed something moving around on a snow ridge, some 150–200 feet from where I was working. Since polar bears were still crossing the island in search of food, we were always keeping one eye open for any danger. I thought at first it was an arctic fox, in its winter white coat, and then realised that it was too big for a fox.

The wolf, as it turned out to be, was obviously as curious about me as I was about it. During the time I was looking towards the wolf, it more than halved the distance between it and where I was standing. All the time watching my every move but without any signs of aggression. When I was finished and turned to go back into the base hut, the wolf took off over the ridge. The next night, again at the 3.00 am observation, the wolf was already on the ridge, waiting for my arrival. This time he approached, getting nearer and nearer, and his confidence appeared to grow with every move. Then whilst still several feet away, he stopped to watch me go me through my routine. At no time did he show any sign of aggression, or fear, just curiosity.

After finishing up the observation and recording all the data readings, I stood to see if he would come closer and he did, but only by a small amount. This repeated for several nights in succession and always the 3.00am observation. After two or three more nights, we had both have gained in confidence in each other's proximity. He would now approach, until just out of hand's reach; the only time he went on his guard was when I went to get a camera out of my pocket. He uttered a low 'whining' growl, until I put the camera back in my pocket. It seems the rules for our relationship were holding nothing in my hands when facing or near him and no attempt at touching. Once we had the rules of contact settled, he would contently follow me around each instrument enclosure, watching everything I did. After these encounters had gone on for quite a few nights, I told my companions at breakfast about the encounters with the wolf that comes to just follow me around. I was immediately harassed with such remarks as "What were you drinking last night?" or "Do you often have these sorts of hallucinations?"

One of them at least decided to test my statement and promised to be there on a future night, to verify my story. On that night, I was near the end of my routine, with the wolf there, all white except for some grey streaks on its back and looking magnificent. The way I was standing at the time, I could not see the base hut, but I heard the hut door bang open. The wolf looked at me and then saw something or someone behind me. He gave a low growl towards the figure behind me, turned and then took off like a rocket. I turned around and saw what had upset the wolf, my companion was holding a camera with a huge telephoto lens attached. But he was able to verify my nightly visitor. I never saw the wolf again, neither did anyone else; although there was now a scramble to do the night observations.

Around this time two factors developed, which were instrumental in getting me moved to a field team on the ice cap. The first was that with the thaw came the resurrection of the mosquitoes, after lying dormant all winter under the ice. I was soon an early victim; the insect stuck its probe into my face and without thinking I tried to brush it away. Anyway, its probe stayed in my face. The result was an allergic reaction, which caused the whole of the left side of my face to swell, so that it was a smooth surface devoid of any facial detail. I ended up on a course of antibiotic medication for the allergic reaction and became a constant target for mosquitoes.

At about this time Kurt Vogtlich was recalled to his job in Switzerland and transferred over his role to John Greenhouse, the Canadian geophysicist. That meant that an assistant was needed to be assigned to work on the project, enabling John to carry on the measurements and free up Kurt, who had to return to his regular employment in Switzerland. Sending me to the Ice cap was seen as the solution to two problems, providing John with an assistant and getting me clear of the mosquitoes.

Once on the ice cap, I was to find the lifestyle very different, instead of a bed in a Jamesway hut, I now shared a two-man tent. Instead of the Weasels to carry stores and supplies, we had to man-haul our own gear on a plastic Pulka sledge. Our routine was to move to a central point for each set of measurements, set up camp there and stay there for the number of days necessary to measure a complete depth set of data. The routine for measuring the ice thickness resistance was to lay out four electrodes. The outer pair were two long steel rods coated with copper. The inner electrodes were porous clay pots, filled with a copper sulphate solution. The power supply and the bridge instrument to measure the resistance were connected between the copper sulphate electrodes. The depth of measurement was directly related to the separation distance between the two outside electrodes, 100 metres apart would approximate to a measurement for a depth of 100 metres.

To measure to a 1000 metre depth, a lot of copper wire had to be laid out in order to connect up the four electrodes. We used army surplus field-telephone assault cable, which was a fairly small reel in size, but weighed over 10kg. I then found out what the assistant was really wanted for, he had to carry the two reels of assault cable. Outwardly a very small load in a rucksack, but in weight over 20 kg. People used to compare my load size with John's which looked huge, his big, full backpack, compared to my little pack.

However, John's load was mainly foam packing, for the instruments and power supply. The total load was little more than the equivalent of one reel of wire. John always consoled me with the remark that he had carried the same two reels across the icecap for Kurt. They had already laid out far more electrode spans than I was likely to have to do. They had completed the major portion of the depth survey.

What John had not had to endure was the effect due to the rising temperature during the day. The rocks that had rolled down on to the ice slopes, and there were hundreds of them, absorbed the heat from the sun and melted their way below the icecap surface. The colder night temperatures quickly froze over the surface water, covering these holes with a layer of ice, leaving the rock at the bottom of a hole, filled with near freezing water.

The concentrated weight on my back gave my whole body an inertial kick any time I suddenly crashed into one of these melt-holes. Following John across the ice slope was at times a real purgatory, because I would repeatedly crash into a succession of these melt pools. As soon as I put my weight on ice covering the melt-holes, the thin ice would collapse, dropping my one leg into a bath of freezing water, then scraping my shinbone up against the sharp ice around the edge of the hole. This resulted in both shins being stripped of most of the skin.

As the days passed, I had to depend on bandages to prevent further injuries. These rock melt-holes had their uses though. They were ready made toilet bowls in which to clean your teeth and wash up for meals. That is if you don't mind freezing cold water. Summer weather was coming to an end, the angle of the sunlight on to the ice cap slopes was no longer as effective. The rock melt-holes slowly disappeared, leaving the newly fallen rocks sitting on the ice slopes' surface.

I am glad to report that at that point my shins started to heal nicely. The daily routine was to move along John's projected line on the ice cap and take depth measurements. However, occasionally, John would deviate from this assigned work to move over to various rock peaks in the glacier to examine and collect small samples. His interest was, I suspected, to look for signs of any deposits of commercial minerals, hence the few samples he did collect. However, he never discussed his geology interests, and I never pressed the subject. Each day we got back to our camp only to find the signs of visitations, from one or a number of arctic foxes. Obviously trying to break into the tent and our supplies. They would leave signs of chewed leather straps on equipment cases and rucksacks, as well as general chaos.

Finally, on the next fine sunny day, we decided to reorganise everything and make everything more secure as well as taking the opportunity to thoroughly dry out all our clothing and sleeping bags in the hot sun. Next morning after ensuring that our camp and its contents was as secure as we could make it against any animal intrusions, we were ready to go. Before we could manage to leave camp, a thick bank of fog descended upon the glacier. It was well past midday before we could make a move.

During the succeeding days, we rushed to try and complete the ice cap depth measurement readings. Incidents did occur which offer some break in the daily monotony. On this occasion John's curiosity had gotten the better of him, he had moved across the glacier towards a rocky outcrop. By the time I looked over in the direction in which he had gone, he had slipped into a small crevasse. In it up to his waist, whilst still hanging on to his ice-axe. The latter was embedded up slope from the point of his plunge into the ice surface. With the sun's heat, this ice was not very firm. I had to drive my axe well and truly into the ice and then reach down to hold the head of John's axe in the ice whilst he hauled himself out of the small crevasse. After that incident he took a lot more care about what was in front of him as well as where he was putting his feet; for the rest of that day and beyond.

Our intention, after the depth measurements were complete, was to move over the ice cap to join up with the glaciology field party in order to move with them, when they returned to the base camp. The weather was now rapidly deteriorating. Our tent would give us very little protection in a real storm. We finally received a radio message informing us that a very big snowstorm was headed our way. The message also suggested we take refuge with the glaciology team. John was at first inclined to disregard their advice and warning. He was convinced he should first complete the final part of his depth measurement task.

We discussed the fact that our small two-man ridge tent would not be capable of surviving a big storm out in the open. In the end, ambition gave way to the reality of the situation. We struck the tent and packed everything on to the Pulka sledge. The journey started well, until the snow started to come down thick and wet, making the hauling of the sledge hard work. Eventually arriving at the glaciology field team's camp, we were met by all three of them Roy, Geoff and Stig. A semi-permanent tent camp had been set up, since with the snowmobile they had quite a range capability for covering their exploratory area. They had set up a big snow wall with a heavy tarpaulin roof covered by snow making it into the form of igloo, inside which they erected their tent.

We managed to squeeze our small tent in alongside theirs for warmth and the extra protection we would need against the impending storm. That night the storm broke, and we were so glad we now had the added protection from 100mph winds and driving snow, as well as plunging temperatures. The storm lasted 10 ten days, during which time we were trapped in our respective tents.

Long before the weather had broken, John was campaigning to get out and try for one more set of profile readings to complete his traverse. Everyone joined in, advising him against trying, pointing out that it would be extremely difficult to lay out a line of electrodes in driving snow and high winds. More to the point, it was highly likely that he would find it impossible to make accurate resistance measurements with his instrumentation in the existing weather conditions. This debate was brought to a conclusive end, when Spencer Apollonio, the expedition leader, ordered everyone back to base camp.

That night the storm cleared, and I stood outside the tent in the crisp, clear evening air. We were only getting the tail end of the long hours of daylight, but still enough to see everything in sharp detail. I gazed across to-wards where I could see the curvature of the ice cap and sit-ting just above it a full moon. This view across our campsite to the edge of the ice cap, partially illuminated by this full moon, was a view I shall remember forever. We jointly stripped the camp, scraping ice off everything and packed it all. Loads that would either fit on the snowmobile, or its trailer, including our Pulka sledge. By midday we were on our way back to base camp, in fine weather all the way. At base camp, we found that plans were well in hand, to close the Ice Cap Station and bring back Alan Gill and Bjorn Holmgren.

Being at the base camp was a little like suddenly being plunged back into the big city, everywhere seemed so crowded. We were soon fully enjoying the extended company, listening to everything and everyone and what they had to say. For myself, I was soon back on the meteorological observations rota, no wolves this time though. In addition, at this time, anyone who had nothing to do was automatically assigned to Gordon Lowther, the archaeologist, for duties digging his ancient Inuit site. Of course, most of the people now on base were gathering their belongings, writing up final reports from their specific data, ready for the journey back to Montreal. During the weeks that followed, all of us had to take our turn as cook. The returning field parties took the opportunity to demonstrate their new culinary skills with recipes they had developed in the field. In the main, the results were reasonably well received. During this time, I sent a message back to Pauline in Montreal with details of when I expected to arrive at the Arctic Institute in Montreal. I received an answering message, stating that she had already been made aware of my arrival details and that she would be there to meet me when I arrived.

Some 10 or 12 of us were earmarked to be in the first group to leave. Because the expedition was operating on a 'shoestring', ours was to be a multi-staged trip back to Montreal. The first stage was to be a pickup from the island by helicopter and transported to the USA coastguard ice-breaker 'Westwind'. Second stage was to be transported, aboard the Westwind, from Devon Island to the USA

171

airbase at Thule in Greenland. Stage three was to be flown in a MATS military aircraft, from Thule airbase to the civil airport at Goose Bay, in Labrador Canada. Stage four, fly by scheduled civil flight from Goose Bay to New York, USA. The final stage was a scheduled shuttle flight from New York to Montreal Airport and a taxi ride down to the Arctic Institute in Montreal.

There was still a lot of time to kill, before departure. In fact, we still had no definite information as to when the US Coastguard ship the Westwind would actually be in the vicinity of Devon Island. Before it was our turn to leave, we had the pleasure of wishing Ross Carswell a safe and peaceful journey back to Alaska, in his 'Super Cub' airplane. It was a sight for sore eyes to see him taking off.

Forget all the stories about sleek-lined aircraft for minimum air resistance, his was just the opposite. With just about everything he owned tied to on the wing struts; his luggage, sleeping bag, aircraft skis, it was all there somewhere, including the balloon tyres. Although he had a passenger seat behind his pilot's seat, this space was taken up by a large drum of extra fuel, which he needed for the distance he had to fly. To get at his extra fuel in flight, he would have to use his mouth to start a syphon flow through the plastic tube from the drum, then push the end of the tube on to a connection tap in his wing tank above the pilot.

We all watched him take off, bouncing over the rough terrain and then heading west. We later learned that he had landed safely, after being challenged as to where he had left USA air space. I have since learned that he later qualified for a commercial pilot's licence and went to work as a pilot for Wein Airlines of Alaska. The rest of us could only wait, 'twiddle our thumbs' and engage in mundane tasks to pass away the time until our turn for 'lift-off'. We finally received the news that the ship was now heading for Devon Island. At last the message came that the ship was within reach of the island and was launching her helicopter, which should be with us within the hour.

Well, of course, the ship had mail on board, which had to be distributed around to those who were remaining on the island, as well as those leaving. The helicopter also brought some fresh food, meat etc., for those wintering on the island. Our final act was to say goodbye to those who were awaiting other means of transport. As well as those who were staying through the winter, for work the next summer. We boarded the helicopter and were whisked on board ship. Then we were underway without further delay, sailing through the strait between Devon and Ellesmere islands, towards Greenland.

All of us assembled on the aft of the ship, to have a group photograph taken for the ship's memoirs. After which we were invited into the officers' mess for coffee. At which time the captain of the ship laid out the rules for our behaviour, since we were not coastguard personnel. He mentioned, that in keeping with all US navy ships, the coastguard ships are also dry, so no alcohol on board. He also mentioned that during the trip to Thule, his ship would be testing their five-inch gun as well, as quick-firing anti-aircraft guns. The ratings would also be tested for rifle firing proficiency.

He emphasised that all this was necessary, to keep training standards up to date. We were then shown to our quarters, after which we were more or less left to our own devices. The weapons testing took place once we were clear of Jones sound and clear of any Inuit settlements. The five-inch gun used big icebergs for distant targets. Helium-filled balloons were used for all the other weapons practice, which was all over in just one day.

As we arrived at the quayside in Thule, the captain assured us that we would be accommodated on board until our air transport was available. However, we would be allowed to use the officers' club and NCOs clubs onshore, in the evenings. Thule was nothing to write home about, just row after row of prefabricated buildings, mounted on concrete blocks. Which, strangely enough, were all painted in light pastel colours. On that first evening, we washed and tidied ourselves up and were all looking pretty 'spic and span', since we were headed for the officers' club. However, as we attempted to enter the officers' club, we were met at the door by a 'major-domo' in evening dress, who informed us that we could not be admitted, unless we were in evening dress. We were disappointed but undaunted, as we moved on to try the NCOs club. Guess what, we were not allowed in for the same reason. One would have thought we were trying to get into the Twenty One club in New York. Instead, we were trying to get into a facility on a front-line military installation that was still on standby.

From then on, we only went ashore to get some exercise and the rest of the time restricted ourselves to the coastguard ship. Until, finally, we had the 'word' to report to the departure hall for MATS transport aircraft. All of us made sure we kept in a close group, so that we did not lose anyone when the time came to board. At that stage we did not know how, or when, we would be informed as to the flight number we would be on, or the departure gate. We stayed in a group, listening for any information over the Tannoy System that might apply to us.

We kept hearing an announcement about a 'crash rescue team'. The conclusion was that it was some team that had been searching for the crew of some downed military aircraft. Naturally, we looked around to see who got up or moved. But no one appeared to respond to the information, to get over to Gate B. We heard this message for the 'crash rescue team' several more times. Then suddenly, a big burly army sergeant rushed up and grabbed two of us by the scruff of our necks, whispering into our ears, "Get over to gate 'B', you are the crash rescue team." Much later we learned that they had to invent some cover story to book a bunch of civilians on a military flight. It was a terrific flight, in that we flew almost the full length of the west coast of Greenland before turning out to sea and heading for Labrador; the views were absolutely amazing.

On arrival at Goose Bay, we found virtually no facilities; it seems that the only civilian flights that regularly used the airport were those that are caught up in weather storms. Or safety problems, that rerouted their flight for a landing at Goose Bay. It was late evening when we arrived, and our connection flight was not until next morning. It was a case of every man for himself, to find a place to sleep. The flight next morning was on a standard passenger aircraft, so we were able to snuggle down in our seats and sleep until we reached New York. As might be expected, there were some wasted hours waiting for a flight to Montreal, that we could get seats on. But in the end, we were aboard and on our way for the last leg of the journey.

At Montreal Airport, people from the Arctic Institute's office were waiting to meet us. They had already arranged taxis to get us to their offices. Everyone was waiting to help us celebrate our return. Amongst them, I was assured, was Pauline waiting for me. It was almost lunchtime by the time we arrived. Anticipating that we would all be both hungry and thirsty, an ample supply of snack foods, bottles of beer and wine was there waiting for us. As the taxi pulled into the driveway of the A.I.N.A. offices, the first person I saw was Pauline standing on the office steps. We were both on a high of anticipation; I was no sooner out of the taxi than I had her in my arms kissing, as though to make up for all the time we had been apart.

We all had to have a hug and a kiss from Pat the office secretary. Then a few group photographs for the newspapers, visitors and, of course, friends and relatives. The road outside was thick with traffic taking fans to the football match at McGill University, all of them wondering what was going on in front of the office. Since by then drinks had been served all around and celebrations were in full swing. The afternoon was hectic and probably we all drank a little too much, but everyone was in a party mood. Although I wanted to take off back to my own apartment with Pauline, it would put a 'few noses' out of joint and so I stuck it out until the main crowd were ready to break up. After that I signalled Pauline and made my rapid goodbyes to everyone, before making a dash for the door. My episode in the Canadian Arctic was now at an end. I had enjoyed it. I had found that the Arctic and Antarctic are very different and that it was necessary to experience both to be able to make that comparison.

Chapter Five

The experience was now over, it was time to get back to work and a normal predictable life. We headed back to my flat, in Kindersley Avenue, it was not the nearest, and Pauline had made a point of mentioning that her flatmate Yvonne was away for the weekend, implying we could go there. It was very obvious that we had both really missed each other. Pauline admitted she had gone through a couple of rough patches. Now that it was all behind us, we could resume discussing our plans for the future. Although I had not actually asked Pauline to marry me, it was something we had both taken for granted. It was now early December, and it would be nice to go home for Christmas and to get married in early January. Having already done most of the planning the previous year and then postponed everything, now it could be all reinstated and actually take place.

In the days that followed, Pauline was tearing her hair out organising wedding invitations as well as deciding who and who not could be on the list. Since we were paying for the wedding ourselves, we decided on 50 guests each. If either of us invited too many relatives, then we would have to forgo some friends; the limit for each was still 50, with no hope of poaching the other's invitations. I was lucky with having a small family and would only have to invite my mother, my brother Albert and his wife Marion. Whereas poor Pauline had dozens of eligible relatives and she had a clear picture of who she wanted to invite and who she did not. The problem was, she immediately had to contend with her mother bleating over the telephone that if we invited so and so and not someone else, the family would be up in arms. We solved the problem by telling her mother that I was footing the bill and spelled out the 50 guests rule for each of us. I added the comment that I had insisted that she first invited all the friends she wanted and then filled up her list with whichever relatives there was room for.

I don't think I was the 'flavour of the month' with my mother-in-law, ever again. There was still the actual reception to arrange, so we got the cooperation of an old friend Pete Britain, a close friend back in England, who was willing to negotiate the details with a couple of hotels in our home area. The outline instruction was 102 guest-places, at so much per head, specifying a low and high cost limit. Pete, being an accountant, this negotiation was water off a duck's back and full details with menus came back without a hitch. Although only just in time to get it to the printer, for inclusion on the invitations. Both of us then rushed around the shops in Montreal, searching for Christmas gifts to take home to our respective families. The big event as far as Pauline was concerned, was shopping for an engagement ring and 'a his and hers wedding ring pair'. We were then able to sit back and relax, although I know Pauline tormented herself with thoughts of things she might have overlooked or forgotten. The final days before heading for the UK were spent browsing around the city, shopping for nothing in particular, really only a futile exercise to kill time.

The evenings were occupied with having dinner at our favourite watering hole, the nightclub on St Catherine's, the 'Indian Room'. A place where there was always live entertainment and first-class food. The flight to UK, when the time came, was like all transatlantic flights boring, more so because we were both high on anticipation of events to come. Just to let us know we were back in England, we landed in thick fog, and as we travelled up from London by train, it was reinforced and fog became smog. I took advantage of the train trip and an empty compartment to correct an earlier omission, that of going down on one knee and asking Pauline to marry me. Luckily, she said yes, although she did ask, "What would you have done if I had said no?" My reply was to the effect that I would have given her the ring as a souvenir, then after the Christmas holiday, I would have gone back to Montreal and signed up for the other two years of the Devon Island Expedition.

She uttered some unprintable remarks, which in essence meant, "Surely, you wouldn't do that to me."

To which I replied, "You would have already made the decision on that point." We both decided not to pursue the subject any further and instead admire the ring, which said it all. Arriving in the centre of Birmingham in thick smog, there was no way we were going to be able to pick up the hire car we had booked. It was a case of searching out the appropriate Midland Red Bus to get us home. That bus literally inched its way forward through the thick fog/smog; it took hours for a very short journey. Getting around whilst the fog lasted was a major problem, since Pauline was staying at her mother's home and I was doing likewise at my mother's home. This meant that one of us had the hire car and the other had to rely on bus rides, which was hardly convenient.

That fog persisted almost up to the Christmas period and if anyone remembers that Christmas of 1962, the weather changed to snow, that was always half melted. That made both walking and driving something less than a pleasure. We had left Montreal with a temperature of minus 18 degrees Fahrenheit, cold, but a dry cold and reasonably comfortable with little wind. That was before our arrival in England, although I have had two years in Antarctica and nearly a year in the Canadian Arctic, I have never felt so bitterly cold as I did that Christmas. The temperature fluctuated around 30 to 32 degrees Fahrenheit with wet snow, and fog, or a mixture of snow and rain; I could just not keep warm.

The snow was still around for the day of our wedding, the 6th of January. When the car arrived with the bride, everyone was worried for her uncle, who was giving the bride away; her father had died some years earlier. He was rather weak on his legs and in a general state of poor health. However, things resolved themselves when two stalwart male guests carried my future wife the short distance from the car to the church steps, to make sure her thin silk slippers did not get soaked in slushy snow. After the service there was the usual traditional photo-session, with the photographer dashing all around, trying to herd people into the groups he planned to photograph. I thought he was finished, then he said he wanted one for the local newspaper and suggested that having my wife in my arms, carrying her across the snow to the car, would make a very good photograph. Well, Pauline at that time was not very heavy, so lifting and carrying her was no problem. What became a problem was my standing in that pose for ages, whilst the photographer tried shots from all the various angles. Throughout all of this, I had to try and keep my footing on the wet snow. I remember my mother-in-law pressing one finger into my back as some sort of support. It did occur to me that if I toppled backwards, I would probably break her finger, but then I had Pauline to consider.

Finally, I was allowed to carry my bride over to the car and ease her into a seat, without falling over. We then all made our way to the reception, after having been informed by the

178

photographer that he would meet us at the reception. At that time, he would have proof prints, from which we could choose those that were to go in our wedding album. The wedding reception was the usual mix of too much food and drink and then plenty of dancing to shake it all up. However, all the guests seemed to be enjoying themselves. We had decided on a honeymoon later in the year and to stay just a couple of days at a hotel in London, so that we could take in a London stage show. The one we booked tickets for, was 'Stop The World, I Want To Get Off', starring Anthony Newley, which seemed an appropriate choice for a newlywed couple at the time.

Having finally agreed on a selection from the proof prints provided for the photos that were our choice to go into our wedding album, we were about ready to leave. It only remained to thank everyone for their wedding gifts and then we would be able to duck out of the festivities and be on our way to London, leaving all the friends and relatives gathered around the photo-proofs, busily choosing the shots they wanted to purchase from the photographer. Then it was away, married and on our way to London for a wedding night in a nice hotel; don't ask me the name, I just do not remember. We both enjoyed the show and bought a recording of it to take back to Montreal. Both hoping that the other did not keep the title in mind, for some subsequent request of theirs.

The ignominy of it all was that our final night in UK was one for which we would again be separated. We both had to go to our respective parents' home, since neither had a second double bedroom. Our hire car had to be returned and then a train to London airport, to catch the late evening flight to Montreal. I don't think either of us relaxed, until we were both in our seats and on our way. Despite the chaos in England, we hoped the Montreal end would be uneventful, since we had already rented a furnished apartment to start our married life. The apartment block in which our chosen apartment was located was the same one in Kindersley Avenue, where I had been previously sharing an apartment with Bill Borthwick, after we had vacated the one on St Catherine's Boulevard.

With a furnished apartment ready and waiting for our occupation, we were essentially all set to begin our life together. For me those first few days back in Montreal were somewhat busy, to say the least. First, I had to go out to Dorval and talk to CAE and then the contract company I was directly employed by. In the meantime, Pauline was back at her job, using every spare minute to write 'thank you' notes to those back in England that had given us wedding presents, many of which we had still to unwrap. CAE's answer for me was favourable, in that they would employ me back with the group I had been previously been working with. They simply instructed me to have my contract company contact them, to agree on a start date. Pauline was relieved about my work news; I think she had a mental image of her being the sole breadwinner, with only one income with which to pay all the bills. Once we were both working, our life settled down to an enjoyable and easy routine. Pauline had her bowl games with the office team once a week, and I had one night training with the rugby club. The other evenings and weekends were spent shopping for all those extras that go to make the place you live in into a 'home'. Our next priority, we decided, was buying ourselves some transport, and after some soul searching and debate we decided to purchase a new VW Beetle. The one we chose was finished in brilliant post office red, which we nicknamed 'The Red Peril'. Friends were quick to point out that with the kind of winters we could expect in Montreal, we would live to regret the choice of a car with an air-cooled engine and no heater.

With a car of our own, we were finally independently mobile; we started shopping in earnest for the extras to make our apartment attractive and comfortable. Amongst our first acquisitions was a second-hand TV, followed by a set of cooking pans and kitchen utensils, plus all the other little items essential in a home. Until we figured we had at last all the essentials and could entertain friends, if and when the occasions occurred. Our social life began to slowly change, now as a married couple we tended to move away from some of the rugby club's more excitable parties and instead to socialise with young couples like ourselves. That did not mean we had given up the 'high life', far from it, we still managed to get invited by our friends to some real wild parties.

Gretchen and Paul, like ourselves a young newly married couple, with a flat on the floor above us in the same apartment block on Kindersley Avenue, became our closest friends. Paul was a cameraman for the National Film Board for Canada, whilst Gretchen was a sub-editor for the Montreal Star newspaper. They were both from New Zealand and always expressed the intention of returning there, once they had their fill of roaming around the world. We, the four of us, would always celebrate family events and birthdays by having a meal together. Sometimes in one or the other flats, or at our favourite watering-hole, the 'Indian Room' night club. Occasionally, one or the other of us would acquire dinner tickets for some big bash or other, such as rugby club dances. On one such occasion, one of us and I cannot remember who, acquired four tickets to a dinner at the Queen Elizabeth Hotel, for the annual presentation of the Canadian Film and Television Awards.

We also socialised with young married couples, associated with the places where we both worked. At CAE, there were three couples that were all from UK, and we used to go on holiday excursions together. Across the border in the USA, mostly summer camping holidays. Although there was one exception, when we all went to New York for the weekend, in order to watch the Easter Parade down Fifth Avenue. That included watching all the women wearing their fantastic hat designs and fashion dresses.

Montreal city was hot and dry, sometimes unbearable during the summer months; the result was most people went elsewhere for summer weekends. The result was that the city was almost a ghost town on hot weekends. This resulted in there being very little road traffic in the city, with most of the people away at some park or campsite in New York State. As the time of year progressed towards the cold weather part of the year, everything changed, as people readied themselves for the snows and ice which were to come. Montreal has real winters, with snow that seems to first fall in November and can then still be around for Easter. But because the cold and the snow came every year, the powers that be were prepared for it. As an example, at the company I worked for, every parking place in the huge car park had a wooden stanchion post holding an electrical power point. Car owners who live in Montreal automatically get sump-heaters fitted into the oil sump of their cars engine, attached to which is a long power lead and this can be plugged into a power supply. Either at home (overnight), or in their employer's car park. This way the oil is kept warm and with it, to a lesser extent, the engine.

Providing your battery is fully charged, your warm-engined car would almost always start, regardless of the air temperature. CAE was also aware that some people drove a worn-out 'clonker' in the winter and kept their good car in the garage. To cater for these people, whose batteries were usually on their last legs, a small trailer was provided, fitted with a block of fully charged batteries with which to 'jump' start the 'clonkers'. On the roads, the main routes were kept continually clear, including sidewalks.

But for lesser routes, where snow blowers were used to blow the snow from the road on to the sidewalks and kerbs, covering adjacent parking spaces there could be problems. In these areas there was usually a notice warning drivers not to park after a certain date, otherwise it could be June before their car was accessible.

The snow made everyone go out and buy new skis, if they did not already own some, and the summer exodus to go camping was now replaced with one where everyone was away skiing. Although lots of people were away, the city never had the same empty look as in the summer. We, for our skiing, used to head across the USA border into the nearest ski areas of Stowe's Jay Peak in Northern Vermont, or Burke Mountain near St Johnsbury.

The first was a big well-developed commercial ski area with plenty of ski-lifts and the necessary eating/drinking facilities. It was well placed to catch most of the weekend skiers coming south from Ontario and Quebec. The second area was Burke Mountain, slightly off the beaten track, with all the ski trails winding down through tree-lined slopes towards a single wooden hut, which housed minimum facilities, which was all that it could offer. The slope was serviced with a single rope tow, to get everyone to the top of the mountain (3000ft); the latter conveniently located between St Johnsbury and Lyndonville. We were able to book into the one motel (then existing) in St Johnsbury and be only 20 minutes' drive away from the slope.

As novice skiers, we both found that Burke Mountain suited our needs much better than the crowded slopes of Jay Peak. The latter had the added attraction for tourist crowds, the Von Trapp lodge (of The Sound of Music fame). In the main, Burke Mountain catered for local family skiers with ski runs to match all levels of skill and experience, without any of the comforts and facilities of the big resort areas. Our VW Beetle was both a blessing and a trial in bad weather, an air cooled-engine meant we never had to worry about our engine coolant freezing-up. With no heater to clear the windscreen, we had to fit clear plastic anti-condensation panels on the windscreen and side windows, which at times was like driving along looking through small portholes, with the rest of the viewing area fogged up. But it came into its own when we had to climb the approach roads to the slopes of Burke Mountain. For that matter, it was ideal in all snow conditions when we had snow tyres on.

Then with the coming of a new summer, and the desire to do more weekend camping, we made the decision to go shopping for all that was necessary to indulge ourselves in that activity. Buying our own gear, tent, sleeping bags, stove, cooking utensils, lantern and all the bits and pieces that go towards organised camping. We had some restriction parameters, in terms of the available packing space in a VW for our camping gear. We did not want to carry anything on the roof, so space had to be allocated to every item, on the basis that there was 'a place for everything' and in turn 'everything had to be in its place'. The key item was to get the right tent, not one with poles that would not fit the width of the car. In the end we selected a roomy frame tent, where the frame folded up into a compact package, with its own canvas bag. The basic plan was to take the bench seat completely out of the back of the car and use the full back space to hold the camping gear.

I cannot remember how many trial and error attempts it took at loading our camping gear, before we achieved a loading that was acceptable, from the getting it out point of view, as well as that of getting it in. We made a few fine adjustments after each of the first trial camping trips. In the end, we were satisfied that we were making the best use of all available space, without having to take ages either packing or unpacking the car.

Life settled down to what you might expect from a very cosmopolitan city, with plenty of night life and entertainment, something always 'on the go'. Pauline and I used to talk about it at nights, mainly when on camping trips, since for all others we were 'shattered', but we used to discuss where our life was going and what sort of environment we would want for our children. Both agreed that it would not be a place like Montreal; it was great for a 'good time' but no place to enjoy family life. However, I began to think over what options we might have, taking into account Pauline's satisfaction with a career as an executive secretary.

It was now apparent that Pauline was very much settled into everything about Montreal and its lifestyle, any suggestion for change would have a 'rocky road' to travel. Change is a situation we have to be ready to face up to and is an accepted part of human existence. It then appeared as though fate was about to expose us to dealing with life's little changes in circumstances and living situations. Some two and a half years after we had established a circle of friends in Montreal, two of the three English couples whom we had met from my working at CAE announced that they were planning to move. In one instance the USA and in the other to British Columbia in western Canada. Peter and Sylvia Anderson were planning to move to the Los Angeles area of California, and

John and Pat Michaels were planning to move to Vancouver. Both men intending to stay with the contract engineering game, until they found something permanent.

It's funny, but there are always times when everything seems organised and running like a well-oiled machine. Everyone is integrated into a tight social activity group, then suddenly someone in the group moves away; all of a sudden the pattern is broken. Everyone suddenly sees their lifestyle changing; you are suddenly aware that the friends you depended on and whose friendship you really valued are suddenly no longer around. Since leaving the USA (many years ago), I have realised that because of the size of the country and the fact that companies freely move their employees around the country, the people in the large cities of the USA shy away from deep friendships, because they know from experience that they are only there a short time and then they are gone.

Pauline, Sylvia and Pat had formed some real friendship bonds; as UK expats in a foreign country, they all seemed to be loath to face up to the idea of losing contact with each other. Outwardly everyone was congratulating them on their plans for a lifestyle change, but inwardly dreading the breakup that was to come.

I was not to be left out of planning lifestyle plans; on a ski trip to Burke Mountain some months earlier, actually on the ski slope, I got talking to one of the locals.

This was Roger Damon, leader of the Vermont Ski Patrol, but more to the point he was the R&D manager for the one major employer in the area, Fairbanks Morse Inc. At that time our conversation was pretty casual; I had said how terrific it would be for me to get a job in the area, then we would not have to fight the traffic jams crossing on to Montreal Island every week. In a similar relaxed mode of conversation, he said that if I ever became serious over moving, he was sure that they could find something for me at Fairbanks. He went on to suggest that I leave my Montreal address with him so as to keep in touch, as it was impossible to predict what opportunities may manifest themselves. I did as he asked and for quite some time forgot all about the open offer.

The ski season was over and we were back to planning camping trips. Possibly the last as a group, since the Andersons were at last doing the early planning for their move. Then a letter came from Roger, in St Johnsbury, saying that an early retirement had created an engineer vacancy and would I like to be considered for the post? If I was interested, to telephone him and he would put the wheels in motion, to arrange for me to come down to St Johnsbury for an interview.

I knew Pauline was disappointed that we were going to lose our closest friends shortly, and it had made her a little unsettled. But I also knew that she was 100% behind the job she was doing and had no thoughts in her head about a move. She loved the 'big city' and all it had to offer. I had jokingly suggested that we could move to Vermont and have all the skiing we wanted, but she had never taken such suggestions seriously. For days I searched for an opportunity to plant the idea of a move and introduce the offer described in Roger's letter. Which was hard, because I do not think she even remembered who Roger Damon was.

Pauline unexpectedly gave me such an opening not that long after the letter arrived. She reminded me that we had discussed the issue of not wanting to bring up a family in a city. During our many discussions she had put forward all kinds of economic arguments. Such as if we moved into the 'boondocks' (countryside), I would have to be certain that I could earn an income enough to support a family. Here in Montreal we have grown used to two incomes. When children grow up in a city, they are more certain to find jobs and not have to leave home to do it.

I realised Pauline had already weighed both sides of an argument in considering the case for and against leaving Montreal. I did not see any way to undermine her main arguments. But in true women's intuitive ways, Pauline said, "You looked pretty disappointed with the arguments against a move to start a family. You cannot keep on moving forever; you have to put down roots somewhere." She continued, "With your kind of work, big cities are the centres for your career advancement. Our friends Pete and John are playing it safe and moving to big cities for job prospects, in one instance Los Angeles and the other Vancouver. What has made you get 'itchy feet', is it because Pete and Sylvia and John and Pat are leaving Montreal?"

"No," I said, "something came in the mail, which simply opened up one possibility." I then showed her Roger's letter and reminded her of how often we had kidded him that we could see ourselves comfortably settling in St Johnsbury to start a family.

Pauline then started to challenge the lack of practical information. "What about salary level and living accommodation? He mentions none of those things."

I tried to explain that all of those things would on the table after an interview and if in the end I was made a job offer. Then I had to shift the 'ball' into Pauline's court, by adding that "Before I can go ahead with an interview, I must know that if I am successful that it is what you want. A move to the USA and life in a very small town, like St Johnsbury, where we would have to make new friends and possibly find a new job for you."

For the next few days my wife was obviously trying to tot-up all the 'fors' and 'against' arguments for the contemplated move. I am sure she was discussing it a lot with close friends at the office. Finally, after all this deliberation, she sat down and said it straight out, yes she liked the idea of moving to Vermont. Go ahead and arrange with Roger, to go down to St Johnsbury for the job interview.

I wonder even now what moved Pauline towards the decision she had made, old-fashioned wife's loyalty, following wherever her husband's work career took him or just a gamble to try anything once. In the weeks that followed, I was on 'tenterhooks' waiting for the day of the interview, still wondering if I would make the right decision. We had established ourselves in a comfortable lifestyle in Montreal, in terms of social life, income and accommodation. Although I was quite prepared to drive down for the interview, Fairbanks had booked me a flight from Montreal to Burlington Vermont and arranged for Fred Fortin, an employee (someone that I would get to know well) to pick me up at the airport and drive me to St Johnsbury. The interview was much as I expected, starting with the director of personnel, who had come from his office in New Jersey. He gave the spiel about the great history of Fairbanks Morse, followed by a review of company benefits and relocation allowances, should I be successful in my application.

Then came the interview with a team comprised of the chief engineer, Roger Damon, and the local personnel manager. The latter was there to tell me about all the St Johnsbury company benefits and rules, the things that would directly affect me. The others were there to find out just how soon I would be up and running, if I was offered a position. They had to relate my background and experience to their requirements and their way of working. For me it was hard to get any clues from their demeanour as to how well was my fit. So, by early afternoon the interview was over and I was on my way back to Burlington airport, with

Fred Fortin, the same man who had picked me up earlier in the day.

My journey to Vermont now over and myself back home in Montreal and our apartment, it was to find that Pauline had cooked a special supper, to be served with wine and all the trimmings. My first remark on arriving home was, "What are we celebrating?" to which she answered, she had a day's holiday owed her and to avoid losing it, had decided on this special meal as a way of using up the time. She could not contain herself in her eagerness to know how the interview had gone and what were my thoughts. I had to tell her in all honesty that I did not really know. It seemed to have gone well, but no one had shown their hand as to which way any decision was going. I gave her all the literature the personnel department, had given me, describing the benefits of living in Vermont as well as the advantages of employment within a division of Colt Industries. Formerly Fairbanks Morse Corporation, but changed after an investment group take-over.

Pauline spent the hours after our meal reading though the standard literature given to all prospective employees, conjuring up vivid images of what life could be like, working for the company they were busy promoting. I discussed with her all the information the personnel director had given me, such as relocation allowances. The formalities with the USA government to get a work permit and visa (green card), before we could move into the USA. I was told that a job offer would make it a matter of routine, and they thought that the whole process would take about six weeks, after a letter of a job offer.

I think that then, for the first time, we really got down to talking about how big the change was going to be for us. I told her that the personnel director had ventured an opinion that she would not have any difficulty getting a position as private secretary. Her background and experience would top-rate her for such a position. We tried to delve into each other's unspoken reservations, about the move, such as they were. I had always felt that Pauline liked the 'big city' and was comfortable with her life in Montreal, that I was pushing her in a direction that was not in line with her innermost wishes. This was despite the many repeated reassurances she kept giving me. Explaining that everything was an extension of the experience of moving from UK, to settle down. Work and normal activities soon pushed the question of a new job into the background, although we both rushed to check the mail each evening for that letter from USA.

Friends asked us how my job application had gone, I could only answer that I did not know, and I guessed that most people assumed a negative result. It was almost four weeks before the long-awaited letter arrived, offering me a position of 'electrical engineer' working on customer controls. The salary offered was somewhat lower than I had expected, but not by too much. There was included a letter we had to take to the US consulate in Montreal, telling us to file a request for work permits and green cards. At the same time make an appointment for an interview and a medical examination. The instructions went on to add that we would be spending a lot of time filling in all the forms required by the US immigration department. The instructions closed with the comments that after we had completed all that was necessary, as already defined, the only delays would be processing the paperwork, investigating our background information and any UK police records. The letter closed and ended by looking forward to receiving an acceptance of their employment offer and specifying a start date in St Johnsbury. Adding that any holdups with the immigration question should be immediately notified to the personnel director.

Well, now we had a firm offer, and it was time to decide whether we would take it up, or whether we would reconsider the idea of a move. It was a strange semi-climax, because we had been the last to make a decision to move away from Montreal. Now here we were, with everything almost 'cut and dried'. Pete and Sylvia were going to Los Angeles in a matter of weeks, and John and Pat would not be far behind with their plans to move to the west coast of Canada. Pete and Sylvia were going on 'speck'. Not really much of a risk, because Pete would be straight into contracting, with one of the aircraft companies on defence contracts. Sylvia was also a design engineer with extensive experience, so they did not expect any problems with her employment.

John and Pat were somewhat different they were moving to Vancouver having decided that it was the place where they wanted to live long-term. They had taken a holiday there and decided it was for them. However, they were moving there without any fixed plans, depending on relatives for support whilst they settled in to a new life there. That night we talked our situation through, until very nearly the dawn of the next day. Weighing the 'pros and cons' for and against the move, and finally decided our original decision was the right one for us. The next day, after work, we settled down to deciding what we could do in the meantime to contribute towards the various tasks we had identified.

The first task, of course, was to find somewhere to live, and we decided that the weekends would be best spent in St Johnsbury, looking for suitable accommodation; we did not expect to succeed in a single visit. That weekend it was beautiful weather for a trip to Vermont, and we looked forward to an enjoyable break, good result or not; we were not to be disappointed. Having not quite appreciated how difficult it would be to find, or even identify, accommodation; that we could rent in the short or medium term. Being the weekend, in a small town, there was no estate agents' offices open and the town only boasted the one. The town was laid out between its two main roadways, Main Street and Railroad Street, and then sprawled out in all directions from that central core.

From Main Street, we eventually focussed our attention on what appeared to be the only apartment block in town, and at odds with all the other buildings, it was a modern brick building. We scouted around the outside of this building, hoping to find someone who could give us information about any apartments that may or may not be vacant. Having just about given up hope of finding anyone, when our luck changed. An old man, whom we had previously seen working in a nearby garden, approached us and enquired as to who we were and what was our interest in the apartments.

Well, as the old man appeared to be of the chatty and friendly type, we told him that I would soon be taking up a job as an engineer at Fairbanks Morse. We were trying to sort out some living accommodation ready for moving down in a few weeks' time. "Goodness me," he said, "you young folk wouldn't want to live in those apartments. They are all filled up anyways and have been for years, with all the rich widows and divorced ladies living off the proceeds." Seeing our look of disappointment, he added, "I think old Spencer, the retired postman, may have one of his flats empty."

He continued, old Spencer had been a bachelor all of his life, then he upped and married the spinster school teacher. She had looked after her father in his old age and so never married until late in life and she was left with the family property. By this time, our new-found source of information had lead us around to the corner of Spring Street and Summer Street, where he pointed out the property across the street junction. There stood a typical

189

wooden white-painted colonial-style family home, set back from the road with a big front lawn. Alongside this home was an impressive three-storey white wooden building, with all the colonial-style trimmings, and we were informed it was over 200 years old. Our guide now pointed to the three-storey structure and added that it was three 8-roomed apartments, one on each level. He thought that the top floor had been occupied by an old lady, who had died some time previously and as far he knew, the flat was still empty. Our new found friend and advisor lived next door to the Spencers and was named Lesley. He went on to advise us to go across to Spencer's house, he was sure the man would be home at that time of day, and ask him about the apartment.

He warned us that they were very 'picky' about who they rented to, so do not be surprised if he turns you down flat. So, with tongue in cheek and fingers crossed, we thanked Lesley for all his advice and ended up by saying that we might end up being neighbours. We crossed the road and rang the Spencer's doorbell. There was some scuffling about in the back of the house and a hurried surveillance through the window curtains, of those who had obviously disturbed his afternoon nap. Up to then we had not thought of our appearance, in flamboyant coloured casual clothing, looking so out of place in this small town, we wished we had gone back to the motel and changed before calling on Spencer.

He came to the door, showing no intention of inviting us inside and with a somewhat hostile attitude, stood on the doorstep, eyeing us up. Finally, after a pause, he asked what was it we were calling about. In the same sort of tone as one would use to a vagrant or gypsy who appeared on your doorstep. I explained that I had just been offered a position as an engineer with Fairbanks Morse and was looking for some accommodation to rent, in advance of moving down from Montreal. The mention of Montreal appeared to increase the negativity of his assessment of the two standing on his doorstep. He mused, "You want somewhere to rent, do you? Well, I have one or two people in town who have also expressed interest in renting the apartment. I will think it over and talk to my wife and ask her opinion.

"You folks staying here the weekend, are you?" to which I answered yes. He went on, "We go to church in the morning, but if you drop by tomorrow in the afternoon, I will give you our answer." Of course, we had not seen inside the apartment and at that time Spencer did not seem inclined to show us until after he had made his decision. But from the size of the building, with each apartment having a complete floor, there must be six or eight rooms at least. It was time to wander around looking at the town again, but this time with the critical eye of a potential resident, paying more attention to the outer limits of the town, which despite its small size appeared to have four churches.

Finally, after the sun had gone down, we made our way back to the town's only motel and ordered a celebratory supper in the restaurant. After roaming all over town during the day, we had no problem sleeping till late the following morning.

The afternoon eventually came around, and we found ourselves once again on Spencer's doorstep. It was only then that I realised that he seemed to conduct all his business on the doorstep, because once again we were not invited into the house. Instead, he simply announced that they would offer us, the apartment and with that lead us towards the building next door. There was one thing we would not be used to and that was the three steep flights of stairs to reach the apartment. As expected, the place was huge compared with what we were used to. An adequate-sized living room, a large dining room, a big breakfast room and kitchen, a bathroom and finally three bedrooms. All rooms with those big high colonial ceilings and eight-foot sash-windows; overall the place was huge. Spencer then took us down into the basement to point that each apartment had its own central heating boiler and electricity meter and, finally, we got down to talking rent money.

We had no idea of what to expect for rent levels in St Johnsbury, which was USA, we had been paying $450 a month in Montreal, but I was hoping that here it would be a little less. I finally broached the subject of rent and asked how much monthly rent he would be asking. With pursed lips and some hesitation, he whispered, "Would $55 a month be too much for you?" I hesitated, so as not to seem over eager, and said that I thought we could manage that, since the heating oil and electricity bills seemed very reasonable. We agreed that we would like to rent from the following weekend. Although we probably wouldn't move in until we had acquired some basic furniture, as we were renting furnished at the present time. Spencer said that would be no problem, and we could come and go as we pleased. He mentioned that there was a good quality furniture store down the hill on Eastern Avenue and the lady who owned the store, would order whatever furniture we wanted.

We drove back to Montreal somewhat elated at finding such spacious accommodation, at an unbelievable rent, right in the centre of town. Of course, in the coming week, we had to tell all our friends about our good luck. Now was the time when we began to think about all the friends we would be losing. We had forged some real close friendships in Montreal and were about to move to where we knew no one. Our friends tried to identify just where in Vermont we planned to live, because in the main most of the people we knew drove straight through the whole of Vermont on their way to visit Boston, or the beaches of South Carolina for vacations. That is except the skiers, and most of them seemed to head for Canon Mountain in New Hampshire. There was the odd facetious answer to these questions, such as, "You remember those bumpy railway line crossings we used to bump across on the way to Lake George, that must have been this St Johnsbury they are on about." Many promised to drop in and visit us on their many excursions into the USA. But since they would be mainly traveling on interstate highways, the likelihood was that they passed the turnoff before they remembered their promise to call in.

We still tried to keep up with all the socialising, but with weekends all taken up with visits to St 'J' to take minor items of furnishings to the apartment, friends and contacts were a low priority. A whole weekend had been spent getting to know Ma Sullivan, the woman who owned the local furniture store that we had been told about, located on Eastern Avenue. With her help sorting through catalogues, we managed to choose the basic furniture we needed to occupy the apartment. She was really a terrific help, and it was hard to imagine how we would have fared without that help. But with it we had orders placed, in minimum time. Having to resort to sleeping bags during these weekend visits was not much of an inconvenience. At least we were slowly getting organised, ready for when we moved. Our weekend visits where becoming so frequent that the border guard, who seemed to be the same one every weekend, decided that instead of filling in forms each weekend, to bring in our belongings from Montreal in 'dribs and drabs', he would wait until we finally crossed over on the day of our entry as permanent residents and do all the paper work in one go.

In between trips to St 'J', we had to get all the US consulate details completed, medical, blood test, form filling and filing etc. Then, finally, the interview and then only the delay, whilst all the forms' information was checked and verified. This included checking whether we had any police record in Canada or the UK. For us, from then on, it was a matter of checking the mail each day when we arrived home from work, to find out whether or not the answer to our application had arrived. True to the forecast, the letter came just two days short of the six weeks from the date we had filed our application, to the receipt of our 'green cards'.

I phoned the Fairbanks Morse personnel department and informed them that I now had all the paperwork necessary to take up employment in the USA. They gave me a start date for the beginning of the next calendar month. The logistics were now complete, and it was now up to us. All the following days were hectic, trying to get to see all our friends and to say goodbye, either by having a meal with them or a social meet-up for a drink. I think that this parting from all our friends was more traumatic than the leaving UK had been for either of us. Whilst we had been arranging the details for our move to USA, details for Pete and Sylvia's move had now matured as well as that for John and Pat. The four of them would be on the move within a few days of our intended move date.

It was decided that we would move across the border to St Johnsbury a week before my employment start date. We needed this time in order to sort out the essentials, like the nearest food stores and petrol station and the best route to my place of employment. The priority would be moving around the furniture in the apartment to some arrangement of our liking. The morning for our move to St Johnsbury and the USA dawned; it sounds like a big move, but in fact it was a mere 150 miles journey by road from Montreal. Our old apartment by that time was devoid of most of our personal belongings. All of which had long since been moved, and we only had our small traveling luggage and those essential items of modern living, which would fit into the back of the VW without any problem.

Once loaded, we handed over the apartment keys and were on our way, saying goodbye to Montreal. It was the end of August and a fine sunny, comfortable day for the journey ahead. By the time we arrived in our new hometown, unloaded our luggage and of course the TV, then did a little shopping for groceries and provisions, the day was just about done. Everywhere we went, people stopped to chat with advice about where everything was in the town and who was who by name. People were extremely friendly to newcomers, it seemed, we would soon learn that St Johnsbury had a 'grapevine' that was second to none. The whole town appeared to know who we were, where we had come from, who we had rented an apartment from. Who would be my immediate work supervisor and even the name of the engineer I would be replacing. By the time we got into the apartment and prepared a meal, it was time to get some shuteye. Both of us worn out from the day's activities and since we had not yet located the TV service provider, we could not have the option of watching TV or sleep.

Next day, after breakfast, we went first to Sullivan's furniture store, because at that moment we had only a double bed plus a kitchen table and four chairs; we wanted to get an idea of when some of the other ordered furniture items might arrive. We had overlooked drapes for all the huge windows, which were obviously going to be a major expense item, so we planned to ask Mrs Sullivan's advice as to where the best source to shop might be. It turned out that most of the things we had ordered would be delivered during the next two or three days and, in fact, some of the items were due that day. The advice on drapes was to get three sets of reasonably priced drapes for the essential privacy needs, which she would get for us, but to leave the general question of drapes until we were settled in and had decided on things, such as colour schemes. Our next stop was to check that the bank account we had opened in town had received the funds we had transferred from our Canadian bank account. We were running out of credit cards and needed to clear some of it.

Without the furnishings, there was very little we could do back at the apartment, except sort out all our kitchen appliances, cutlery, crockery and stow it away in the kitchen cupboards. Another priority task was to sign up with the local TV connection company, so that we could have some TV viewing that evening. Whilst we had been busy doing some organising in the apartment, we had failed to see the note that had been slipped under our apartment door. It was from a Carol and Ray Dimmick, and the writer went on to say that I would be working with Ray and they thought it would nice to invite us around to their house for supper that evening. The note ended up with directions as to how to get to their home from our apartment. Pauline asked me whether or not I remembered the name from people I met at the interview. I said I thought it was that of the man who was to be my immediate supervisor.

So, with our evening meal already sorted and having more or less identified the shops we needed to know in town, clothes, groceries, haberdashery, furniture, gift items, and all the rest, we decided to explore what the nearest adjacent towns had to offer.

Well, Lyndonville was the nearest; this was a smaller town than St Johnsbury with fewer shops. Its main claim to fame, from people who had told us about the town, was that it had a small floodlit ski slope in the centre of town, which was where all the school children ended up after school in the winter. For shops Lyndonville was a disappointment, although we made note of a furniture store that had one or two items that attracted our attention. We made a mental note to return to take a closer look at what this furniture store had to offer that we had not seen at Sullivan's. Our attention was then focussed on the next nearby town some 10 miles away; this was Littleton, which was not in Vermont at all. In fact, it was just over the state border in New Hampshire. Littleton was a nice place to browse around, with most of its shops geared to the needs of visitors and tourists.

Having enjoyed a couple of hours browsing around, we decided it was time we headed home and got cleaned up for the invite out. It was easy to find Carol and Ray's house, just one small street block away, and the house was a typical 200-year-old colonial town house. Carol answered the door with Ray, whom I recognised immediately, standing immediately behind her. They both lead us through the house into the garden (yard) and introduced us to their two pre-school aged sons. Ray asked me what I wanted to drink, and Carol latched on to Pauline and led her inside the house, leaving Ray to entertain me whilst overseeing the meat, which was cooking on the barbecue. Ray reappeared from indoors with two beers and after casting an eye over the barbecue, indicated a couple of seats in the shade, where we sat to down our drinks. It was at that time that I was made aware of the fact that Ray was an addicted chain smoker; in the short interval of time since we had arrived, he had already lit and stubbed out three cigarettes. Ray was a heavyset muscular man of about five feet nine inches in height and during conversation he mentioned that he had served in the US Marine Corp. Followed by a period as a lifeguard, on Florida's sunny beaches; this, of course, was all before he was married.

He seemed to deliberately avoid the subject of work, stating that he originally had been one of three sons. The first of the two brothers was killed in World War II, and the second was electrocuted whilst working as an engineer on the high voltage cross-country transmission lines. It seemed that most of the established people of St Johnsbury owned holiday homes on the shores of Joe's Pond and in the summer used to move up to the pond for their weekend water activities. As I was later to find out, Joe's Pond was a couple of miles from town. I could never understand why people would move up for the weekend, when it was just a small car journey away. Anyway, Ray said that they would be up at the Pond the coming weekend, and we might like to visit them and get in some water skiing. He assured us that he would provide the instruction. We gladly accepted an invitation that included some water-skiing, which neither of us had ever indulged in before.

People in St Johnsbury seemed immensely friendly and willing to do anything to help us, the strangers from Montreal. I had to get new US tax plates for our car within a month of entry, and since I had a free day, I decided I would drive over to Montpelier to get it done. The clerk at the tax office remarked that I would be glad to get rid of the Quebec plates. When I asked why, he replied, "Well, Quebec drivers have such a bad reputation here in Vermont that the moment a car with Quebec plates on enters Vermont, the state troopers follow it, until its clear of the state." We now had a bright red car with bright green tax plates. Still it was a good job done, because I may not have had another opportunity to drive over to the state capital before the time limit was up.

By Friday of that week we were shipshape and comfortable, with most of the unpacking complete; we had not had any wardrobes delivered as yet and that was of some inconvenience. Tomorrow was the day Ray and his wife had invited us up to Joe's Pond, so no apartment chores to be scheduled for that day. We located Joe's Pond on the map and drove to its perimeter by simply following the map. But once we were in the proximity of the Pond, with a holiday cabin on every bit of the shoreline, our navigating problems came home to roost. We went over Ray's directions for when we had reached the Pond, disagreeing with each other about the bit of the shoreline Ray's instruction started from. After several false starts, we finally parked just off the road near a sign which announced for the 'Dimmock's' follow the pointer, indicating a path down to the shoreline. Ray and Carol were in swimming gear and suggested we would like to change in to swim-gear before getting involved with anything else. They had one of their boys with them, who was about three years old and who had a length of soft rope tied around his waist, with the other end secured to the corner of the cabin. Carol explained the rope saying, "Given the chance he would be off into the water before anyone could stop him; we even have to keep it on him when in the boat for the same reason."

Once we were changed, everyone was keen to get us out in the boat and enjoy our first attempts at skiing on water. We did the take-off from a sitting position on the boat jetty. With both of us, our first attempts at getting up on to the skis was less than successful. But eventually we both made it, with Ray starting with wide sweeps of the lake, in order to avoid us having to ride over the turbulent waters created by the boat. Then when each of us thought we had made it, Ray decided to prove that we were not there yet. He started cutting the size of the sweeps, until he eventually was in a line that forced the skier over the turbulent backwash of the boat. It was now time for us both to experience several good duckings and the loss of our skis. It was then back to the boat jetty to relaunch on skis. On one of these returns to the jetty, Pauline decided she had her fill and was going to stay behind with Carol and her roped-up son. She would help get the barbecue organised and added that I could stay till I had my fill of duckings.

Ray decided that I was getting a little bit overconfident, after defeating his gentle tactics repeatedly. So, he opened the throttle on the boat and I could really feel that extra pull on my arms. Before I could get use to the extra speed, he cut back almost parallel to my direction of travel, allowing the towrope to go slack. There I was flying through the air, head over heels into the swirling water created by his boat's manoeuvre, with me still in the water holding on to my skis. Ray suggested that I should try learning to get up on my skis in the water, there would not always be a nice handy boat jetty to launch from. He explained how to sit back in the water, lined up on my skis and added that to pull me up out of the water he would have to give the boat a lot of throttle and there would be a sudden jerk on my arms. He continued by telling me I must not let my arms be jerked out straight, that would send me head first forward over my skis. I must keep my crouched position, holding the tow rope with my skis angled up out of the water. The idea was for me to come upright in the same attitude, more or less, that I was holding in the water. He said, "Want to give it a go?" I nodded and braced my arms ready to counteract the jerk he had warned me about. He hit the throttle and by 'gosh or by golly' I was up and moving ahead. We tried the manoeuvre several times again, and I eventually got the hang of what he had been telling me.

I guess Ray could see that I was beginning to look tired and suggested that it was time we got back to Carol and Pauline, because he was sure that by now all the 'eats' were ready. A pleasant sunny evening and there we were, having a barbecued supper and drinks with new friends, having been in town barely one week. When we left, we were profuse in our thanks to them, for inviting us to such a glorious introduction to the social life of St Johnsbury. Their reply was simply to point out that since Ray and I would be working together, it seemed appropriate that Carol and Pauline should have the opportunity to get to know one another. From that day on, Carol and Ray and their family were our closest friends for the rest of our life in Vermont. Ray's parting remark was, "Don't be late Monday, your first day," (with a big grin on his face).

Chapter Six

This was to be the first day of my new job, for Pauline and me it was the hinge-pin on which our decision to settle in Vermont was based, which for us both was seen as a life-changing decision. With hindsight, looking back at it all, everyone was so friendly and helpful from day one and seemed to remain that way throughout the time we lived there. Of all places that I have visited or lived, St Johnsbury was the only place I have ever really regretted leaving. Our apartment was on Summer Street, so I could not have been nearer, from the point of view of traveling to work each day, simply a walk to the end of Summer Street. From the end of Summer Street, it was a short distance down a narrow slip road to the company plant, on the main road out of town going north.

On the opposite side of the road was the trade school; this was the school for those who wanted an alternative to attending high school. This school taught basic academic subjects up to minimum standard. Then filled in with trade courses, electrical wiring, house construction trades, engineering drafting and a few others. On down the hill to the front entrance of Fairbanks Morse, a company that had been extremely rich at its peak. A stock market takeover by an investment group (asset strippers) and their reorganisation left it the poorest and least effective member of the new corporation. From being a successful family-owned company, rich in cash assets, it now found itself without any working capital and earmarked for closure, due to the need for new plant and modernisation. The company had been started by two brothers, Thaddeus and Erasmus Fairbanks, who after inventing a platform scale to replace the old-fashioned balance beam, found a ready market amongst farm and bulk food shippers worldwide.

With the advent of World War II, they had been joined by Charles Morse, who provided the commercial drive and business acumen, which eventually lead to his becoming a partner in the company. By this time, they had expanded into many industries, diesels, gas engines. The needs of the war led them to apply their manufacturing capacity to wherever there was an opportunity. Expanding into a diverse mix of industries, including railways and tank engines. All this bygone prosperity meant that the front building was everything one would expect for a rich 200-year-old business. Because the land sloped downwards away from the road, the main offices, the machine shops and huge foundry were not apparent to the casual visitor.

I made my way up to the reception desk, feeling very strange and out of my depth. After giving my name and adding that I was a new engineer joining the company, I received an immediate reply, to the effect that Mr Dimmick was expecting me and would be with me in a matter of minutes. Ray appeared as forecast from a door somewhere beyond the reception desk, and his opening remark was, have you gotten rid of all the muscle pains after your violent introduction to water skiing. I said yes, which was not quite true. The engineering department was more or less standard, a large open-plan office, with a small enclosed office at one end housing the chief engineer and his secretary. A group of about six desks outside that office was the accommodation for Ray and the product engineers, the remainder of the office space was filled with drawing boards for draftsmen, who were already busy creating, or amending, product drawings.

Ray led the way into the chief engineer's office and introduced me to the chief engineer, whom it seemed would be retiring the end of that year. After the usual informal chitchat with the introductions, the chief engineer turned to introduce another man in the office, saying, "Jim, this is Les, one of our controls engineers, who retires in a few weeks and is the engineer you are here to replace. He will have only a few weeks to put you in the picture as to what is required of you and pass on some of his 'know-how'." He went on to spell out that for the rest of that day Ray would be taking me around the various department offices and introducing me to the people I would be working with. Tomorrow he would assign someone to take me around the machine shops and foundry.

By the time we were out of the chief engineer's office it was lunch time. I already knew that those who lived nearby went home to lunch, so I took off in one direction and Ray in another, promising to meet up again after lunch. Over lunch I imparted as much as I had learned about the company and its workings, which was almost nothing, to Pauline. After I was finished, Pauline informed me she was going with Carol to meet some of the other wives and get tuned in to the town 'grapevine'. After lunch was over and we were back on site, I was just about to speak to Ray, when he interrupted me mid-sentence. With a very serious expression on his face, he informed me that I had two visitors in reception who wanted to talk to me. I went through to reception and the receptionist said from behind a file folder which she was holding to cover her mouth, "There are two gentlemen from the FBI who wish to speak with you." Well, in an instant, I was trying to organise my thoughts, in an attempt to understand why they wanted to speak to me. Had I inadvertently made a false statement on the documents I had completed for entry into the USA? I could think of nothing to explain why they might want to interview me.

If I was confused and left guessing, you can use your imagination to figure out what was going through the minds of everyone at Fairbanks Morse. Who was this criminal we have hired, we have never before had a visit from the FBI? As I walked across the reception lobby, the two agents stood up, both smiling and one said, "Mr Fellows?" to which I nodded assent. They both looked like the film image, young athletic types in well-tailored suits. The senior agent introduced himself, then he repeated my name in full, "Mr James Walter Fellows?" to which I again nodded in assent. He went on to explain that they were here on a routine matter, the details of which were essentially that a man named Peter Anderson had applied for employment in the USA defence industry, for which security clearance was required. They went on to state he had recently moved to California from Montreal and had given my name and address as one of his character references. They followed on with a list of simple questions, how long had I known him, did I know him socially as well as in an employment capacity, and they continued with a series of minor questions, ticking them off a list as they progressed. Finally, it was all over, they shook hands and thanked me for my cooperation, and I saw them off the premises.

Back in the office, Ray was immediately there, no doubt detailed off to ascertain exactly what had transpired during my interview by the FBI. When I told Ray what it was all about, he could hardly stop laughing, his response was to the effect that how could the FBI send agents up from Boston, almost 200 miles, just to verify the information filled out on a form by someone in California and not just one agent but two. We walked together back into the engineering department amidst all the guarded whispers, Ray whispered back to me, "The town grapevine going to have a 'heyday' with this one." Of course, as we went from department to department introducing me, Ray was determined to 'milk' the incident for all it was worth, with such remarks as, "What can you really think about a new hire, who on his first day on site, is called in for interrogation by the FBI?"

I can honestly say I was glad when the first day was over, doubly sure that I will have forgotten half of the names of people I had been introduced to that day. At home, Pauline was full of all the information she had gleaned from the other wives. Including an assurance that she could get a medical records secretary's job, at Brightlook Hospital, just a few hundred yards from our apartment. She intended not to lose any time, but to go there and apply the very next day.

We watched TV that night and switched over to the local town-station broadcast channel, operated by the local trade school. This covered upcoming local events, as well as the town gossip and town events. There was nothing we could identify with, so we switched back to regular TV and, of course, the endless interruptions for advertising.

The next day, my tour of the machine shops and foundry was more relaxed and interesting. I was looking forward to it and enjoyed it much more than my first day. Some of the machine bays were huge, with good reason, the company weighed huge 'container cars' on platform scales, rail cars that could carry grain, cement and any other commodity that could be loaded as a fluidised material. These large platform scales could be installed under sections of a branch railway line to weigh engines, container cars for grain and other cereals, molten-steel bottle-cars, coal wagons and endless others. These platform-type scales were so huge that they required levers that could be 30–40 feet in length. These had to be suspended at each end on hardened steel-knife edges, riding in 'V' block steel bearings. For the scale to be accurate, the distance between knife-edges, on each lever, had to be measured and machined to very fine tolerances. For this they needed special long-bed monster machines. Where the machinist with his milling and broaching tools (a small machine in itself), would ride on a pair of precision lead screws for the full length of the cast lever, between each face that had to be milled flat and precision bored then broached for each 'knife-edge'.

The foundry was another eye-opener; it was huge, as well it need be, to cast some of the huge levers required for those long platform scales. Like all old foundries, the floor was deep in fettling dust and casting sand that never seemed to get fully cleared. I really enjoyed my day, as well as meeting up with one or two people. People who could be of help, should I ever come up against a casting or machining problem on the equipment orders I would eventually be involved with. A wise old engineer had once told me that obtaining the solution to any problem is finding the right person who really understands what the real nature of the problem is. Whilst I was down in the machine shop, I was recruited to join the local branch of Kiwanas, a fraternal/charitable society similar to the 'Round Table' in UK. It was suggested that it would be a good opportunity to meet men of the town, other than those I worked with.

Pauline got the job at Brightlook Hospital as a medical records secretary and was due to start work the following week. Things were beginning to fall into place, all part of the essential task of settling in. I was becoming more aware each day, just how ill-equipped a new engineer is to function productively, no matter how experienced he is of other companies' practices. Experience seldom applies for the first few weeks in a new job. In my first few weeks, I seemed to spend my life trying to find out who I could contact. A necessary adjunct to get customers operation details, or prices, or a service engineer's report on a problem. It seemed as if at every turn there was someone or some department that I had to identify or locate, for even the minutest piece of information. The only place where that didn't apply was in the lab, with Les working on an actual problem. As the weeks passed, I began to find my feet and feel a little more confident on the job.

At least one event will stay in my memory for ever. It started as a routine day, and I was lining up some questions I needed answering about a customer's operation. It was in connection with an equipment order I was dealing with and had already learned that you call up the sales-office that took the order. If possible, I wanted to speak to the actual salesman. So, I put in a call to the Dallas sales office, introduced myself and explained who I was. To be greeted with the reply, "Oh, you are the new engineer we have been hearing about. Well, you have a lot to live up to; Les was highly regarded here, both personally and as a good engineer."

I had just started to discuss the information I needed and had quoted the order number, when there was the sound of a pandemonium at the other end of the phone. The man on the line started shouting questions to others who were in the same office. But I was unable to grasp the nature of the incident that had caused all the excitement. Eventually, I heard the phone being dropped on the desk with the line still live. I then began to understand that something had happened outside their office building, which they were trying to get information about. Eventually, someone came back on the line and said they would get back to me later, as everything was in turmoil in the office at that time. Naturally, I asked what had happened; he replied, "Someone just shot President Kennedy."

I asked, "Is he dead?"

The reply was that, "We do not know for sure, but it's highly likely, call you back later today," and then the phone went dead. So, admittedly, it was on the phone, but I had an instant on the spot report about the assassination of President Kennedy in Dallas Texas in September 1963. An event I well have good reasons to remember. By the time the Dallas office called back, we were getting full coverage on National TV, with the confirmation that he actually died from gunshot wounds. Well, after that, every time I touched that specific order's documentation, it was a constant reminder. Although I did not need further contact with that sales office, the one contact was all I needed.

Things were settling down now, and we were both feeling very confident about the way things were shaping up both with jobs and social life. So much so that we discussed the idea of a touring holiday in UK, with plenty of opportunities to visit family and friends. However, before I continue with that story, I need to fill in a bit of background information that had some bearing on our holiday plans. Remember, I mentioned earlier that the town had a 'grapevine' system second-to-none, for if someone dropped a pin on Main Street, people on Railroad Street would be reporting on the event before it hit the ground. At that time the company was running a big advertising campaign, promoting all the new technology they had brought to the weighing industry and were continuing to do so. As a part of this campaign, which they advertised nationally, all regional sales offices, local sales offices and manufacturing locations were invited to enter an idea for a product enhancement. The winning idea would be developed into a working device to improve controls on weighing applications, and there would be a prize of $500, which in 1963 was a reasonable sum of money, for the winner.

The chief engineer circulated a memo stating that he expected it to be won by someone not only from the St Johnsbury plant but from his department. Well, plans for our UK holiday were maturing, and we started sorting out the details. One of which was acquiring new luggage, as our old stuff had reached the end of its useful life. Around the same time, having in mind the design competition, I started playing with a switching device. Which basically consisted of a glass-encapsulated micro-switch and a miniature actuating bar magnet, together with a ferrous metal flag that could be mounted so as to interrupt the magnetic field. The idea being that when a Tare-beam came to balance, the ferrous blade would block the magnetic field and the microswitch would open. There were a few other sophistications to ensure that the field cut-off was a sharp line, to give weighing accuracy. When I had it finished, I figured it was an idea for a low cost cut-off control, for use with a basic balance beam on small platform scales. I didn't really think it could win, because it was so simple and basic. Surely, with all of the other departments across the country offering competing entries, there was going to be some stiff competition. Well, I handed in my design and then forgot about the whole issue; no one seemed to have any idea of when the winner would be announced.

Some weeks later, we were going into a local store to choose some new luggage and having made our selection, we went up to the cash desk to pay. Whilst I was thus engaged, Pauline was chatting to some woman whom she seemed to know well, probably one of the wives from the plant, so I thought. Once we were clear of the store, Pauline burst out with, "Did you hear what she said? 'So you are spending your ill-gotten gains already!' She thinks you have already been told that you have won the design prize." I assured her that her friend was just guessing, no one knows yet, or else I would know. She was just making conversation, or more likely probing to see what we knew. Well, we went on our grand holiday to UK and having thoroughly enjoyed it, were now back in harness in St Johnsbury. It was now some nine weeks since Pauline's acquaintance had made the remark about us spending our ill-gotten gains already.

At midday of that day, I was called into the chief engineer's office, who presented me with a big white envelope, and if it had not been for the big grin on his face, I might have thought they were my termination notice. "Go on, open it," he said. I then tore open the envelope and took out a single sheet letter and a cheque made out for $500. The letter was from Mr Isaacson, president of Fairbanks Morse Inc, and had an address in Fairlawn New Jersey. It said that a panel of judges had deemed my entry the winner on the basis of intuitive innovation, applicability to the product line and potentially low cost. That it would require very little further development before an application was possible. I handed the letter to the chief engineer to read, but he waved it away, he had obviously read a copy, but added, "You better go and show it to Ray."

I went over to Ray, he grinned and said, "So now you finally know."

"As well as the rest of town," I said, but the decision was made in Fairlawn. His muttered reply was something about people floating between St Johnsbury and Fairlawn; the result was the whole town virtually, had known the result for over eight weeks. Ray congratulated me on winning the design competition, but in the months following, no attempt was made to apply my design in any way.

I began to realise that it had been a PR scheme, attempting to focus everyone's attention on the product line and the need for continued innovation. I continued to work on customer orders, but at the same time would have liked to have worked with Roger Damon's group. Developing improved or completely new products. Roger was the manager of R&D and a key man in the organisation.

I guess it was a constant interest in new ideas that started me ordering copies of the Harry Diamond Laboratories reports, a government research agency. They had been researching the application of Coanda Flow theory for fluids, to produce digital switching devices of a fairly small geometry. These could be assembled into control circuits that would have normally have been restricted to electrical devices. These new control circuits would operate on pressurised air or gas. At pressures as low as 20 inches of water-gauge (0.722 psi). The flow would be in tiny passageways, typically of the order of 0.020 x 0.030 inches in width and depth. Peak operating speeds were the speed of sound, as opposed to electrical devices, where the limit was the speed of an electron.

At that time low-voltage integrated circuits had not yet come to fruition. Everyone felt that there was a big future for fluidic controls (fluidics was the name adopted for the new technology). By 1966 the 'pundits' were forecasting markets in the millions of dollars, yet by that time no one had yet launched a commercial application. Early in 1966, a sales engineer at the corporate offices in Fairlawn, having heard that I was playing with some of these devices, some of my own manufacture and others that I had purchased, suggested that this technology might be applied to some of our systems in chemical plants, where a fire or explosion hazard might exist; such plants relied on 'Underwriters' Laboratories'. Before any plant could obtain insurance cover, it had to be inspected and passed as safe by UL; this inspection was always after the plant had been completed. UL would often turn down electrical controls on the basis that there was not enough protection from 'spark' hazards and refuse approval for insurance of the plant. To avoid these costly situations, chemical plant engineers would often play safe and use hydraulic or pneumatic controls. With the latter devices, any sequential controls were either bulky, slow or extremely costly. What was needed was some sort of switching device that was low-powered, fairly fast and intrinsically safe from spark hazards. Fluidics appeared to offer all of those attributes as a switching device that could be applied to sequential controls.

My reply to the Fairlawn office was that the devices available on the market were still unproven and the long-term reliability unknown. Surely, we would not wish to risk such a system on our customer; a customer would certainly not wish to invest in untried system controls. But the salesman would not be put off, he was dealing with a company who had several plants handling a material that was potentially both a fire and an explosion hazard. They have been having so many problems in getting UL approval, they want to try something new, and they fully appreciate all the risks they are taking. If we did not do it for them, he was sure they would find some other company that was willing to take the order. Well, I was over a barrel and if we accepted the order, I would literally have to build a prototype system that would essentially be sold to the customer. There had been no commercial fluidic systems sold to industry up to that date, this would be the first. Well, the end result was that I settled on using a device that was more fully understood than the Coanda devices for this working prototype, although final systems would be expected to use the Coanda devices. The outcome of all this was, I designed a full batching by weight system that would potentially be the first commercial application of fluidics control systems in the USA. The company started to apply for patents in my name, and I was granted US patents 3343616 and 3407890. In June 1966, I presented a paper to a meeting of the American Society of Mechanical Engineers at their meeting in Chicago, titled

FLUIDICS IN WEIGHING SYSTEMS CONTROLS. Following all the publicity about our system, Mr Isaacson, president of Fairbanks Corporation, sent me another letter with a cheque for $100 and said that he had read with interest the paper I had presented at the ASME meeting and had heard how well it had been received. In keeping with company policy of awarding a $100 honorarium to engineers who presented papers before professional societies, please accept the enclosed cheque. In the following months, I received a flow of $50 cheques, one for each patent filed, one for each patent granted and one for each license granted on the patent. All this time, of course, the development, testing and installation of the system had to be progressed to its conclusion.

After the initial system using turbulence amplifiers, subsequent repeat orders were re-engineered, and the system used Coanda Flow devices, the complete circuit manufactured as a compact integrated circuit, some 7x5x2 inches. Which was considerably more compact than the individual components connected by plastic tubing would have been. Then the crash came, the advent of very low voltage digital circuits put an end to the dreams of huge markets for fluidic controls. The life of the technology was virtually at an end by 1968. There was still a specialist market for fire and explosion hazard control systems, but low voltage meant the sparks would be cool enough so that they could not ignite most hazardous materials.

Of course, with all the fluidics publicity, I became 'the flavour of the month'. So, when in early 1967, a team from corporate headquarters decided to take advantage of the 'brain drain' raids on the UK for engineers, having heard from other companies that the quality of hires from the UK was extremely high, they decided to invest in some for St Johnsbury. It seems the director of human resources thought that having me along would give them an edge, when attempting to convince an applicant to come 'on board'. In London we were ensconced in luxury rooms, with a suite of well-equipped interview rooms, the whole thing was organised on a grand scale. All the client-hirers had to do was interview likely prospects. Each enterprise seeking new hires were handed some 1500 résumés that the agency staff had received and matched to each of their clients. Which meant that every application was seen by many client companies. In fact, the final applicants would probably be interviewed by several interested employers. Our first few days were spent sorting through this pile of applications, to get down to the small number we would like to interview.

I soon realised that sorting through applicants for a job was no easy task; okay, I could match qualifications and experience against the needs in the St Johnsbury plant. I was pretty adept at sorting the ones that said they had done things from those that claimed they had those skills. The plant we were hiring for was very much a hands-on place, without too much formal structure; these people would have to be capable of seeking solutions for themselves. We needed to know fairly reliably who had those qualities and is a team player who can be relied on as an individual. Well, we finally whittled the list down to 12 individuals, interviewed them and hired the lot. A pretty good package was offered to them, moving costs, including furnishings and belongings for married couples, a generous settling in allowance and fairly good salary levels. I was left alone with them to relate my experience and problems settling in St Johnsbury. For them to question me about my settling in experiences and to answer any questions they had or had forgotten to ask at the interview. This often meant I had to go back to the Fairlawn Team to get the answers if it related to their hire details. Of course, all these people I was talking to did not yet know that they would all receive an offer, which would be made by mail before we left England.

At a time prior to the recruiting visit to England, Pauline and I had jointly decided to buy some land and eventually have a house built on it. With that objective in view, we purchased an isolated plot of land (2.27 acres) on Rocky Ridge, some 2.8 miles from town. The land offered an absolutely glorious view, right over to the mountains of New Hampshire, and at the time only two other families were living up on the ridge. We had mentioned it to a friend, who was the assistant manager at the bank where we had our account, and his only comment was, "Well, do not forget to let us loan you the money when you are ready to build."

The new hires from UK started to arrive and obviously some took longer to wind up their affairs in UK. As was the case with a couple, one of the more mature married couples, unlike the others in their early to late twenties. The company human resources team lined up rental accommodation for all the couples as they arrived, giving the early arrivals more than one choice and leaving the late arrivals with limited choice. There were some amusing sidelines to their effect on the local populace; one example was all the young women in their twenties (remember this was the 60s) wearing mini-skirts. This in a little town they had nicknamed 'Hicksville' when they first arrived. They caused a riot amongst the male population, who 'ogled' these half-naked English girls. They encountered their first real problem when their husbands took them to the St Johnsbury House hotel and ordered drinks. The old barman insisted that the women appeared to be dressed as schoolgirls; therefore, by law he was bound to ask then for a driving license or other identity to verify their age.

In the meantime, whilst all this was going on, I had approached the Citizens Bank, where I had an account, and arranged a meeting with the bank manager to discuss a loan to build my house. I went to that meeting convinced that it would be all a formality and that I would get my loan. Imagine my surprise when, without asking me to sit down, the manager informed me that the bank had decided not to loan me the money I had asked for. I did ask why and was told it was a bank decision. I was madder than hell and immediately moved my account to the other bank in town, which was Howards Bank. This was an accomplished fact when the new arrivals asked me which was the best bank. So as each new arrival asked the same question, I always told them that I had recently moved to Howards Bank, having been let down on a personal banking issue by Citizens Bank; pretty well all chose the same bank.

Sometime later in the year, I was to be allowed to gloat at Citizens Bank expense, when the main 'investment advisory' company in the town threw a cocktail party to promote their services. The guests included the bank managers, the moneyed people of the town and all the new English arrivals. At this party, the bank manager of Citizens Bank was busy praising the loan facilities that it could offer its clients for house mortgages, small business loans and loans for home construction. I jumped at the opportunity and asked in a loud voice, so that everyone could hear, "I asked you for a loan to build my house on Rocky Ridge, you refused the request for a loan without giving any reasons whatsoever. I moved my account to the Howards Bank and within days was granted the needed loan." Although most people in town knew the answer, they wanted to hear it from the bank manager's lips. He seemed uncertain of his ground, but in the end he said he was acting on direct instructions from one of the bank's senior directors to deny the loan. He admitted that, "It has probably been one of the biggest mistakes the bank has ever made, and we now realise that it could cost us many millions in loan business over the long term."

The director at the root of all this was financing the building of a group of houses on land he had acquired between the centre of town and Rocky Ridge and saw these new arrivals from UK as his clients for the purchase of houses in his new development. As well as others who had moved into the area to work at Fairbanks Morse. He reasoned that if I built on Rocky Ridge, many more would follow suit, and therefore, it was not in the best interests of Citizens Bank to grant the loan request. Whilst the manager of Citizens Bank was making his confession, the manager of Howards Bank was grinning like a 'Cheshire cat'. Smug with the knowledge that almost all the new arrivals had taken out bank loans to purchase cars and at least half had signed up for mortgages to buy a house. The whole room revelled in the discomfort my remarks had caused Citizens Bank's manager, who had never been very popular at best.

The new English crowd soon settled in; it was obvious that as a group they would soon be a power to be reckoned with. Many were already holding key positions in the planned reorganisation structure demanded by the new corporate management, whose offices were in Connecticut. Ever since the stock market takeover of Fairbanks Morse Inc, the new owners had reorganised itself with a new corporate identity, under the name of one of Fairbanks Morse old acquisitions, the well-known name of 'Colt Firearms'. The re-named group became Colt Industries, owning the whole of the Fairbanks Morse industrial empire. All the capital which had made Fairbanks Morse such a rich and stable company was transferred to the assets of Colt Industries. This left the weighing systems operation at St Johnsbury without operating capital of any kind and earmarked for disposal consideration by the parent organisation. The reasons given for such a consideration was that it was an out-of-date plant with very limited life expectancy. After closure the residue of the company business could be moved to Fairlawn New Jersey.

But Colt Industries had misjudged 'Vermonters', who formed a committee of people from St Johnsbury and the surrounds, those who depended on the plant for the town's survival. They put together a paper, asking very exact details of why the existing plant did not fit in with Colt Industries' requirements. What were the details of a manufacturing plant that met those requirements? The Colt Industries reply was almost flamboyant, since they really wanted to bury Fairbanks Morse. They said that it would have to be single-level building, with a one direction flow of product. Meaning that raw materials would have to be delivered at one end of the building and finished product taken away at the other end. All machinery would have to be new and fit for purpose and where necessary, purpose-built. They ended by saying that they could not invest that sort of capital for a rebuild on the company's present order book. The committee made Colt Industries come out in public and announce that they definitely would not shut down the St Johnsbury manufacturing if a modern fully equipped plant became available. The committee proposed to Colt Industries that it would build a new plant to their specifications and lease it fully equipped to Colt Industries. Colt had no alternative but to accept the terms for keeping manufacturing in St Johnsbury. To cut a long story short, the committee, the town, the area, with support from the state, all pulling together, raised the capital and leased a new plant to Colt Industries in under three years. As a result, manufacturing is still in operation at St Johnsbury and the old plant is the site of a large modern motel.

Well, to get back to my story, we had the house built on Rocky Ridge and, as expected, the view from our living room window was straight across to the snow-covered peaks of the mountains in New Hampshire. The town of St Johnsbury was just a glow of light in the bottom of the valley at night. Our son Paul was born some weeks before the house was finished, and I remember him at the hospital, where he was in a fairly large crib and used to always scoot tight up into the corner. No matter how many times you pulled him into the middle, he still scooted to the corner, so that in the end the nurses christened him 'Scooter', a name that stuck for months. We moved into the house about a month later. My fame with fluidics meant that I used to get the odd call from headhunters, asking if I was interested in moving and, of course, a regular one from our biggest competitor. So, the idea of moving must have been lying dormant in my mind for some time, I am not quite sure.

In our time in St Johnsbury we had made many dear, real friends, and we tended to socialise as much with the locals as with the now not so new English arrivals. The activities were varied and typical of the area; in the summer it was camping, swimming and barbecues, and in the winter, skiing and house parties. The Kiwanis activities took up a lot of my time at first, for they used to run a charity auction each year on the town TV channel. Which meant all Kiwanis were busy either canvassing local businesses to donate goods for the auction or dressing up and taking part in the actual auction on TV. One big project, which was again an annual event, was the resurfacing of the walls of the town swimming pool with chlorinated rubber paint to reseal them. Although I was not a resident at the time, I was told about how everyone had donated their labour and skills. Everyone, the doctors from the local hospital to proprietors of the local businesses, all helped to build the swimming pool. Swimming and swimming parties were popular events in the summer. The summer brought the urge out in everyone to get outdoors. Vermonters were keen hunting and fishing people and spent a great deal of time outdoors.

Often, Pauline and I would team up with a local group, known as the Kingdom Kampers, and spend a few days away, either camping, or pony trekking, or a mixture of both. There was also the swimming parties and barbecues at the Kiwanis pool. In the summer there was always invites from friends to weekend barbecues, or water-skiing at Joes Pond, or Miles Pond, with friends who had holiday homes there. Winter brought its own problems, because snow was usually on the ground from late November through to Easter. This brought travel problems, which Vermonters were well used to coping with, out came the snow tyres and chains. My solution for the VW Beetle, was to fit retread tyres to all four wheels, but these were no ordinary retreads. They were what the locals nicknamed 'Sandpaper' treads, for when the tyres are re-moulded, the face of the tread is covered with hardwood sawdust. When it came out of the mould, the sawdust was brushed away, leaving a pattern of holes across the face of the tyre.

Once the snow-covered roads had been scraped by the snow plough, the town spread a generous cover of fine grit, and first time out with the new retreads, the holes became filled with this fine grit. Cars with these tyres coped well with hard-packed snow and ice, and I sometimes felt that the Beetle with those tyres on could almost climb trees. They were a blessing when travelling up to the ski slopes on Burke Mountain and elsewhere. Of course, if you have snow, then you have to enjoy it, so everyone in Vermont skied, from the schoolchildren to the grandparents. Of course, for Pauline and I this was all before our son Paul was born; after that event our activities had to be moderated. Pauline still managed to allow me to get in a few hours on the slope and maintain the ability.

Even though our house was 2.8 miles upwards from the centre of St Johnsbury, with the last part being a fairly steep final mile, I only remember one occasion when the slope had not been ploughed clear, by seven o'clock in the morning. Because of the steepness of the road, we did get fewer visitors in the winter, and friends would make all sort of excuses why they had failed to visit. We knew that some were afraid of running over the edge of the road and taking the 'quick way into town'. Excluding the winter situation, we now socialised with our married friends, and there were always visitors at the house, in the evenings and weekends. I was home most evenings before five o' clock, and often Pauline would meet me in the car with a picnic supper and we would head for a local state park, to eat supper in the sunshine.

Time had brought changes in the management structure; the chief engineer and the position was gone and in its place was appointed a 'vice president of engineering'. Colt Industries had appointed a man of their own choice. However, the man came in under a shadow, the source of his appointment was a corporate vice president named Scot, a name that was one changed from his original German name. He was a one-time officer in the German forces (possibly air force) and his choice for the St Johnsbury post was Carl Rexroth, an ex-captain of the German air force, who had seen action over Stalingrad in 1941. The general opinion on the grapevine was that Scot had got him appointed and he would only survive while Scot was around to protect him. Carl had taken over the position and seemed an efficient administrator, in that he immediately set about moving people about to set up his vision for the engineering management structure. Most of the UK hires seemed to gain from the restructuring.

Of course, as time went on, some people thought they had been 'pushed out' of the control circle and talked of a move. The first to go was one of the English families, actually the man was the oldest engineer that had been hired. His move was not straight forward or just dissatisfaction. He and his wife had been attending a church in another town and had become deeply involved with the activities of this church. The result was that they decided to move their family and to seek employment in the town where the church was located.

The other move was a 'single' engineer, who thought he should have had an appointment awarded to someone else. He resigned and moved to Connecticut, where he thought there would be more opportunities. In the meantime, my immediate boss was

Herr Rexroth, as some called him. At first we seemed to work well together. But as time passed, it became apparent that we didn't see eye to eye on many things. If something had to be done to move a customer on and there was no one available to do it, I would do it to save time and keep faith with the customer. He disapproved of such actions and would remind me that I was part of the management team and as such should delegate work. Most of the time it was minor changes on drawings, without which work was being held up on the shop floor; we did not have enough draftsmen to keep up with the workload and Rexroth knew this. It was easier to brand me as a poor manager, instead of resolving the real issue. I used to argue that one had to be flexible in our size of organisation, with the work as well as with people. Most times we worked and cooperated with each other effectively on the main workload issues.

Occasionally, we were on opposite ends of an issue, and it seems that such an issue came to a head. Sometime earlier, he had claimed that some people from within engineering had withheld vital information from him. Information that would have prevented a fatal flaw in the design of a special diecasting machine, the procurement of which was his responsibility. Which in the end cost the company a lot of money. I supported the claims of those who said they had given him the information. However, in the end, he appeared to have taken an attitude that in my position I should have supported him in his claim and strengthened his position. I began to feel that my position was weak and I should review my options.

The following day I was summoned to Rexroth's office, and the receptionist passed me the message that the director of human resources from Fairlawn was also in Rexroth's office. Rexroth spoke to me first and said that he had made an official complaint over my weakness as a manager. He could not afford to have me in such a small team, that I was not a strong team player, as demonstrated by my stance over the recent issue in engineering. He had therefore demanded that action be taken to correct the situation, which was now in the hands of the human resources department.

Rexroth then left the office, and J B Kennard outstretched his hands and said, "What am I to do? He can do no wrong as far as Colt Industries are concerned, and he can sack you on half a dozen weak charges, but what he wants is you off-site. As far as I am concerned, your best bet is to resign of your own accord, he wants to fire you. I have warned him that such an action won't make him very popular. He has agreed that if I can persuade you to resign, he will accept that as a solution."

I had no way out and no alternative, so it was go and hide somewhere, whilst I reviewed all my options. Rexroth knew that I had received several firm offers quite recently but had not acted upon them, one from Texas Instruments and one from Avery Labels, two very different types of companies. Also, a director of Fairbanks Morse, who had retired before the big changes, suggested I join him. He was negotiating the takeover of a company that Vermont state funds had supported, where the principals had done a bunk over the border into Quebec, leaving the company insolvent. Vermont wanted someone to start up the business again and bring it back into production, and at least one state senator was backing him as the preferred candidate. I knew the history of the plant and that the previous boss had absconded with the company funds, and I knew that there was a viable product. They were into moulding plastic heels for women's and men's shoes and the fashion for women, with very high platform soles. Heels like the Japanese geishas wore, an ideal product for a plastic moulding operation. But I would need to invest some money, which I did not have and therefore, had to decline the offer.

I did not have time to waste, so I started to write volumes of application letters, and after 200-some letters and 5 interviews, I had 3 job offers. None of which really employed my experience or were of an equivalent position. Now it came down to location, one was Boston and another in Connecticut. Then a surprise call from an old salesman, who had previously worked for Fairbanks Morse and had since moved to a position with Hobart Corporation, changed my prospects. He had talked about my abilities to their director of research and had mentioned that I was thinking of moving. The director of research had said that he would like to talk to me and would I telephone to make an appointment. Well, I decided I still had time before I had to give an answer to either of the other offers.

In the meantime, whilst my attention was focussed on a new job and family problems, the situation had developed at the office and had progressed more rapidly than I could have foreseen. I received the management's decision, my resignation was the only option. I answered, "Then that's it and I will take the only option I have."

J B Kennard's reply was, "The action will be effective from end of office hours today." Then changing his tone, he said, "I am sorry, Jim, after what you have done for this company, but if we argue against his claimed dispute with you, he is going to win."

I went back home and told Pauline, I did not want her to hear it from the town grapevine. She took it fairly calmly and said, "Are you worried?" and I said, "Not really." I said that I had received some promising information about a possible offer from a Hobart Corporation of a position with them, and I am going to phone now to make an appointment to talk to them. As well as that, I have other plans in hand and it may mean money is a little tight until we get back on an even keel with everything. The call was made to Hobart and an appointment made for the following week, and we both realised that so much might depend on its outcome.

Those intervening days we spent time talking to each other about issues one or the other may not have noticed. Pauline eventually got into her stride and revealed many home truths to me. I guess things had gotten so hectic during the past months that we had not been seriously talking to each other, as much as we might have. She said that she became very unsettled and even depressed once we moved up to the house, which was a little isolated. There was so much time when no one was around, and unless she put Paul in the car and took off into town, she had contact with no one during the day. I answered that there are bound to be some restrictions and the responsibility of having to look after a very new baby. Pauline seemed in the mood for 'home truths' and had now gotten the bit between her teeth. She said that she was basically a city girl and enjoyed city life, she had grown up in Birmingham and then moved to Montreal, another big city, which she had enjoyed very much. She had recalled that her mother always had to up roots and move to another station whenever the army decided to move her father. In the end, her mother rebelled against so many moves and stayed in her own home. Somehow Pauline related all this to my making her move to Vermont and then from the apartment to the house on Rocky Ridge.

I guess with Pauline being so unsettled about everything, I asked straight out that if she didn't like it living where she was, where would she like to live? Did that also mean she actually wanted to move? Of course, her next question was, where to? I foolishly said that would depend on where any new job was located. Which, of course, gave rise to a sarcastic comment. I said realistically I could apply for dozens of jobs in all sorts of locations. The conversation with Pauline had given me a lot to think about and something to feel guilty about.

The day of the appointment came quickly and after a long drive to Boston airport, it was only a short flight to Dayton, a town that I dubbed the US version of Birmingham, UK. This was because it was a hub of manufacturing covering, domestic appliances, cars, aircraft and railroad engines, and it was also the home of Wright Paterson Air Force Base, which alone employed over 5000 civilians. Typically an American-style of town, with wide roads, big housing developments and hordes of fast food outlets.

The interview was early morning; considering that I had to fly in and then make it to their offices, I made it with not too much of a margin in hand. Ed Boshinski, who was the director of the Dayton Research Division of Dayton Scale, which in turn was a division of Hobart Corporation, met me by the reception desk and led me into his office. He asked me if I wanted a coffee and enquired after what sort of a journey I had coming over from Vermont and how was the old Fairbanks Morse business doing. The chitchat complete, with me settled with a cup of coffee, he started to fill me in with what they had in mind for my day's interview. He started by saying that he would be joined shortly by his boss, who was the managing director of Dayton Scale. He confided in me that "This man has forgotten more about scales than what we both had jointly learned", implying that the man's comments should be listened to seriously. "He knows what sort of a person we are looking for, and if the past is anything to go by, he will know if you are our man by the time we have had lunch." Ed went on to say they wanted to have a quick chat with me, then a quick tour around the scale factory. After which he would then like me to spend the rest of the time going around the labs and model shop, talking to as many of the model makers, technicians and engineers as there was time for.

Ed's boss was a jovial man with a mass of glistening white hair, which gave a clue to mature age, but in every other way he looked like someone who looked after himself, and in later years I learned how; he was a golf fanatic. He impressed me as a good judge of men, making instant judgements on virtually short contacts. They did not seem to be particularly asking questions about my capability in areas they might be interested in. A few questions were pertinent to the design of mechanical scales, such as pendulum design and lever multiples, understandable since they appeared to be moving towards electronic weighing. I said that although the Fairlawn Division of Fairbanks Morse main products lines were 'Loadcell' based systems, the Vermont plant was only involved in the fabrication of platform and conveyor scales, bin structures and lever systems. They were never involved with the electronics, although their R&D group were heavily involved with the development of digital readout systems, for loadcell applications.

We talked about our competitors and their competitors and broadly discussed the structure of their development efforts. He said their big development efforts were to find some new technology that will put them ahead of their competition. As an example of that they launched their first weighing, pricing and labelling machine, with the labelling and price calculations based on National Cash Register components. "From there on, industry pressures forced us to find something faster than the old cash register parts, something along the lines of a simple electronic computer, but computers were costing millions. Our problem was, how could we build a simple price/weight computer at a cost we could live with? It only required to compute the answer, to weight multiplied by price per unit weight, a simple multiplication problem." Well, it seemed Ed came up with the idea of designing a simple computer based on 13-pole telephone relays. They took the design to IBM and asked them if they could volume manufacture them for Dayton Scale (Hobart acquired Dayton Scale from IBM). After studying the design, they said it was impractical and they should look to transistorised systems.

So, Hobart manufactured them and that had so far given them a 10-year lead over their competitors, who only now were offering transistorised systems. In their newest systems, they had 10 years of operating knowledge embedded in their designs, which the competition lacked. They said, "We also keep our minds open to any new innovations we can build into our existing product line. To have them ready for when marketing tells us that they need something new to go to a product show with, or to fight off a competitor's advertising campaign. We in the labs here, have to be ready with a few of these ideas completed up to a finished prototype. So that when the requirement arises, we can respond with some form of a solution."

Ed told me that his boss's son was working as a line foreman in the factory to learn the business and he would guide the factory tour. He was not long out of university, but he was a 'hands on' man like his old man. The scale factory was fairly easy to comprehend in that they were manufacturing weighing equipment and the equipment associated with their specialist applications, which were different from what I was leaving behind. Dayton Scale specialised in automatic weigh, price and labelling systems for the foods industries and supermarkets, as well as certain select high-precision weighing devices he had mentioned. In this regard, they had supplied weighing systems to weigh banknotes for the Federal Reserve Bank, as a faster means than machine counting. On the other hand, Fairbanks Morse specialised in huge process weighing systems, for measuring and batching of chemicals and ingredients for food products in massive volumes. Ingredients in tonnes at a time, fed by screw feeds and conveyor belts into vast mixer tanks and retorts, there was large difference in size and concept. I enjoyed the trip around the factory and as I headed back to Ed's office for stage three of my day, and I began to gain a little confidence.

I still could not be sure just how much 'my friendly salesman' knew about my final parting from Fairbanks Morse. If anything, how much had he passed on to Ed and his boss. Ed steered me into the labs and handed me over to the first engineer that came within range and then he left. I went around the model shop, first admiring some of the machines they had, that in UK would only have been found in a major production toolroom. I talked to some of the model makers about what sort of work they did, and the reply was, "Everything you might want a prototype of. Sometimes we even have to cut parts from a solid block of metal that in production would be cast or die-cast." I wandered around the various workbenches, talking about what they were doing and what was it for, what would be the end result. They all seemed to be team players and appeared to get on well with each other on a personal basis. To give them their due, they appeared to be digging out what I really did know and what I professed to know. I was to find out later in my life that talking to this bunch was the real interview.

When lunch time came around, Ed came over to collect me, and I should have noticed then that he had a few quiet words with two or three people, before he followed me out. At lunch Ed's boss wanted to know what I thought of the Dayton Scale operation, and I said I was very impressed. I did mention that his son could not restrain himself, as we toured the factory, from pointing out that

220

this scale and that scale were designed by his dad. Almost having to add that most of the scales were his father's design. Ed asked what I thought of his lab team, and I said I thought he had a good, balanced mix that was almost autonomous and he agreed. After the usual friendly banter that goes on with lunch, Ed's boss shook my hand and gave a nod to Ed and then upped and left, although I don't know what else I expected him to say. I thought there would be some mention in the context of the interview I had just attended.

Well, Ed interrupted my thoughts with the bombshell remark, "Well, Jim, how would you like to come and work with us?" He said that he had talked to some of the people in the lab, and they all agreed that I would fit in to the team and get along with everybody. We then got down to details of how the transition from Vermont to Ohio would be handled. Hobart would cover the full costs of my removal from St Johnsbury to Dayton and would put me up in a downtown hotel for the first four weeks with them. Which would give me long enough to find and lease a suitable apartment for myself and my family. I explained that my wife would be looking after the sale of our Vermont home, and the completion of that sale would decide when I would have to take time off to move my family. He then said that they would specify all the arrangements, cash help and a start date in a letter that should be with me in the next couple of days. On the plane back to Vermont, I was on one hand elated that I had landed the job, but on the other guilty of how much of a load I was putting on my wife, pregnant as she was.

Back home on the ridge and glad to see Pauline's positive reaction to a positive result, I realised that she had not yet grasped that we would be apart for several weeks, until the house was sold and after the days needed to organise a move. All the English crowd in St Johnsbury promised they would rally around and make sure Pauline was not lonely, not without help when she needed it, and I was confident that they would all do as promised.

When the all-important letter arrived with a start date, I was able to fix the date I would have to leave St Johnsbury, with an 1100 mile drive ahead of me. The VW Beetle I would leave with Pauline, and I would take the slightly larger 1600 VW estate-car, which would have more room for my luggage and essentials. It would take me two full days, more or less, was my estimate, with an overnight stop at a motel at the end of the first day. I would be arriving in Dayton on a Friday evening and would have to amuse myself on my own for the whole weekend, an ordeal that I did not relish. Parting, even though only for a few weeks, was a wrench for both of us, and I guess we put on a brave face for each other's sake. I checked over all the details for her to operate on her own, access to money, how to contact me, who to call in town when she needed help, as well as access to all the title-papers to sell the house.

That early morning parting, after a farewell hug in the early morning mist, was one of the most painful in my life. I wound my way down the hillside of Rocky Ridge into the town. It was only a short trip, but I seemed to be taking extra note of every detail of the view, I guess inwardly aware that I was leaving it all behind forever.

Chapter Seven

Once clear of Vermont, I headed west on to the interstate highway across the top of New York State towards Ohio. The scenery changed to an endless strip of concrete, disappearing over an ever-present sun-dazzled horizon. I made a point of stopping regularly to have a coffee, find a toilet and walk around for a 20-minute break and where necessary top up with fuel. The concrete highway glistened in the sun and seemed to keep me mesmerised with its straightness and the lack of any scenic detail. Somewhere around 8.00 pm, having covered more than half of the total distance of my journey, I pulled over into a motel carpark and checked in for the night. There was a small coffee shop on site, selling fast food such as burgers and pizzas etc., so after satisfying my hunger, I turned in for the night and slept undisturbed till daylight.

I was on my way early, for I did not want to get caught in the evening rush hour traffic whilst looking for my hotel in Dayton; my plan was to arrive Dayton 4.00–5.00 pm in the evening. I arrived in town on schedule and after a few false attempts, finally located the hotel, which was small, obviously designed to suit the business crowd of sales people and service engineers that flooded into Dayton every week. Having arrived in Dayton on a Friday with no idea what I would find to do with my spare time during the next few days on my lonesome, my misgivings were further strengthened by a salesman whom I met in the hotel bar and who said, "Hey Mac, you are not going to spend the weekend here, God man! In this part of town they roll up the sidewalks at 6 pm." I was soon to find out what he meant about 'that part of town' and in the end did not stray too far from the hotel. That is until the Monday, when I would drive to my place of work for the first time.

Once I got into my hotel room, my first action was to call Pauline on the telephone and get her news, if any. She wanted to know how the drive had gone and what I thought of Dayton now that I was there. Her news was that an estate agent had called and said she had two prospects who might be interested in buying the house and wanted to bring one of them over on Saturday. For me that meant the next day, so things were moving. We chatted for an hour about everything and nothing, just content to hear each other; for someone who was six months pregnant, she sounded over the moon. I told her that there did not seem to be anywhere to go in the evening near the hotel and that I intended to watch TV and get some reading time in. Finally, we ended our conversation with a mutual promise to call the following evening. It was only when that phone went down on the cradle that I suddenly felt really alone and a little lost. The cure was to go down into the restaurant for a leisurely meal and a quiet drink, after which I intended to find something to watch on TV.

Monday turned out to be a hectic one; first problem was finding my way to the 'research labs' from my hotel and then finding a parking space in their rather small car park. Both were experiences that tended to amplify my feelings of insecurity with a new job in a totally different environment. The familiar face of Ed Boshinski soon dispelled most of those feelings, and we spent most of the day discussing the priorities for the projects in hand. Plus, the philosophy in operation, for deciding which were long-term goals and which were short-term.

The sales team seemed to be pretty good at feeding back to the lab engineers comments from customers about features they thought might be useful additions to this or that product. It usually took a few meetings between the labs and marketing to sort the 'chaff from the wheat'. Since a lot of ideas were either outlandish pipe dreams or just not on for 'cost versus benefits' score. The good ideas were added to the development list, either as a 'long or short term' project. It was from amongst these short-term projects that the marketing team expected to be able to go to trade exhibitions with a 'new shine' on any particular individual product. This meant that marketing could come along and, out of the blue, say they wanted something new for this or that product. It then had to be available by the date of one or the other big trade exhibitions. This unpredictable demand had led to a way of operating the work schedules in the labs. A fully demonstrable prototype of each new idea would be produced, as its turn came up on the development program, and it was then put into storage. Of course, these working prototypes would then accumulate, so that when marketing made their demands, they had a range of fully developed ideas to help their various standard products. Then, of course, 'the proverbial would hit the fan'; they would request two or three models of the selected idea, which would have to be identical to the tooled-up product, there could be no 'lash-ups'. These prototypes all came under the heading of what was intended to be available in five years or less, and the rest were working prototypes for long-term work in developing completely new products.

We then talked about any ideas I already had for improving some of the equipment peripherals and a suggestion that I look at how 'fluidic' technology could be applied to dishwashers, replacing moving parts. By the end of the week, I had totally settled in, initially helping other engineers with their projects, as just another pair of hands, or maybe a brain. Of course, all of this with the help of the regular nightly telephone calls to talk to Pauline. Eventually, as the weeks progressed, I moved on to my own projects.

My spare time was spent searching for a suitable apartment we could rent as a home for the short term, until the baby was here and manageable. I finally put a deposit on a four-bedroomed apartment close to Paterson Air Force Base, on the south side of town so as to be close to where I was working. Then came the good news from Pauline, that she had sold the house and would be closing the sale the following week. I immediately conferred with my new boss Ed Boshinski about having time off to return to Vermont, to close out the sale and then help with the packing up of our belongings, bearing in mind that Pauline was now very pregnant. Ed agreed without hesitation and offered to meet the very pregnant Pauline with baby Paul off the plane and drive them from the airport to our newly rented apartment. Meanwhile, I would be driving Pauline's VW Beetle from Vermont to Dayton, Ohio.

The following week I flew back to Vermont to organise the move, which with the help of my new employers would be relatively straightforward and painless. The moving contractor was a full service one, that would pack 'everything' into designed packaging and unload and set up everything at the other end of its journey. Pauline assured me that the house sale details were all sorted and were ready for signing. Ed would meet the flight Pauline was booked on and drive her to our Yorktown Colony apartment. Needless to say, Pauline was glad to see me, even after such a short separation; despite the fact that we had talked to each other on the telephone almost every night, I had sorely missed the two of them. That first evening back on the ridge was a very nostalgic one; here I was leaving the house we had built to our own tastes and after only a year, here we were leaving it all behind to move on. We avoided the subjects related to the new problems we might have to face. Concentrating on bolstering each other's confidence, that we would find solutions to any problems, as and when they occurred. The following day our potential house buyer arrived with our sales agent, who introduced everyone. Our buyers were a young Chinese couple, who were about to move to St Johnsbury. They disappointed me straightaway, by saying that they would be having the cocktail bar in the family room removed and replaced with a bookcase. It seemed that they would only be living there for two or three years. After all the formalities of contract signing were completed and a day and time set for the exchange of contracts, I spent a few days giving toilets and bathrooms a thorough cleaning, as well as the stove and ovens. During this time Pauline was fully occupied with our 18-month-old toddler Paul and the impending newcomer. Despite all of the moving activity, she was in high spirits, quite flattered that my boss would be meeting her at the Dayton Airport to drive her to our apartment, in the York Town Colony Apartments.

By the end of a week back home, the sale had been closed and the purchase money was in our bank account. The movers confirmed that their vehicle would be with us early the following Monday morning. The weekend was spent sorting out the clothes that we needed to have with us in suitcases to cover the period of the move. After that, it was time to say goodbye to all the people in town who had befriended us since our arrival. Pauline was reduced to tears at the prospect of some particularly close friends she would probably not be seeing again. Remember, I mentioned that we lived some 2.8 miles from the centre of the town of St Johnsbury, up a steep hillside winding trail, to an area known as Rocky Ridge.

Monday had a startling beginning with a telephone call at 7.45 am from our nearest neighbour, who lived lower down the ridge. Fighting off the fog of deep sleep, I picked up the telephone and a voice said, "Hi, it's Carol. A big tractor-trailer rig is parked on the trail across from my place. It appears the driver and his companion got out of the cab to check out exactly where your house was in the thick early morning mist. Unfortunately, all my dogs were out loose and in a playful mood and figured the two men, who were afraid of dogs, wanted to play. At this moment, they have your driver and his companion pinned up against the retaining wall in the bend leading up to your house; they need your help to get away from the dogs." I informed Carol that I would be right down, as soon as I could get some clothes on.

At this point I think I should explain that Carol bred German Shepherds and at the time had a dozen young ones on hand. Once dressed, I rushed down the track and found two men cowering before a pack of 12 enthusiastic young German Shepherds. I searched for Donka (the mother who normally kept them under control) and on finding her, led her away and told her to call her 'pups'. But they were having too much fun already and were not about to give it up that easily. I decided to try an alternative ruse and picking up a short piece of wood, waved it in the direction of the pups and then threw it as far as I could. Seven or eight of the pups took off after the piece of wood, but the other four or five kept the two men pinned in the bend of the stone wall. One of the dogs brought the piece of wood back to me, and I realised I now had to get the attention of the dogs that remained behind. After first telling the two frightened men, "As soon as I draw the dogs away, run for your truck cab." I then teased the dogs closest to them with the piece of wood, before hurling it down the hillside. They took off after it and with some slight hesitation the others followed. Then luckily, Donka joined in and after collecting the piece of wood between her teeth, she led them all the way down the hillside.

The men got back into the driving cab of their truck and moved their rig up in front of our house and positioned it ready for loading. Whilst the truck crew unloaded their packing materials, we brewed some coffee and made a pile of buttered toast. Over coffee the men admitted that the dogs had never really appeared to be a danger, just big, full of energy, and after the experience, they were none the worse. As the day progressed, I was impressed at how systematic and efficiently they worked. Going from room to room and packing the contents of each room, into specially designed boxes. Clothes were taken from the wardrobes and hung straight into 'wardrobe' boxes, and all crockery, cooking utensils, ornaments, drapes, bedding, all had their own special packing and boxes. It was so efficient that in a couple of hours they had broken the back of the workload and moved on to wrapping the furnishings with padding and crush-protection materials to protect it all. When they had finally loaded all the furniture and fitted all the filled boxes into their trailer, creating a compact travel package with no spaces, it was still only mid-afternoon.

So, it was decided to have Pauline fly that evening, if it could be arranged with Ed, back in Dayton. The arrangements all organised, I drove Pauline to the airport, having first confirmed that Ed would be at the airport to meet her flight and drive her plus little Paul to the apartment. Since I had been living there, the apartment contained the basics necessary to survive until our possessions and furnishings arrived in two days' time.

I was aware of some great sense of loss as I drove away, all the stress and tensions one feels when leaving home and security. Looking back on my life, I can once again repeat and honestly say, that of all the places I have travelled to, Vermont is the only place I regretted leaving, but 'past is past' and we all have to move on. Back on the ridge, I tidied up the house ready for the new owner, before leaving to hand the keys over to the sales agent. For the airport Pauline had Paul on a short safety rein, so that he could not run around, and she would be traveling with a minimum of hand luggage. Once all that miscellaneous details had been completed, I drove my young son and a very 'pregnant' wife Pauline, together with their immediate luggage, to the airport in time for a 7.00 pm flight. Not long after that I was on my way and headed for Dayton, Ohio, a distance of about 1100 miles; I am not sure of the exact figure.

My plan was to drive as many hours as I could, hoping to drive for a few hours that evening before checking into a motel, then after a few hours' sleep, get back on the road, around 6.00 am. I checked into a motel around midnight and got into bed and fell asleep, without any thought of food. After some sleep, I felt really refreshed and after checking out of the motel, decided to put off breakfast for at least three hours. The sheer boredom of such a long drive was the main problem I had mainly to cope with. The monotony of unchanging scenery and, for most of the time, following an endless strip of glaring white concrete was a constant threat. That evening I checked into another motel and after some food and a shower, slept for a solid eight hours. Again, I decided to check out of the motel and get breakfast en route, hoping to average 50–60 mph for the whole trip.

I reached Dayton around 8.30 am and headed straight for the York Town Colony Apartment complex. My son Paul was crawling around the lounge floor, exploring his new home, totally wrapped up in his own activities and not taking any particular notice of his daddy's arrival. Pauline, of course, was all over me, with a kiss and a hug and obviously relieved that my journey had been uneventful. She asked all the usual questions, such as had I been able to find reasonable motels en route and how had I coped with the monotony of such a long drive. I asked how well her journey had gone, to which she answered that it had all been pretty straightforward. That Ed had been an 'angel', even calling at a supermarket to let her get some essential food items. She added that the journey had tired her, being pregnant and all that, and now she felt that she was short on energy.

We chatted about this and that, including an observation that people in Dayton are not familiar with the use of safety harnesses and reins to keep small children away from danger. Her use of a safety rein to lead Paul along elicited many passing remarks such as, "Fancy leading a child around on a rein like a dog on a lead."

I answered, "Don't worry about it, they may have reason to wish they had used one when their child dashes from them into oncoming traffic."

Having had lunch and fed Paul, who was a delight at his age and great fun, so much so that Pauline remarked, "Yes, you tire him out so that I can get him to sleep; he seems to have the energy that I need and more."

I telephoned Ed and thanked him for picking up Pauline at the airport and helping her to get settled and promised to be back in the office the following Monday.

The movers arrived on schedule just before lunch and once again demonstrated their efficient operating methods as they proceeded to repeat the procedure they demonstrated in the Vermont house, but now in reverse. Working room by room, placing the furniture first and then unpacking boxes and placing their contents into the appropriate wardrobes and cupboards, until everything had been unpacked and the apartment looked so organised one would be excused for thinking we were already in residence. Okay, we may move around some of furnishings, from personal choice, and into different rooms, but here we were, settled in with all our possessions and ready to get on with living our new life, including the expectation of a new addition to the family in three to four months' time.

My hours started at 7.30 am, but this resulted in my finishing time being 16.30 hours, allowing me to be home with Pauline and Paul before 5.00 pm. We took advantage of this to eat out in evenings or fit in shopping trips. This gave Pauline a break from little Paul and the four walls of the apartment, where she was trapped all day or most of the time. We did have an outdoor swimming pool and a children's paddling pool in the apartment complex. Pauline was able to organise her day so that in the afternoons she could lay on a lounger at the paddling pool, allowing little Paul to have a splash around.

Quickly settling into my job and having a variety of assignments, from exploring 'fluidics' applications to replace moving parts in dishwashers, to a re-inking device for application to a new label printer they were developing. Another key assignment was solving a dashpot problem, with current weighing machines involved in their automatic wrap-weigh-label systems. It seemed that some important customers were trying to push the system beyond its original design limit, to increase their productivity. The first project involving 'fluidics' called for a device to replace the rotating spray arm with an annular configuration of a bistable 'Coanda Flow' devices. But this had to operate within the legal demands of government regulations for large-scale dishwashing machines, which specifies the volume of water the dishes are exposed to in a washing cycle. The project was abandoned after early prototypes showed that it would be difficult to arrive at a design configuration that would meet requirements for volume flow of water within available pressure supply limits. The second project ended up producing a mobius-loop ink ribbon with a re-inking system. A prototype printer was built based on pulsed-magnetic type stepper-wheels, unique at the time.

However, before any production thoughts could even be contemplated for the project, low-cost mechanisms from the far east obsoleted the design concept and offered very low-price alternatives. The low-cost electro-mech printing mechanisms manufactured by Seiko in Japan offered a better solution to our needs, and in in the end they flooded the market with their product. This to the extent, there could be no production strategy which could result in a one-off price that could compete with the Japanese mechanism prices, so another project was dead.

By this time, I was getting more admin and supervisory work and my life was taking on a different focus. Electronics was by this time becoming a prominent factor in Hobart's product line. Instead of trying to expand an existing department into an operating division, Hobart's executive management planned to find an existing electronics company and buy it as a going operation. The acquired company would then become another operating division of Hobart Corporation. Rumours floating around suggested that Ed was to be the man they had selected to head up the new division. I found myself assigning resources together with most of the day-to-day management of the lab facility, assigning work tasks to the toolmakers and model-makers in the workshop, assigning technician and model-maker support to the various project engineers. My working hours meant that I had plenty of time to spend with my wife and baby son, both evenings and weekends.

We had also made many new friends in the apartment complex where we were living. Yorktown Colony Apartments was very close to Wright Patterson Air Force Base, which employed many thousands of civilian workers and was the home for many US Air Force Commands. These apartments were favoured by air force, newly married couples, mainly commissioned air crew. Pauline managed to easily get baby sitters from amongst these friends. We could, therefore, manage to have the occasional evening out at one of the area's cinemas; or in one instance, for Pauline's birthday, a prominent area night club. Time was now getting very short, towards when we had to start planning for the new arrival. Pauline had found herself a local doctor and was having regular check-ups and had been assured that everything was going to be fine. Although this was her second pregnancy, she appeared to be more than a little nervous about the impending experience.

We had arrived in Dayton in June, now it was early October and Pauline's delivery date was looming ever closer, and the event was beginning to get more attention than problems at work. I had suggested that Pauline might like to have her mother over with her, but the suggestion wasn't immediately taken up. However later, when we had to build baby Paul into the picture and the need for help in the days immediately following the birth, these additional factors swayed Pauline's decision, having her mother stay with us was a real solution. With a four-bedroom apartment, accommodation was no problem. As might be expected, her mother was more than ready for another trip over the 'pond'. My mother-in-law arrived over in early September and was soon comfortably settled into our spacious apartment.

As might be expected, the big day dawned at 4.00 am in the morning. Pauline woke me with the announcement, "I think I have started labour pains, we had better make haste to the hospital." We grabbed her previously prepared hospital bag and headed into the 'crisp morning air' (cold, I mean). As with a lot of prosperous cities in USA that were the crossroads in a massive rail network, Dayton had its own maze of level crossings. To get from our

231

location and across town to the hospital, we would have to cross a wide span of level crossings. I was fearful that the shaking Pauline would get might precipitate the birth before we reached the hospital.

Before leaving the apartment we had called her doctor, who said he would meet her at the hospital. Whenever I think of my daughter, I am reminded of that journey across those acres of rail crossings. Every bumpy rail is firmly embedded in my memory, accompanied by the cries of warning from Pauline. I had big visions of having to deliver a baby in the car, whilst parked in that maze of railway lines. Despite the hazard, we got to the hospital without any mishap; her own doctor arriving not long after us. At this hospital, in those days, it was not the practice for the fathers to be allowed to be present at the birth. So, when Pauline was taken away to the delivery room, I was parked off in a side waiting room. After her doctor had examined her and the nurses had helped her into bed, the doctor came into the waiting room to inform me that there was no panic and nothing was going to happen yet awhile. The doctor and I were sitting, talking over a cup of coffee, for what seemed a very short space of time. Then a nurse came rushing into the waiting room, announcing that the doctor was needed.

I walked backwards and forwards across that waiting room floor for what seemed hours, but what was really very much less, without anyone coming to enlighten me as to what was going on. The door finally opened and in came the doctor with a big grin all over his face, saying, "It's all over and you are the proud father of a healthy little baby girl." Then adding, "Your wife is fine, a little tired and exhausted with the effort, as might be expected." He led me into the delivery room and there was Pauline looking 'proud as punch' with her new baby in her arms. After we had something like 15 minutes together to talk in private, the doctor came back and suggested that I get off to wherever I was going. To let Pauline get some sleep, which she needed more than anything else at the moment. I reluctantly left Pauline, promising to come back in the late afternoon.

My original plan envisaged my being at the hospital most of the morning and not at my desk, before early afternoon. Yet here I was at 7.30 am in the morning and it was all over. I did consider going back to the apartment. But the thought of having to while away all those hours, until it was time to go back and see Pauline, with nothing to occupy my mind, was too daunting so I headed into the office. Of course, everyone was surprised to see me, the predominating remark was, "False alarm, was it?" to which I readily replied, "No, it's all over," and left it at that. I called Pauline's mother to inquire about Paul's health and temper and was assured that he was fine; I gave her chapter and verse of everything that had happened since leaving the apartment. I added that I was going to see her on my own that evening and that I would take her, with baby Paul, to see Pauline and the new baby the following day. An arrangement she seemed to accept without comment. It was a good strategy, to get involved in work and get my mind off any imagined problems that might occur under the circumstances.

I drove to the hospital straight from the office and arrived there sometime around 4.30 in the afternoon to find that Pauline was sitting up in bed, breastfeeding our daughter. I told her that I had put her mother in the picture about everything that had gone on that morning. I eventually got to cuddle my new baby daughter, such tiny hands and feet, but so perfect in every detail. I asked how long they intended to keep her in hospital and how she was feeling; she told me it would probably be three days and went to say that she felt fine but was very tired. I told her that her mother and Paul would not be coming to visit until next day, and I think she was a little relieved with that information. For myself I was reluctant to leave, but after the nurse had given me endless hints that it was time I left, giving Pauline a last kiss and a hug, I allowed myself to be shown the way out. The next evening, I collected some flowers, little Paul and Edith (my mother-in-law) and headed for the hospital to visit my wife and new baby daughter.

We all got to hold the new baby, even Paul, with a little help from his grandmother. Pauline had obviously had a little sleep and looked much better for it. We all talked our heads off for about an hour, before I realised that Pauline was beginning to look tired and was trying to settle herself back in bed with sleep in mind. We said our goodbyes with plenty of hugs and kisses and a few tears from Paul, who did not want to leave his 'mommy'. By the time I had ushered everyone out of the ward, we had all been there for over two hours, leaving a very tired but happy Pauline to finally get some more sleep.

When my wife was finally discharged to bring home the new baby, I really got an introduction to the commercial aspect of medical care in the USA. Before they would release my wife and daughter into my care, I had to produce proof of valid medical insurance that would fully cover any bills from the hospital. I took a couple of days off from work to see that Pauline had whatever was needed, but having Edith there made me somewhat surplus to requirements. Weeks passed and Pauline's mother returned to UK, remarking that she expected to find things very different back home in Birmingham but was looking forward to seeing the rest of her family.

For us the passing weeks became months, and all this time baby Pamela was growing into a beautiful baby girl, with a very happy and cheerful disposition. We were now well settled in the York Town Colony Apartments. Although I started work at 7.30 am, my workday finished at 4.30 pm, which meant that we could drive out for a family meal or a shopping trip to one of the many big shopping malls in the area, on any evening of our choice. We had the apartment complex swimming pools. Pauline was able to take the children there during the day, and I would join them in the evenings when I got home. In our new situation I saw much more of my family on a daily basis, and we were able to spend more time together, which had to be a plus. Pauline had made many friends in the apartment complex amongst the new wives of American officers based at the nearby Wright-Paterson Air Force Base. Mother-in-law was already making overtures about coming over for another visit, but we were already planning a visit to the UK, to introduce our two offspring to my mother and Pauline's extensive family.

Our daughter's first birthday was soon upon us, and she was always happily whizzing around the apartment in a wheeled walker, either being chased by brother Paul or chasing him. We began to talk about buying a house now that our situation appeared stable and more or less permanent. Pauline seemed to have settled down to being a full-time mother to two young children. For myself I found the 'research division' something that I could get involved in and progress my position in a positive direction towards supervision and management. Buying our own home would offer a more stable home life than living in an apartment complex. With the latter, people were continually moving in and out, you no sooner made new friends only to find they are suddenly gone. This time our choice was to be a second or third time owner, and with this in mind we spent endless weekends driving around housing estates within easy reach of everywhere we had established as our 'lifestyle patch' and, of course, my work.

We finally chose an area close to Wright State University (where I was currently attending evening classes). After looking over two-storey and split-level houses, we finally made an offer on a 75-foot ranch house and when all the legal and mortgage details were complete, eventually moved in. Surprise, surprise, one of our new next-door neighbours turned out to be English, a fact we were not aware of at the time of settling on which house to buy. Tom Pinkerton was English; however, his wife Denise was French. Tom a retired air force wing commander and his wife a consultant on international law. Tom and Denise had no children, his wife was barren, so it would appear they compensated by living a very active social life and keeping two dogs. Before moving to Dayton, Tom was still in the Royal Air Force and held the appointment of British air attaché in Washington. Pauline soon established a strong friendship with another neighbour further along Brown Bark Drive, the road our house was in. Louise was in her second marriage, with two teenage sons from a former marriage (not living with her) and two daughters from the present marriage. The eldest daughter was in high school and the younger needed special schooling, because she was a Down syndrome child. Once in the new house, whenever I could not find Pauline, I knew that the first place to look was at Louise's house.

We were soon moved in, busy making all the changes people usually make in order to put their personal stamp on a new home. We joined the local social/swimming club and had a great deal of fun, teaching our two new offspring to swim, although they had already been introduced to swimming in the apartment complex, which had two pools. With eating out two or three times a week and weekends at the swimming club, life became very relaxed and satisfying. In the following couple of years, we made a holiday trip to see the families in UK. We also made a trip to stay with the Mariners, friends from Vermont who had moved to Northern New York state. We managed the odd camping holiday, which was not so easy with two small children, despite the fact that they took to camping like ducks take to water.

After getting established in her new home, Pauline used to accept quite a few invitations to the air force base, socialising and shopping at the base PX, with the air force wives she had made friends with. This developed into a group, that were exclusively the English wives married to American air force officers. Of course, although I never found out until much later, these wives would drool with envy over one or the other whose husband was being posted to UK or had resigned and they were both moving to UK. They would forever be re-telling stories of their recent holidays in UK, and it was fairly obvious that they were all 'homesick', which made one wonder why they had ever come over in the first place.

Whilst all this was going on in the background, my role at the 'research centre' was developing whilst Ed (as the director of research) assigned the work projects to specific engineers. I would allocate technician support and model-shop time to those work projects. It was a loose sort of model-shop management role, which eventually developed to a full manager role. Then a 'bomb' landed, Pauline succumbed to a series of acute bouts of depression, during which she was unable to function and was hospitalised. The homesick attitudes of her recent close group for friends appeared to have played a significant role in the way she was feeling. Her doctor did not think that it was other than a crutch on which to lean all the blame and was sure there was a deeper underlying problem yet to be identified. After three weeks in hospital, Pauline came home and invited Edith, her mother, to be with her when she came home, which was probably the biggest mistake of my life. Her doctor had warned me not to make any drastic lifestyle-changing decisions because of Pauline's illness. I would find that in the long run, radical lifestyle changes have very little positive influence on an illness such as Pauline was suffering from. That was sound advice that I ignored and for which I would eventually pay the penalty.

But to get on with the story, Pauline appeared to be in fine spirit; firstly, because she was back with her children and secondly, because she had her mother with her to help out. I guess Edith had been with us for about four weeks, when she announced that she would like to have a private conversation with me about Pauline's problem and her future. I had furnished a small room at the back of the garage as my study and figured that would be a suitable place to have our conversation without being overheard. To get the ordeal over with, I took an afternoon off work and invited Edith into my study. I guess at first she didn't really know what to say, or rather the exact words to open the dialogue, conveying the message she intended to impart to me. In the end, after a meaningful silence, she just blurted out, "Pauline is homesick and she wants to come home and live with me!"

I was ready to query anything and everything she would say, but faced with this short statement issued in this manner, one that appeared to be placing the content beyond question, or query, I said, "Just what are you saying, that she wants a divorce or what?" She replied that she thought that her daughter needed to come home for a time, until she could sort herself out, at the very least. I led Edith back to the lounge, to where we had left Pauline sitting, and I said, "Do you know what your mother has just said?" in response she just nodded her head. I then said, "Are you asking for a divorce, is that it?"

She started crying and said, "No, no, I want us all to go, you and the children." Covering her face and still sobbing, she then composed herself and continued. "I have moved three times to where ever you wanted to move, surely you can make this one move for me." She sat back a little more composed now after she had her say.

At first I was struck dumb for an answer, but eventually some realities clicked into place and I said, "For starters, I am under contract to give three months' notice before I can quit." Then I went on to say that I would have to sell the house, probably at a loss and that is all we would have to live on until I could get a job. It was a difficult conversation and I went on to state that, even if I agreed to your proposal and you and the children left as soon as possible with your mother, it would be six months before I could have everything wound up and able to join you. Her answer was simply, "I want us all to go now, you will soon find a job, you always do!"

My reply was, "Pauline I am 45 and in England they do 'not bend over backwards' to offer 45 and plus year olds a job." I continued, "Particularly now when half the country is on a three-day work week (it was the early 1970s)." I decided that I would have to sleep on it and would give my answer in the morning.

I was 'floored' by what Edith had conveyed to me, as being Pauline's wishes and then to have Pauline confirm them with just a nod of her head. I knew from things Pauline had told me about teenage relationships with her mother that Edith had been a very domineering mother, not allowing either her or her brother to think for themselves on day-to-day life issues. I wondered if Pauline, in her present depressed condition, was being led to a decision that was not entirely her own. The statement she had made, about having made three lifestyle-changing moves to fit in with my career moves I knew was true and that realisation made me feel a little guilty. These feelings made me think that she did have a case, to have me make a move of her choice, that fitted lifestyle changes she wanted.

The next morning, I announced that I agreed in principle to what they proposed and would make arrangements for Pauline and the children to fly with Edith to UK as soon as such arrangements could be implemented. I further added that I would not be able to go with them, but would join them in about six months' time. This was the time I would need to terminate my employment, sell the house, dispose of the bulk of our furnishings and goods, as well as the cars. They, neither Edith nor Pauline, made any comment; to all intents and purposes, it appeared as though they had heard the answer they wanted. By the end of the following week, I had booked flights from Dayton via Chicago to Birmingham Airport. Also arranged for her brother Charles to pick them up at the airport and drive them to the family home. In the following days, conversation seemed to be reduced to essentials, everyone was scared of saying too much, if they said anything. It was a strange and impossible atmosphere to exist in.

I guess the worst day of my life was when I took them to the airport, Edith stayed close to Pauline, who seemed to be keeping a distance between us. Either from feelings of guilt or to hide what she really felt. I hugged the children for a long time, half believing that this might be the last time I would see them, then finally released them and watched as they disappeared down the route to the boarding gate. When they finally disappeared, I felt my whole world had collapsed. I could not even contemplate how I was going back to an empty house alone, or how to cope. I could not call on friends, because I had told no one of the plans and certainly could not have listened to them debate the pros and cons of what had transpired. I now faced a weekend completely on my own, brooding over the predicament I found myself in. The right moment would have to be chosen to tell Ed (my boss) what had happened. Of my decision to end my employment contract and eventually move back to England to join Pauline and the children. That weekend was the loneliest period of my life, and to this day I do not know how I got through it. The conflicting arguments that ran backwards through my mind as to who was blame for what had happened and why. On the Monday morning, by the time I was ready to leave for the office, I had convinced myself that life must go on and that I had to put my own life back together, whatever the cost.

Chapter Eight

It had been almost a month now since Pauline left with the children, to start a new life back home with her mother. A move that I can now admit nearly shattered my whole life and future. The first few days back at work were difficult, part of me wanted to shout it out to everyone. That my wife had packed up and left me and accept everyone's condolences, constructive or otherwise, and put on the brave face as the victim of the situation. But I knew that the situation was much more complex and that I was going to make the utmost effort to save my marriage and keep my family together. I must have admitted at the time that I had not made a very positive start, sending them all on their way, away from me.

My first positive action was to have a long and detailed discussion with Ed, my boss, and tell the whole story, starting with details of Pauline's periods of deep depression, my decision to bring her mother to the USA to look after her, and then the shattering decision that they had handed me. That Pauline's mother intended to take Pauline and the children home with her, as this was her understanding of what Pauline wanted. They had said that they wanted me to leave everything behind and come to UK. However, the way that part of the message was delivered lacked conviction and sincerity and sounded like a feeble peace offering. Yet I had committed myself to the undertaking, that as soon as I was able to wind up our affairs in the USA, I would join them in UK. That was of itself a path strewn with many intangibles and countless pitfalls.

I would be 45 by that time, not a good age to go looking for a job in UK. Add to that that the UK had its industry on three-day weeks, how would I convince people in UK that I had given up a career position in USA to join the unemployed in UK for very good reasons? Ed saw my point of view and accepted that I was attempting to prevent my family fragmenting; after all, I had two very small children to take into account. He promised me all the help and support he could muster. Those early days were not easy to deal with, well-meaning people would come up to me and confide that they had gone through a similar situation and a divorce had been the only workable solution in the end. Whilst others, who had tried my solution, related that they ended up losing everything in the end. They were all well-meaning, but I guess in my frame of mind, I was closed to reason and reality issues, something I would have to wrestle with as time progressed. I buried myself in my work and planning the early actions towards the final move in a few months' time. I established a routine of a weekly telephone calls to Pauline. The early ones had a strained almost forced level of conversation, and I quickly realised that her doctor in UK had put her on some form of strong medication, which inhibited her conversation.

As the weeks passed, Pauline started to sound like her old confident self, she had found herself secretarial work with a 'temps' agency, moving around different companies in the Birmingham area. Focus was on discussing the things that I thought should come first, on my action list. The top of which was to sort out which of our belongings we would ship to UK. We reasoned that to move furnishings and appliances was not on, as furniture would probably not suit a smaller UK home and appliances would be of the wrong power rating. So, we settled on all clothing and bedding, children's toys, wedding presents, family memorabilia, photo albums and family pictures. It was left to me to decide on how best the transfer could be organised, so that there was no bottleneck at the UK end. Having sorted everything out on lists and then divided the same lists into package lots, I followed that task with a search of Hobart sites for some cardboard shipping cases that would suit the size of shipments I wanted to handle. Next stop was to go out to the freight area of the airport and get the lowdown on costs and any problems that might arise with shipping the size of packages I had in mind. I identified the best days to ship to the destination airport in UK and how collection could be handled at that end.

When it was all organised, I called Pauline and said that I would ship one box per week and the boxes would be of a size that could be fitted into a small van. Shipping one box each Wednesday from Dayton airport, it would be in the UK customs sheds at Birmingham Airport by Friday, ready for her collection. The first box was air freighted the following week and her brother, using his VW bus, helped her collect it. Everything worked like clockwork in those first weeks and later Pauline bought herself a small R4 Renault van, which relieved her brother of the collection chore. As the number of boxes shipped mounted up, a storage problem at the UK end arose, which had not been planned for. In the end, both her mother and her brother had all the spare space in their homes packed solid with the big boxes of air freight.

In parallel with all the air freight activity, I now had to arrange to sell the house, dispose of three motor-vehicles. Sell off or give away all the household goods that would not be going to the UK and arrange a short-term apartment rental for when the house was sold. Having not yet decided when to offer my resignation, I mentioned the fact to Ed. He asked me to hang on as he had something in mind that might tide me over whilst I was looking for a job in UK.

I quickly got a bite for the sale of the house, it seemed an air force major had been posted to Wright Patterson Air Base with his family and was looking for a house in my area. Things quickly moved on to my advantage, with the signing of a sales contract. Having completed the air freighting of belongings that were going to be shipped to UK, I could hand over the property as soon as the furniture and those items one accumulates in a house could be disposed of. What could be sold was, and the rest was given away to friends and neighbours, or taken to the Salvation Army shop/warehouse. Within a couple of weeks, I was ready to move into a small apartment back at the Yorktown Colony Apartments. In the meantime, I had maintained my weekly calls to Pauline in the UK, never being sure about her depression problems. It was something she would never discuss with me, and my relationship with Edith preluded any likelihood of my getting information from that source. But since she seemed to be regularly working, I had to assume that her bouts of depression were at least under control. For me, work was the only way I could keep any sense of focus on what I was trying to do in my private life, the more complex the better.

A particular problem came into the labs whilst Ed was on vacation, where the users in Germany for the company's wrap-weigh and labelling systems were seeking a solution for higher throughput. One that was beyond the possibility with existing weighing scales, due to the maximum throughput the scale damping device would allow. The damping dashpot was adjusted to allow the fastest cycle time, consistent with the demands of the weighing accuracy; this damped the weight mass oscillations to two and half cycles before balance. All efforts on the spot to reduce the cycle time to balance, by changing operating fluids and modifying fluid flow clearances, had failed. To my mind we had to somehow allow maximum fluid velocity on the inertial downstroke, but somehow slow down the fluid velocity of the other half of the cycle up to the balance point, to reduce overshoot and further cycles.

Although digital fluidics technology had faded from the public view, there were still technical papers being published, about related aspects of control for fluid flow. One such paper described the application of 'squeeze films' as a means of converting turbulent fluid flow to a more uniform and lower velocity laminar flow. Using these ideas, a new dashpot was designed, wherein the fluid on the downstroke had the normal path for the fluid to move. However, this path was blocked for the return stroke and instead was forced between two circular plates, with only a minuscule gap between them. Using the equations in the published paper, a little Fortran and some time on a 'Timeshare' computer service, we optimised the gap between plates for our application. A scale platform tracking device allowed us to view the balance cycle on an oscilloscope. We found that we could reduce the number of cycles to bring a weight to balance, from the standard two and half cycles to one and a half cycles within the same weighing accuracy. After some extensive testing to validate reliability and repeatability, we manufactured a number of these special dashpots and sent them off to Germany for their evaluation.

The answer came back that as far as they were concerned, we had solved their problem. In the main, we were involved in the core activity of exploring the new technologies and materials as they related to the existing product lines of the corporation. My spare time after moving out of house, which had been occupied by packing and moving chores, now hung heavy on my day. Although I went with friends from the labs, for drinks or to visit friends for meals or a barbecue, there was still a lot of spare evenings with nothing to do.

This problem was solved by joining a 'square dance club', and once I had the hang of things, I was able to go with them on visits to other clubs in the area, including weekend gatherings. A new member like myself had no partner and dancers got paired off with whoever is available. Over time this settled down, to being the same person on each occasion. In my case it was Lucy, a senior surgery nurse from one of the big hospitals in Dayton. During our travels to and from the various clubs we visited, we got plenty of time to discuss our private lives. Lucy had just got through a divorce that had shaken her self-confidence to its foundations; her husband had left her and four children for a much younger woman. As a devout Catholic, she had always accepted that marriage was for life.

She had the strong conviction that people are of the opinion that the children are unaffected by divorce, that they adjust to the new circumstances easily. She said that if her children are anything to go by, then that idea could not be farther from the truth. She went on to say that her oldest son had sworn that if his farther ever came near the house, he would kill him. He moved out of the family home to live with a girlfriend to emphasise his statement. An older daughter, who was already living with a partner, said that she never wanted to see her father ever again and that she regretted that she had to live on the same planet as him.

Then, of course, I started to share my problems and her immediate reaction was that I should do everything possible to patch things up, for the sake of my two children, if for no other reason. I guess the way I told it things, it sounded like my wife had taken off with the children and her mother, leaving me high and dry. I eventually managed to get her to understand that I was already planning to join my wife in the UK, for a new start. That I needed time to wind up my affairs and job in the USA before I could join her and the children. At times I would lose Lucy to another club member, who had suddenly appeared on the scene, and end up with a different partner. However, I still saw Lucy, at a lot of the club's activities, throughout the many weeks prior to my take-off for UK. I heard later, from friends at the club that I kept in touch with, that Lucy had eventually married one of her partners from the club and that they had moved to Florida.

Getting back to my situation and plans for relocating to UK, I had decided to have a two-week holiday, combining a visit to be with my wife and children with exploring the UK job market as well as getting a few job applications out and maybe an interview, ahead of my final arrival in UK. The Hobart management had suggested (under Ed's influence) that I might be interested in working with the technical department of the UK division for a few weeks whilst I was searching for a UK job. This would help me and provide them with a direct contact to troubleshoot some problems they were having with their plastic film wrapping machines. These are used to wrap meat trays as well as fresh vegetables and fruit packs. The machines had already had modification upgrade kits fitted to address the problems as reported. As these machines were used for high volume packing operations, in packing sheds located on huge vegetable farms in rural areas, other factors appeared to be involved. It was feared that either the machines were not being operated correctly, or that the UK maintenance teams had not fitted and adjusted the modification kits correctly. The idea was that I should visit these problem sites, to either correct the installation and adjustments, or report in detail just what the nature of the operator problems were.

I told Pauline about my visit plans, and she seemed enthusiastic and was looking forward to it, saying she could hardly wait to see me again after so long. She went on to say that she would be working during the day, but then I would be involved in job hunting, so we could concentrate on family evenings together. Back in the office Ed broached the subject of my move back to UK many times, asking the same question, 'had I really thought it all through?' He and everyone in the lab were quoting examples of neighbours or acquaintances who had 'upped stakes and moved back to the "old country" to solve marriage problems and failed'. I would be 45 years old by the time I was back in UK, not a good age to start looking for a new job in what was a deflated job market. I must admit vague fears about the outcome of a job search did keep coming to the forefront of my mind at times.

However, it was press on with both work and play to fill in the time before my holiday visit to Pauline and the children. The day for my departure to UK, on holiday, could not come to quickly enough, and I arranged with Pauline to pick me up at the airport in her little Renault R4 van. I will never forget seeing Pauline waiting for me at the barrier, as I came out of the customs and immigration area; she looked positively radiant, appearing excited and on top form. So that when we finally were able to kiss and hug, it seemed ages before we even spoke a single word. As we drove to her mother's house, she filled in the details for the rest of her day. She had to get back to her work by the afternoon, but she would be home around teatime. Edith's greeting, when I arrived, was somewhat reserved, or one might even say frosty, but I did not care, I was there to be with Pauline and my children.

That evening was destined to be one of the very few that I was to spend with my wife. From that day on, her mother arranged a series of visits to various members of her family, or to the families of her sister's, of which there were four. All were purported to be important occasions that Pauline could not afford to miss (according to her mother). As might be expected, I was not invited to any of these occasions, and I was to learn sometime later that it was at the request of the relations that I was not invited. The family understood from Edith that I was the root of all Pauline's problems. From the point of view of getting to spend important hours with Pauline, to make up for the time we had been separated, my holiday was a total failure, and the job search did not fare much better. I had targeted the companies that were involved in the technologies in which I had expertise and to whom I reasoned I had something to offer, from the level of the research we had done into those various emerging technologies.

At the top end, typical replies were "We do not hire managers from outside the company, we promote from within our own ranks". This was after I specifically pointed out that I was looking for any level of engineering opportunity. I was also exposed to what seemed, at that time, to be a widespread attitude against American ideas of industrial management and operation. I was told on several occasions that with my long-term USA background, they did not feel that I would fit in with their organisation. In total, the results for the time spent on job-search was essentially 'nil' and boded ill for my planned return to UK. I returned to the USA after a failed holiday, with the conviction that the 'wedge' Edith had driven between myself and Pauline left me with only one option, divorce and cancellation of my move to UK.

I guess to everyone I met, I was essentially preoccupied with my problems, not good company to work with or socialise with. So, when I met up with Lucy again at the 'Square Dance Club' and told her of what had transpired during my visit to UK, she took it upon herself to counsel me in what were the real issues. Firstly, she said I had to put the children first in whatever decisions I made and that divorce was not in their best interest. The real problem I had to solve was breaking my wife free of the dominating influence her mother exerted over her life. She went on to advise that my first priority, when I returned to UK, would be to get a home of my own and put as much distance as possible between my wife and her mother. I guess talking to Lucy helped me get things straight in my mind. I instinctively felt that what she had said made sense and put me back on course with my plans.

At the back of my mind, there was always the fear that I was not going to find work back in UK, and it did put a damper on any positive thinking. When I first called Pauline by telephone, I did not mention anything about the job-search and the results. For her part, she was effusive in her apologies for the very little time we had together. More or less glossing over the whole issue, with the remark that, "You know what Mom is like over family and will never take no for an answer." She seemed to consider that as a sufficient explanation. Life became more stable during my last weeks in the USA. Ed made an offer that he would keep my job open for me for three months, so that if things did not work out, I could bail out and come back.

Two days before I was to leave for UK, the people in the lab threw a surprise farewell party at a local night club. This cheered me up no end and made me sure I would miss many, who had become close friends. One of my friends from the lab arranged to take me up to the airport to catch the UK overnight flight, and Lucy turned up to wish me farewell and good luck. It was with an air of finality that I boarded the aircraft, convinced in my own mind that I would never be coming back to work in USA, despite Ed's offer. I only have vague memories of those first few days on arrival in UK and the installation of myself at the home of my mother-in-law. In those early days my relationship with Edith alternated between good and the occasional armed truce, on some issues. Those first few days I focussed on spending as much time as possible together with Pauline and the children; to this end Pauline had taken a few days off work so that we could get away on our own and discuss plans for the future.

I told Pauline about the work Hobart had given me to tide me over the first three months and that it would mean living in London Monday to Friday, only having weekends with her and the children. This she accepted as one of the things we would have to cope with before life settled down. That few days cleared the anguish of our long separation and welded us back together as a married couple, with a family.

Edith's house was only a two-bedroomed house and prior to my arrival, Edith had the one bedroom with a double bed, whilst Pauline had a single bed in the other bedroom, and the two children shared a single bed in the same room.

My arrival caused an upheaval in that arrangement, which was solved by Pauline and I occupying the double bed and Edith the single bed in the other bedroom with the children. My luggage had to be stowed away all over the house, and many things have never seen the light of day since, such was the necessity to utilise every nook and cranny in the limited cupboard and wardrobe space. Before leaving for London, I talked to Edith about my plans were, once the work in London was organised. I would devote one weekend with Pauline to search for a house we could buy, information she took without any comment.

The B&B which the Hobart sales team had booked for me was located in the Muswell Hill area of London, which at that time was a pretty run-down area of London. First impressions horrified me, the bedroom looked like it could do with a good clean and the sparse kitchenette area looked like it was never cleaned and was more than basic. All the lights everywhere were bare bulbs and overall, the light level was so low, one could hardly see whether or not the place was clean anyways. That week I went out over the local area wrapping machines, to get a first-hand insight into some of the problems they were having. Long before that week had ended, I knew that there was no way I was going to spend half my life in such a crummy B&B. So, before the week was up, I phoned the UK sales manager and told him that if that was the best accommodation they could provide, I was finished. He said to leave it with him and by the following Monday I was booked into a small B&B/hotel that catered for salesmen and other business travellers.

My new accommodation was comfortable with a good food, not that I would be there for more than breakfast, but it was to be where I would spend half my life for the coming weeks. It soon became apparent that I would not be spending that many nights in my new comfortable B&B. Most of the problem machines were located in the rural areas of Lincolnshire, on farms and in isolated farm-packing sheds, which meant overnights stays in those areas in most instances. My second weekend away from London was the one we planned on for house-hunting. Before we set out on that task, Pauline said that her mother had informed her that a house had come on the market on the opposite side of the road from her, that the asking price was very reasonable and well within our budget. Edith had suggested we look at this house first before looking elsewhere, but Pauline knew my answer to that one long before I said an emphatic no! We started looking first in the Sutton Coldfield area, but nothing seemed to satisfy Pauline's requirements for layout or facilities amongst those that were in a price range we could afford.

By late afternoon of the Saturday, we were still no nearer deciding on possible buys, so I suggested that we look at the village of Shenstone, which was close to the motorway network for me travelling to and from London, and that we pick a house that met our basic requirements. The intention being a short-term solution, so everything did not have to be perfect. We looked at two or three houses in the village and finally settled on one in Schoolfields Road, arranging with the owner to come back the following day for a detailed look over the property. As it happened the owner of the house was a solicitor, whose main business was in property conveyancing, and he said he could also arrange an endowment mortgage, if we were interested.

The weekend ended with us committed to buying the house in Shenstone, an announcement which as expected brought some cutting comments from Edith. She excelled herself in pointing out, "You are both stupid, you are going to spend all that money on a house in Shenstone. I have pointed you towards a perfectly adequate family home that you could have bought for a fraction of the cost you are now facing." She continued, "It is in a location which is served by regular bus routes and has nearby schools for the children." Not about to get into any deep discussion on the subject, I informed her that the decision was made jointly by Pauline and myself, and we were prepared to live with any mistake we may be making.

I went back to London on the Monday, elated by the thoughts that things were finally moving in our favour and in a short time we would be able to move into our own home. Once I got out amongst the Lincolnshire problem machines, I soon established that the majority of their problems were that all the operations were using wrapping film that held high levels of static electricity. Levels I had never encountered before, and I realised that on the 500-feet reels, such static could reach a very high level. Approved suppliers of film for automatic wrapping machines have either zero static or a very low level. They understand the problems static on film causes in automatic wrapping machines.

Almost all of the Lincolnshire area machines were at one time production sites using manual or semi-manual film wrapping of perishable produce packages. They had used suppliers of film who had ignored the high level of static on their roll film, selling simply on the basis of price. These packers had continued to use the same film suppliers as they had used for manual packaging. They expected the automatic machine suppliers to be able to adjust their machines to use all or any of their film supplies. Much of what I was seeing was substandard film, and although Hobart UK had done everything they could to cope with the problem film, from an extreme range of machine adjustments, to fitting special adapter kits, it was not working.

All automatic film wrapping machines are designed to run using film manufactured to an industry specification. The use of film outside that specification was prone to a wide range of wrapping faults, machine downtime and lost production. It suggested that the Hobart UK sales team were remiss in some cases, for not spelling out that the machines would only be guaranteed and supported using film manufactured to the industry standard specification.

Having identified the problem, I headed back to London and loaded up my car with reels of approved film. Then re-visited each working site one by one and at each site removed the offending film, replacing it with approved reel. In some cases, where on site people had not played around and altered all the key adjustments, I was able to start a trouble-free packaging run. Right before the owner's or manager's eyes, demonstrating how trouble-free and straightforward the solution was. At other sites, I had to open up all the adjustments and recalibrate the machine from square one, before loading the approved film and then a round of final adjustments before starting a packaging run.

All this time I kept backtracking to make sure that the machines I had already set running were still running with no breakdown or faulty packages. Also, to make any final adjustments if and where necessary. This revisiting of sites to ensure that the machines were still working meant that I soon developed a good working relationship with the owners and managers and was able to convince them that using approved film sources was in their own interest, even if the cost was higher.

Once the main core of machines in the rural areas were up and working, I had to move on to troubleshooting the isolated small number of problem machines. That had been fitted with conversion kits to address a particular problem, such as loose packages, due to the packs moving out of position during the wrap cycle.

Here there were signs poor initial setup, and then moving every adjustment, until they did not know where the set-up should be. My approach had to start with getting the machine back to a standard configuration. Adjusted to run as such, then loading a known quality of film and checking the wrap cycle through each stage. In some cases, results appeared to be problem-free. So what had gone wrong? By going back to a known sample of faulty film,

I was able to produce some faulty, loose packages and started to get an insight into the problems of what had gone wrong.

The local maintenance team had treated the symptoms of the problem rather the cause. Seeing that the packages were moving out of position at some stages of a wrap cycle, they had wrongly concluded that they had a machine that would not hold the adjustment settings through long hours of operation. They had then fitted a conversion kit, to force the packages into the correct position at each stage of the wrap cycle. So, the conversion kit was continually fighting the static drag on the wrap film, and the result was a mixture good and bad packages, during a day's packaging. Bad packages had to be corrected by hand wrapping, involving extra labour and cost. Once they had gone down the conversion kit route, no one seems to have looked at the film quality they were using. They had therefore failed to find the real solution, which was using approved quality film. These cases was publicised around all the area maintenance teams, with the result that a lot of problem sites suddenly dropped off the list. It seemed that widespread use of poor low-cost film, from questionable sources with a high static electricity content, was a real problem in the UK.

During the many weeks of all this dashing around the country, resolving wrapping machine problems, things were happening on the home front which had to be dealt with on the weekends. Finalising the purchase of the house, shopping for basic furnishings and then the final the move, for which I did take extra time off from work. It was a time of chaos and near panic for all involved, but somehow we worked through it all. I had a company car, which came in handy with all the dashing about, tying up loose ends, as well as collecting the smaller items and moving everybody on the day of the move.

I remember that day in particular, because Edith had undertaken to put the two children in the back of the car. Having successfully installed Pamela in her 'child seat', she then attempted to do the same with Paul, who was not in a very cooperative mood, to say the least. Edith roughly pushed him into the back of the car against all his protestations, with the closing remark, "Just like your b****y father," no doubt a comment on my lack of cooperation with some of her suggestions.

Somehow we moved in, we had most of the furniture we had ordered. Except for the dining room, so meals were on a miscellany of rickety tables and a couple of old chairs and some small boxes for the two children to sit on. We signed up the two children at the village school, which was quite close by the house, and Pauline had made contact with a woman in the village for after school. This woman had organised a local scheme to look after small children in her own home, until their parents came home from work. I went back to London feeling pretty good about the house move and began to look forward to the days when I could live there seven days a week, knowing that when that time came I would face some real employment problems.

I had been so busy in London that I had very little time to spend on job search, other than answer advertisements in the national newspapers. It was soon apparent that the economy downturn in the early 1970s had severely suppressed the job market, added to which no one seemed to be anxious to hire a 45 year old. It was near the time when I would have to think about ending the relationship with Hobart UK that Ed suddenly arrived at the London office. He was there to tie up some company business issue, the nature of which I was not a party to. He left a message for me to meet him for dinner that day. I arrived on time for dinner with Ed at his hotel and eager to hear what he had to say, once we were at our table. He broached the subject of my situation and asked how things were going for me. Adding that the London office people had told him that I was having no luck finding a job, for after I was finished with them. He also said he had heard from the guys in the lab the details of just how badly things had gone for me on my two-week holiday visit and that I had actually considered a divorce. He then dropped his own bombshell, Hobart Corp had purchased an electronics manufacturing company and wanted Ed to run the operation. He had flown over to offer me his position in the Dayton Research Division, believing that my problem in the UK would prompt my return to work in the USA. I thanked Ed and told him just how much I appreciated his offer, but said I was committed to what I had started. One way or another, I was going to make it work for me and my family. He applauded my resolve and said he hoped that everything worked out. He did, however, say that he would hold the position open for a further month in case I had second thoughts.

The week before I was due to sever my connections, the Hobart UK sales manager called me into his office and said that since I had not yet found employment, he was interested in offering me a technical support role with the national sales team. The role was to support major sales presentations to the then emerging supermarket chains, to sell our wrap-weigh-labelling systems into these emerging organisations. He said that the position would be London-based and as I was already used to commuting to and from my home in Shenstone, that should not be a problem.

As a divorced man, I suspect a home and family did not rate too high on his list of priorities, so as not to appear as dismissing the idea out of hand, I said I would like time to think about it. My immediate answer was that I would get in touch with him as soon as I had reached a decision on the offer. I had already made a lot of new friends whilst working in London. On that final day I realised just how much I would miss that camaraderie of working in a team, particularly since I was now moving into the isolated world of the unemployed.

That first weekend at home was somewhat tense. Pauline knew I was worried about job prospects, and I knew she was feeling guilty for having triggered events that put me in that situation. One or two happenings had taken place since we had first moved into the house. The first of which was that we had become close friends with one of our nearby neighbours, Dick and Ella Yates. We used to go out to dinner together, whilst their daughter Louise, who was 16 at the time, looked after little Pamela and Paul.

Dick had an engineering background and had up to the time we first met them been a director of a company manufacturing plastic powder coating systems for metal components. A takeover of the company, which he had opposed, ended with his being forced out of the company. His response was the setting up of his own operation in a small factory, doing contract powder coating for low volume metal component manufacturers. He had been in the RAF and I had been in the army and with similar working histories. We had a lot in common, with the result that whenever we were able, we used to take off down the pub and 'chew' over old times. At such times I filled him in on the details of what brought me to Shenstone and the temporary work arrangement with my USA employers, which kept me in London Monday through Friday.

He agreed with my assessment that once I finished in London, I would not find it easy to find a decent engineering position, particularly at 45 years of age. He was only three years older and had faced the same problem, prompting him to try and build-up a one man business with a widely fluctuating workload; 'feast and famine' as he described it. Once he knew I was through in London, he asked whether or not I had made any plans for attacking my employment problem. He suggested that whilst I was searching for jobs, he could give me some casual time at his little factory, helping load the powder-coated parts on to the oven conveyor. He admitted he could not pay me a lot, but at least it would put groceries on the table and occupy my mind whilst waiting for employment enquiries' replies. Having seen all my own problems in his own situation, he was able to suggest a viable strategy, "Do not start off applying for engineer positions straightaway, decisions and offers only come after several letters, interviews and second interviews.

"Instead," he said, "look at the 'Technical Salesmen' adverts, there are plenty of them in the newspapers. The salaries are not so good, but it is something you could live on, whilst you apply for the engineering job you really want. The salesman network is a great industrial grapevine and often you will hear about job openings before they get in the newspapers, or are released to agencies. On top of that, you will have a company car, an essential convenience to get to job interviews with."

That seemed a sound strategy and without one of my own, I was keen to follow it up, having seen the large number of technical sales adverts in the national newspaper. I suspect in a lot of cases, the word 'technical' was added to the title to dress the job up bit, and I already knew there was a big turnover of people in sales jobs. I started helping Dick during the day and writing after-sales jobs at night and when answers came through, most of which were nothing, I would discuss the pros and cons with Dick.

He warned that many jobs for salesmen are from companies with questionable products and do not last long. Eventually, a job turned up based in nearby Burton-on-Trent. Dick looked at the letterhead and said that he had done some powder coating for that company, they supply controls and communication equipment to British Steel Corporation and the National Coal Board. I applied and some ten days later a letter came offering me an interview. I showed the letter to Dick, and when he read that the interview was in late afternoon, he offered to drive me to the interview, an offer I readily accepted. Well, to cut a long story short, I got the job, mainly I suspect because that the other salesman that I would have to work with decided that my broad technical background might prove useful. The product was a self-contained 'loud hailer' or 'Tannoy system' and their primary customers were National Coal

Board sites, British Steel sites and the various sites for British Leyland Cars.

We both, myself and one other salesman, spent most of our working days in our cars, driving between a British Leyland site in Oxford, or midland area mines, or steelworks spread throughout the UK. At most customer sites, union rules dictated that a site porter had to transport the equipment from the main gate to the point of installation. A union millwright had then to drill any mounting holes, followed by an electrician who had to connect the units to mains supplies. Then we could do the final calibration and any extension connections required to marry the units, into an existing system. Yes, we not only had to sell the equipment, we were also expected to connect it all up on site. Brian, the other salesman, had been with the company for several years and with this status tended to be the man that did the sales pitches at corporate offices level. This was where totally new systems for new sites were discussed. My roll was seen as look after replacement and additional equipment for all the existing established sales sites. This meant that throughout any week, I would be dashing between sites to satisfy what in sales terms were minor requirements, which had to be serviced to keep the customer happy. In real terms, this did not bring in much profit for the company, so that in some ways I was a 'Mr Fix-it'. The distances between different sites meant that it was more often than not an overnight away, or at the very least a very late arrival home and straight to bed. In this job I was not destined to see much of my family except on weekends, and it was hardly the life we had envisaged, when I moved back from London.

But it was employment and was the best on offer, as far as I was concerned. It paid the bills, if 'only just', but it was a job that I held on to for nearly three years, whilst I still constantly scanned the job market for some sort of career opening. Motorway rest areas and their catering establishments were a popular place for salesmen to meet up to collect new assignments via another salesman from the same company. Or with your sales manager to report any sales result. These places were also a great place to swap pieces of information about jobs that were being offered, salesmen are always 'all ears'.

They pick up all kinds of information and, of course, many other categories of business travellers also use all of these facilities. So, it was on such an occasion that I had pulled off the motorway for a coffee and a break. The time of year meant that the facilities were crowded by families with children coming or going on holiday; seats in restaurants were at a premium. As luck would have it, I sat next to Henry Merryweather.

Although people are reluctant to discuss any current business, they readily discuss their past, and it seemed Henry had quite an impressive one. He had started work as an apprentice in the shipyards of Hull and gained a HNC in mechanical engineering. Without going into all the ins and outs of his related working life, he eventually managed to get into Cambridge, where he worked up his HNC to BSc level. Then on to do a master's in computer graphics.

By that time the government had sponsored the creation of the Computer Aided Design Centre in Cambridge to develop and enhance the spread of CAD throughout UK industry. Henry joined the centre, to do a PhD thesis on the CAD design and analysis of fluid flow impellers, a component of vital importance in jet engines. By the time I had arrived in UK, the centre had been running for some time and had developed all sorts of connections in industry. Many of its leading researchers had now set themselves up as independent consultants to industry. Whilst others were attempting to float their own companies offering CAD services and software to the industry in general. Henry Merryweather was in the latter category; he was in the process of setting up his own CAD service company.

As I related my work history in UK, Canada and USA to him, we sort of established a common discussion platform. When I said that I had seen some early efforts in CAD before leaving USA, but had not seen any real hardware to support the potential. The next question was why had I moved my career aims from engineering to marketing.

When I told him that I had been unable to get any engineering opening and that technical sales was my only option, he looked very thoughtful for a few moments and then said, "I have an appointment now, but here is my phone number and office address. Give me a call and make an appointment to meet, I think we could have some mutual interests." Well, I was curious as to what he had in mind, but he had not given any clue, so I had no way of gauging whether it would be worth making an appointment to speak to him.

At the end of the day, in my hotel room, I was going through notes and paperwork, amongst which was Henry's business card with telephone numbers, both office and home. Although he suggested I called him at the office, I did not think he would mind being called at home. I dialled the home number and my luck was in, because he was home to take the call. I suggested that I would be passing Rugby on the following Monday, on my way to Oxford, and could call at his office in the early afternoon for a chat. Henry was pleased I called and said, "Why not make it in time for lunch and then we could talk over a pub-lunch somewhere." I agreed with the suggestion and noted the arrangement in my appointments book. That evening I mulled over what Henry might have in mind, trying to assess what sort of work offer I might be willing to consider. I did not want something that was not significantly better than what I was already doing, in terms of work interest and future growth.

Always away at my job, with very little time to dwell on what my family was doing. The days and evenings spent together, either watching the children play in the garden of our recent Dayton home or eating out as a family, two or three times a week, was now sorely missed.

Whilst I had been working, Pauline had become a private secretary to the managing director of a company, whose offices were right there on the edge of the village. The office location was virtually within walking distance. Their business was the supply of educational materials to schools and colleges in the whole of the UK. We had also replaced her old Renault-4 van with a SAAB 99, a few years old, but in top condition. So that she had safe transport to ferry the children to their various activities and dental appointments. The children were now firmly established at the local infant school and doing fairly well, with all the logistics of their life falling on Pauline's shoulders. I was never home at a time, when I could have proved useful, but somehow she managed it all without complaint.

The house was fairly shipshape, although we had earmarked one or two items as priorities for me to see to, when I had any spare time. There was the back-garden that needed all the old plants of the previous tenant digging out. The garden, which was very overgrown, needed totally reorganising to be manageable alongside full-time employment. To this was added the need to have a new central heating boiler fitted, to get away from an unreliable pilot light dependency problem. Then there was the task of checking out the possibility of break in the sewer pipe under the back-garden. In order to ascertain whether that was a problem, suspected on the basis of smell nearby.

256

We were both in full-time employment and both had our spare time utilisation programmed for the future. When I was home in time, I always would make a point of going into the children's room to give them a hug and a goodnight kiss. My children were at that fun age where I would have loved to have had more time with them and felt that I was missing the most important part of their lives. I guess this was one of penalties of earning a living in England. With 'run of the mill' jobs, you had to put the hours in to make ends meet. Well, to get back to the other part of my story, the day of my meeting dawned, and I turned up at the Rugby Offices of Henry Merryweather, ready for lunch and whatever transpired.

They occupied a floor in a large building, which was owned by a national central heating company and was located conveniently right on the approach road into Rugby. The staff consisted of a woman who functioned as company secretary, plus two programmers, who were not present at that time, and Henry as the MD. The moment I came into the office, Henry grabbed his jacket, said something to the secretary and motioned me towards the door. We drove to what was obviously the favourite pub, since the two programmers were already in there busy with their lunch, not taking any particular attention of who was with Henry. Drinks were ordered and then I waited for Henry to open the conversation, I guess he was searching for some way to lead into what he had in mind. In the end he must have decided on going right back to the start.

He said he had let it be known to visitors to the CAD centre that he was thinking of setting up a CAD services company and was looking for partners and investors. An acquaintance of his happened to visit during these early days, adding did I know Colin Southgate, a former project manager with ICL before they went 'belly up'. A man who, together with like minds from his project team, started the Software Sciences Company. Their marketable commodity was computer programming and the skills needed to program software needed by systems-oriented organisations. They focussed these skills on contracting out programming teams to individual businesses, focussing on banks, airlines and oil companies.

They had a ready source of programmers of known quality and ability from those that were made redundant by ICL, who were only too willing to go to work for Software Sciences. The company prospered rapidly, continued Henry, and now Colin was looking for something to invest in, that complemented what he was already doing. He was willing to finance Henry's idea, as a subsidiary of Software Sciences and would carry us for at least a year and hopefully by then we would to be earning some significant income. The company was to be known as Software Sciences Engineering, and I would well remember the name Colin Southgate in the future years. Because he was in time destined to be the future chairman of Thorne EMI and later chairman of National Power. However, at that time he was a man on the way up.

Computer equipment with less power than today's desktop computers, costing from 100,000 to over a million pounds, was the only available hardware at the time. So, SSE assets would be computer hardware, they had yet to launch services that would make money. Having covered the start-up background, he went on to cover the sort of services they had explored that would make money. His first service to be explored was 'projector image inspection', where precision optics project a sharp magnified shadow image of a component on to a screen, which had all the tolerance zones drawn around the projected image at the scale of projection. These drawn images have to be very accurate and to produce manually were extremely costly, but such systems allowed QA inspectors to quickly inspect complex components, on a fast pass or fail basis.

Because there are components that have minute tolerances, where the projection magnification would have to very large and the drawn image accurate to almost impossible limits, this inspection method was not available to very small and varied precision parts. Henry had been in touch with Kodak over a series of plastic cameras planned. Where all components were plastic-moulded parts, and they wanted to use Projection Image Inspection for all preproduction runs and the inspection image to be CAD printed on mylar sheet. This meant drawing with CAD each and every component and then adding the tolerance zone outlines on each, then for printing it was only necessary to specify the projection scale to produce inspection images.

It was a big task and work that Henry was about to bid for, including the assembly of these components as a CAD assembly. In order to check for where tolerance zone interferences could be detected, on assembly. Although Henry discussed several other ideas for services with CAD, the KODAK camera project was the one he intended to launch with. At the same time, he wished to canvas other large companies requiring high precision printed images for Projector Image Inspection. He then got down to the nitty gritty of the role I could fit into, firstly he needed someone on the marketing side to canvas for service work. "But since we were a start-up company, everybody has to be flexible. We want you to run prints of projection images for delivery to customers. We would also want you to help input component data into CAD software to create CAD images; in other words, everyone is expected to function as a jack-of-all-trades, within their capabilities that is."

Well, by this time we were about to be thrown out of the pub, so we ended with a promise that I would think things over and decide whether or not I wanted to come on board. All the way to Oxford, my mind was in a turmoil, trying to pigeonhole the various categories of information I had been exposed to. Plus, attempt to make an assessment whether, or not, CAD had an immediate future. I already knew that the CAD software capabilities was way ahead of the hardware available; all of which had insufficient memory and processor speeds below that needed. Another hardware deficiency was the slow development of display screens, the current ones being either too slow or of too low a resolution. Of course, the answer to all this was a technology has to start somewhere, but will supporters be willing to buy systems and hardware that is at the bottom end of a development cycle? But for me it was the promise of a new challenge and if the money was right, I saw no reason for not joining them in their gamble on the future of CAD.

Before joining Henry's new enterprise, I wanted to get in a family holiday on the limited funds I had available. When considering my options, my neighbour and now close friend, Dick Yates, offered me the use of a caravan. Which he had on site at Saundersfoot in Pembrokeshire. That holiday was a milestone for the family, because Saundersfoot became established as our favourite holiday resort; one we would head for each year, until the children were of mid-teens age. Initially, we found ourselves a nearby caravan site and then later moved on to renting a family apartment near the seafront.

Chapter Nine

Well, I had made up my mind that if I was ever going to find a new career path, CAD seemed to be the new horizon for me to aim for. On reaching that conclusion, joining Henry's new start-up enterprise was as good a place as any to make a new start. The Myson Company building had at least five floors; we shared one floor with a 'job centre' operation. Our part of that floor was divided up into three work spaces, a reception area, an office for the MD, which also functioned as the business office, and the 'general' open-plan office. Up to the time of my arrival on the scene, Henry had to do all the racing around the country in a car, to obtain CAD work that would keep his start-up company afloat. The publicity that had been given to the potential for CAD systems to speed up product development and vastly reduce design errors had made a lot of the larger industrial companies wake up.

They began to take notice, but at that time promises were way ahead of what could be achieved. The right hardware in terms of display screens and fast computer processors was just not yet available. The software capabilities were simply ahead of their time. It would be a long time before the hardware technology caught up with the demands about to be made on it by the needs of CAD. That first week Henry gave me a briefing me on the work that might be found; top of the list was specialist companies wanting custom CAD software services focussing on their own specific needs. There were others who wanted to buy CAD design services, to produce drawings for them. Added to these were people who wanted CAD plotting services, particularly in the area of dimensional inspection, using precision projector systems. At the bottom of the list were those machining companies who had converted their machines for NC operation. Now they needed someone to write post-processors to match the software they intended to use, with the instruction set of their particular machine.

Once I was on the road doing the canvassing for work, Henry would be released and then able to concentrate as much effort as possible to produce a company product. This would be in concept a multi-discipline 2D CAD system, the core software for which he had been working on for some time. Well, my career venture into the yet infant area of CAD took off in late 1979, and in the following years I learned all about CAD from the ground up, my involvement continually expanding as CAD capabilities developed. Lack of capital investment and cashflow problems held back the market penetration by new UK-based start-ups in CAD. These new enterprises were all in danger of being eventually overtaken by the well-financed efforts of USA-based CAD enterprises. Such competitors as Compervision, Unigraphics, Intergraph, to name but a few early front runners. This even though many of the ideas and capabilities in UK CAD software were ahead of the field.

The growing emphasis on computer-based solutions, for everything from accounting, stock control, NC machining and CAD, meant that all the big corporations were looking for takeover opportunities amongst the recent start-ups. BOC was such a company, who felt that they were too dependent on the industrial gases market alone and should diversify into other business areas. They acquired Colin Southgate's group of small companies 'Software Sciences' and amalgamated them with other computer capabilities they had acquired, to form their Computer Services Division. They appointed Colin Southgate as head of that division. The immediate effect of the BOC takeover on Henry's enterprise was that we had to physically move from our offices in Rugby to BOC premises on an industrial estate near Daventry.

Despite government grants to leading UK companies, to encourage the take-up of CAD, the cost of hardware in UK and the lack of a will to adopt new ideas kept the growth of CAD in UK to a minimum for many years. In 1983 BOC appointed a new CEO, an American, to take over the reins of business. He decided that the organisation should concentrate on its core business, industrial gases and sell off all enterprises outside of that category. He charged Colin Southgate with the task of finding a buyer for the whole of BOC Computer Services Division. Colin was able to negotiate an acceptable deal with the Thorn EMI group of companies, for all activities with the exception of the still struggling CAD start-up.

It was decided, at board level, that the CAD venture should be either 'wound up' or disposed of via a management buyout. Henry and most of the others, who could borrow money against their mortgages, proposed to Colin Southgate a management buyout, which he agreed to. My mortgage was both so recent, as well as being an endowment-type mortgage, that I was certain I would not be able to borrow against it. So, myself and two or three others that could not contribute cash to the buyout, were marked for redundancy. This was to be effective the date of the BOC disposal of the division.

Once again I found myself without a job, but in a slightly different situation to the move from the USA. On this occasion I intended to make use of the many contacts I had made within the UK CAD industry. I knew there was a lot of 'one-off' commissions or contract work to be had from many of these people. The contract work was a fluctuating demand on my time, sometimes only requiring one or two days. Therefore, I used the spare time to write a book about CAD/CAM systems, 'a guide for managers and company executives'. The book was aimed at people who might want to put together their own system, since at that time there were no off-the-shelf system packages.

The book was published in 1984 and such was the rapid development in computing technology, it was virtually out of date by the date of publication. Sales of it were not very robust, because everyone was borrowing a copy from their local library. In the end I used the book as lead-in, for consultancy and sponsored seminar opportunities. This initiative led to some CAD seminars in Brazil and a short consultancy assignment, followed by an offer of CAD system manager with one of the Thorn EMI divisions.

During that interim period, I made many forays around the country, doing all kinds of contract assignments for the earlier industry contacts I had made. Work ranging from CAD demonstrations at industrial shows, writing confidential internal company reports associated with CAD, producing CAD graphics for a publicity agency that served the UK CAD industry, carrying out internal CAD performance studies and anything else that I could get paid for.

It was during one of these forays that I called into a plant owned by the Thorn EMI group, located in Rugeley Staffordshire. A plant whose effort was divided 50% on defence work and 50% on industrial work; the latter mainly for British Steel. It seemed that they had implemented a small CAD system to deal with their customer's wiring design and data storage and the storage of that information. The arrival of a new MD opened up an opportunity for me. It seemed that the man managing the CAD and the new

MD did not see eye to eye. It was pointed out that the CAD manager was at that time working out a three-month notice. He was leaving to take up an appointment with the company that had supplied the CAD software.

At an interview, the MD confided that in his opinion the CAD was not working well, despite the opinions of the CAD manager and the assurances of the software supplier. He wanted someone to come in as an independent examiner, to do a complete appraisal of the work achieved to date and write a detailed fault and reliability report of the software. I accepted the commission, and the report was submitted to the software company involved, who immediately rejected the findings. Claiming that it simply said what it was intended to say without very little supporting evidence. It was produced by an independent source, hired to write a report with those conclusions.

After some discussion, a joint decision was concluded that I should join Thorn EMI as the replacement CAD manager, reporting directly to the MD, initially on contract for one month. During that month I would examine and record in detail every error that showed up during the day-to-day operation. Also, I would study and evaluate the errors that had occurred on work completed in the immediate past. Another, more detailed, report was then sent to the software provider, with a request that they study each of the faults identified and on a mutually agreed date come on site. The purpose of the latter was to demonstrate that in each case recorded, we were in error in claiming a fault, by completing fault-free operations.

The software company requested time to prepare their 'defence' demonstration. After a number of cancellations and re-scheduling, they arrived on site, prepared to admit that we had identified several major deficiencies in the software. The rest of the faults they claimed to either have fixed, or were down to operator method failure. Eventually, all parties agreed that the software company would have six months to correct the major faults identified and demonstrated, that I would work closely with them until these results were achieved. My status was changed to that of a fully employed member of staff, on a mutual three-month notice contract, still reporting directly to the MD.

I then gained approval and finance for designing a completely new CAD system, based on Intergraph hardware. All the CAD operators were retrained, and I also was given approval to hire and train a younger man, who could takeover eventually from me as the CAD system manager. The working role went very well, except for the fact that reporting direct to the MD did tend to isolate me from the other managers. The relationship did have its advantage, in that I did get to play a major role in the CAD 'user-group activities', which took me to group meetings in the USA to chase up software changes and corrections.

In one instance I was allowed to take some of my annual holiday entitlement and present some CAD seminars in Brazil, an opportunity that arose as a direct result of the book I had written. It transpired that an American management training enterprise, which ran training seminars in Brazil, had contracted a CAD consultant based in UK to present a seminar. This man had fallen ill and was unable to present the planned CAD seminar, in San Paulo. He had been chosen on the basis of a book he had written and had suggested myself as a possible alternative candidate to present the seminar. The cash was attractive, as were the expenses and as I would be using part of my holiday entitlement, time off was not a problem. I flew to Rio, where I was allowed two days to recover, before flying on to San Paulo to deliver the seminar. The seminar was delivered in English, with live translation, and all went well; the organisers seemed pleased with the results and feedback from the attendees was positive.

In fact, the promotors asked if I would stay over and present the same seminar again, to which I agreed. My MD, on my return, passed the comment, "Was I thinking of becoming a regular presenter at these worldwide events?" but I assured him that this was just 'one-off'.

Then in the summer of 1989, I was diagnosed as needing 'coronary bypass surgery', after visiting my doctor, complaining of 'tightness in my chest' whilst swimming. Well, as my salary package included BUPA insurance cover, it was scheduled and completed in just a few weeks; the result was I felt fine. I was off work and receiving physiotherapy for a total of eight weeks and then back in harness with a vengeance. Comments in the background at the office suggested that everyone expected me to take early retirement and let my younger assistant take over.

In the ensuing few years, Thorn EMI, like every other enterprise, was examining its future role in defence work, versus its other activities and decided to sell off the Rugeley operation, resulting in some management changes. This included the resignation of the MD, and a large segment of the staff were given notice of redundancy. This prompted actions by the remaining senior managers, for a reshuffle of reporting roles. As I was considered to be one of the outgoing MD's men, I was marked for redundancy (because of age and health issues, they said); a decision which they rapidly implemented.

So come 1991, I was again on the job market, but this time again contacts were to play a big part in finding me a job. My activities in the Intergraph Users Group meant that I had regular encounters with the CAD manager for Metro-Cammell Carriage & Rail Company. When he heard of my situation, he said that his assistant manager was planning to retire in a few weeks; if I was interested, he would discuss with his boss the possibility of my filling the post.

I was by this time 67 and no longer driven by career ambition and a job was a job, with which to pay the bills, and I knew that their CAD system was a big one with a busy role in user support. In the end I was hired and had no sooner moved into the role than a GEC/Alsthom partnership took over the Metro-Cammell company, bringing in its own managers to take over all the key admin rolls. In the early days the new administration didn't appear to have much effect on normal operations, including the CAD. Then the company won the contract to build all the rolling stock for the new channel tunnel train. The new admin really went to town on this one and a new state-of-the-art CAD design studio was planned and implemented at huge expense. New CAD designers had to be trained and new suites of software supported, so that the CAD management team were hard put to support everything, including the new design centre.

At the same time as all this was going on, GEC was negotiating with Alsthom train manufacturing operation in France, a working partnership to build trains in UK. On the surface this appeared to be a 50–50 partnership, but as time progressed the GEC directors appeared to be sleeping partners. The French directors of Alsthom slowly moved into all the key administration positions and, ever so slowly at first, completely took control of the train design and building operation. Whilst all this was going on, we were busy designing the channel tunnel trains. With the Birmingham plant building the rolling stock, the German division designing and building the Bogie assemblies, and the Spanish division building the rolling stock body shells.

On the CAD operation, up to this point, the three divisions had been using MicroStation 2D/3D CAD software, and the exchange of CAD data was no problem. At about the halfway design stage and with the French directors now in full control, they gave the order that the three divisions of the design team must implement the CAD package they were using in France. This was a French-owned software package that had been developed for the aircraft industry and known as CATIA. It was a massive software package and would cost millions to implement. At a meeting of everyone involved, it was decided that we could not completely switch CAD packages at such an advanced design stage.

The plan was to run the two software packages in parallel and use conversion files to pass the design data from the MicroStation data into the CATIA software and slowly build up a full CATIA model of the train design. This meant that the design workload doubled and bottlenecks kept upsetting the planned schedule. Added to this the conversion software did not always pass on the MicroStation data correctly and left gaps in the CATIA model. On site IBM were hired as consultants to manage the implementation of the CATIA software and had to deal with all of the ongoing problems, the on-site CAD team being fully involved in completing the design with the existing software implementation.

Well, the train was designed and built and by that time I was ready to retire from a working life. True to expectations, the French directors took full control of the Birmingham train building facility and moved it 'lock stock and barrel' to their engineering site at La Rochelle. The huge Birmingham site was sold off to developers! The final five years that I was with GEC/Alsthom was on a contract basis, which meant that I was earning much more money than as a company employee. This allowed me to put a lot of money into my retirement pension to boost it to something I could live on. I had enjoyed the pressure of new train projects and would be lost for something to take its place once I had retired and I knew it.

Chapter Ten

Whilst my working life was pursuing its course, my family life was seeing many changes. Pauline no longer worked for a company in the village and instead now worked as a receptionist, at a Lichfield Council run IT training centre. My daughter Pamela had in 1987 decided that she wanted to go back to college in the USA, and in 1993 she married someone she met in college and now had three daughters and a son of her own, now all living in North Carolina. My son Paul had no such plans to relocate to the USA, and in 1995 he married a girl from Lichfield, and they now had quite a large family of their own, a daughter and three sons. So here I was in the year 2000, retired and the proud relative of eight grandchildren (not knowing at the time that an additional grandson would be born in 2009).

That summer I concentrated on maintenance jobs in the house and garden; at the end of each day I would go to Lichfield to drive Pauline home, after she had finished work. It wasn't always straight home, sometimes we would go for a drive, some shopping or to eat out. I shared household chores with Pauline, took turns to cook a meal and was quite willing to extend my efforts to whatever else was needed. Because I had a small white beard and that first summer I was usually wearing a blue double breasted blazer, Pauline's office companions used to shout to her that 'Captain Birdseye' had arrived, as soon as I pulled on to the car park. I guess there would have been some resemblance if I had been wearing a peaked cap, which I never did.

With opening of the new art college, its literature boasting a wide range of student programs, I was able to pursue my plan to develop some retirement hobbies and had to organise my day around various class schedules. To these classes, I added another activity, I joined a local ramblers club and twice a week took part on day-long walks into the Derbyshire or the Staffordshire countryside. This did mean that I was not always back in time to drive Pauline home from the office, but she was able to use the train and did not mind the occasional break from routine. Life now focussed on home and wife; we fitted in plenty of vacation time, either to the USA to visit our daughter and family, or at our favourite Saundersfoot holiday destination. On the odd occasion a holiday in Scotland, for some reason we were not interested in any European holidays.

Now as grandparents we were always in demand, to babysit our son's children, on a fairly regular basis. Which was fun and enjoyable, when they were small, but once they were nearly teenagers, it was an exhausting experience. Trying to keep pace with teenage exuberance was exhausting to say the least, and we did not look forward to the occasions.

Sometime, in or around the time I retired, Pauline was attending hospital to have blood tests on a fairly regular basis. She passed the whole situation off as a procedure to monitor her kidney function, whilst she was taking certain medications for depression. In 2002 I went with Pauline to hear a verdict on her kidney condition and was dismayed to be told that her kidney function had been deteriorating for some time. It had now reached a level where talk about dialysis had to be entered into and if possible a transplant.

In early 2003, Pauline opted for a form of self-dialysis on the basis that she would have more control over her life. So throughout the spring and summer months, she would go on endless coach trips to here, there, everywhere. Either with me or with close women friends, and learn to manage her self-dialysis, whilst travelling away from home base. That summer we rented a cottage for two weeks down in Wales, where she was able to carry out her self-dialysis and indulge in all the usual activities that couples of pensionable age indulge in.

Pauline seemed on top form throughout the year, until late December, then one day there she was suddenly on the floor, writhing in agony and complaining of terrible pains in her abdominal cavity. She was rushed into hospital and prepped for exploratory surgery, the consultants believed that possibly some tissue where the connection for self-dialysis was made had twisted and was the source of the pain. The result of the exploratory surgery was negative, they found nothing to explain the source of the violent pains.

Her nurses said that on the day of the surgery, she had undergone a dialysis treatment and had been given an ECG test to check her heart function; all treatments and test results were perfectly normal. The two days recovering from the surgery meant that she found it impossible to get any prolonged sleep, and during my visits she was always drifting in and out of consciousness, from the effects of medication. On the second day the nurses had settled her into a big comfortable armchair by her bedside; propped into a comfortable position, with a number of cushions so that she could sleep. When I arrived, she was snoring away and knowing how badly she had needed to sleep, I did not have the heart to awaken her. Instead, I spent hours walking backwards and forwards between the restaurant and the ward, only to find her still asleep.

Finally, at about 6:30 in the evening of December 18th, her doctor and a surgical consultant briefed me as to the situation, saying that she was still asleep and in about half an hour the nurses would put her back into bed. Adding that they planned another minor exploratory surgery on her stomach, to be sure that they had not missed something. After the briefing, I said goodnight to the staff and drove home and had only just entered my home, when the phone rang with a message stating, could I quickly return to the hospital as there was a problem with my wife. I called my son and asked him to drive me over to the hospital, fearing what the problem might be. We arrived at the ward and were met by a senior staff nurse, who briefed us on what had happened since my leaving the hospital. Her statement was that when the nurses went to put my wife into bed, they found that she was unconscious. They immediately summoned the crash-resuscitation team, but it was all to no avail, and Pauline was pronounced dead.

Pauline had been cleaned up and put back in bed; when I saw her, she looked very peaceful, almost smiling. Paul and I said our goodbyes and left. We were both completely drained of emotion, it was so unexpected and unexplained. Travelling back home was a silent ordeal, each of us wrapped up with our thoughts and emotions. Paul stayed till the early hours of the morning; he had been very close to his mother and he took her passing extremely hard, crying intermittently. Finally, Paul drove back to his home, but I could not even think of sleep; the house now seemed almost hostile it was no longer a home and a refuge. I do not know how I got through those early morning hours. Come daybreak I knew that a lot of arrangements had to be made, and the first task was to get our daughter Pamela over from the USA. Luckily for me, she was over in less than two days; without her support I am sure that I would have come apart. Having Pamela staying in the house was all that kept me sane and able to function.

Pauline had been in middle of preparations for Christmas, baking cakes, sorting Christmas cards into piles for posting, it was all around me. Reminding me of the truth that she would not be here for this Christmas or any other. The funeral came and went, leaving me in a daze; I cannot even remember what Pamela and I did that Christmas. Pauline died December 18th, 2003, and from then onwards I could hardly bear to be in the house that had been our home. I would come in to sleep and then leave as soon as it was daylight; I don't really remember how I passed the intervening hours.

Finally, it was time for Pamela to fly back to her family, and somehow seeing her leave made me make up my mind to pull myself together and get on with my own life. It took many weeks, but finally I got back on an even keel and began once again to socialise with my friends and neighbours. Married friends and neighbours rallied around straight after the funeral, inviting me for meals or to join them on a social night out. It was noticeable that as the weeks passed the invites that were a regular event before you were widowed, now lapsed and became infrequent, because you were always the odd one out in the group. After a few weeks, the invites disappeared altogether, and I was left to explore the lonely life of a bachelor pensioner. You really understand how much your wife meant to you, after she is no longer around; I certainly did, and she left a big hole in my life that will never heal.

The year 2004 was well progressed by the time I had come to terms with the fact that I was now facing life on my own, for what would turn out to be another seven years. The years where you would telephone some friend to have someone to talk to. Only to have them reply, "Can I call you back, I have something on at the moment?" They seldom called back. Then I would go into Lichfield, drinking endless cups, in various coffee shops, in the hope that I would meet someone I knew and could talk to.

Gradually, I overcame these hurdles in life, and it started with joining up with a little group of pensioner artists, who used to meet up every Wednesday afternoon to enjoy the others' company, painting whatever they could turn their hand to. I then the joined the local U3A group, that used to meet up one day a month for lunch. Then Friday Friends in Shenstone, the village pensioner group. These met up every Friday, in the Village Hall, to spend the day together, for morning coffee then a cooked lunch. After which everyone indulged in a wide range of organised activities that filled the day.

For holidays, I joined up with two or three friends to go on regular walking holidays in the Black Forest area of Germany and to the various wine festivals, in the Rhine valley. So very slowly my activity and involvement level were upped to a maximum during the daylight hours. However, the time always came around to the evenings, where you went home alone to an empty house to realise what real loneliness is, with only a television to break the eternal silence. The years went by and I flew over to the USA regularly, to spend a couple of weeks with my daughter Pamela, just a short interlude in a lonely life.

The day dawned when I had to take stock of my future, instead of letting it wander aimlessly. Obviously, I needed to downsize from a three-bedroomed house to something of a more manageable size, but to what? A one-bedroomed apartment in a quiet area or some form of sheltered accommodation? Then there was the new vogue of retirement villages that were appearing all over the country. At the bottom of the list was to just a move into a conventional 'care home', where there was staff to look after the facilities and you. I investigated them all. I could not see anything that I could identify with, until I applied to the St John's Hospital in Lichfield, a charity, who owned a group of small one-bedroomed accommodations. These they rented to deserving retired long-time residents of Lichfield, who were able to look after themselves without help.

At about the same time as my application to Saint John's was under consideration, the local branch of the Staffordshire Regimental Association was organising a visit by some members to visit the Royal Hospital in Chelsea. This to attend their Founders' Day Parade and talk to some of the Chelsea pensioners. Although we did not have a current ex-regimental member living in the Chelsea Hospital, we had some in earlier years, and the advice was that I should go and take a look at it, as one of my alternative solutions. In the end I decided to travel down to London, with two other members of the regimental association, to watch the 'Founders' Day Parade' and afterwards have a few drinks with the pensioners themselves.

That visit sowed the seed of interest, and within a few days, I had submitted the application forms to be considered for entry to the Royal Hospital as a Chelsea pensioner.

The day soon dawned when I was invited down to London for a four-day trial, living the life of a Chelsea pensioner. It was four days for me to decide whether this was what I wanted and at the same time an opportunity for the hospital executives to decide whether I met all their criteria and should, or should not, be offered a place. I still had the house and selling that, if I was offered a place at the Royal Hospital, some might think, would be like burning your bridges behind you. My reasoning was that to keep all your options open would not be making a decision with any real conviction behind it.

I had already had one offer for the house, and although it required me to move out quickly, once the sale had been agreed, I thought I could cope with it. I entered on the four-day trial with a completely open mind and although the accommodation was very compact, with shared toilet facilities, I could live with that in the short term, knowing that new en suite accommodation was being built, which would mean only tolerating the initial conditions for about two years. I came away from that four-day visit with some very positive conclusions, about how it fitted in with my ideas for a future. A letter duly arrived from the Royal Hospital Chelsea Hospital, offering me an entry date of the 24th of October, 2011; accepting that date would depend on whether or not I could sell my house and sort myself out by then.

I decided to accept the offer that had been made for the house but cringed at the thought of having to clear out completely in just a few days. The offer was from a woman, very recently divorced with a 10 year old son. I arranged with a nearby neighbour, a B&B rental, to cover the two weeks before I would be moving to the Royal Hospital Chelsea. After first hiring a storage unit that could hold the contents of a three-bedroomed house. My son Paul helped me move a lot of the large furniture pieces, by hiring a decent-sized van for a couple of days. The remainder was taken in small loads to the storage unit, using my own VW car, with the rear seats folded down. Another day clearing up the house and it was all done, I was ready to hand over the house and move in my B&B accommodation.

Leaving a house that has been your home for over 30 years is a big transition and had quite an effect on me at first; a mixture of nostalgia, old memories of life in that house, the lost feeling of security that had been strong before leaving the house. Knowing that I was leaving friends in the village who had rallied around and invited me to evening meals so frequently that I seldom had to resort to the fast food outlets or pubs in Lichfield for a meal. That final two weeks passed very quickly, and all of a sudden, it seemed I was being driven by Paul in my old car (which I had transferred with DVLA to him) to London and the beginning of a new life as a Chelsea pensioner.

It was almost like joining the army again, particularly the uniform issue. However, whilst new serving soldiers are mainly upright and slender, pensioners come in all shapes and statures, particularly around the middle. In years gone by the hospital was run along strictly military lines, with respect to military discipline and rules of dress and behaviour. The organisation was much like that of the military; pensioners were divided into four companies, with a captain of invalids responsible for each company. These in their turn were broken down into 'wards' of 36 berths under the old accommodation system and 20 after the remodelling project is complete. A ward and berth number gave the final location of any pensioner; discipline and military ethos are the responsibility of an RSM and adjutant.

The overall operation of the Royal Hospital Chelsea is administered by board of commissioners and a governor who represents the queen. The formal military organisation that had existed in bygone days is now more relaxed and replaced with company representatives, ward representatives and their assistants. The dress code is blue uniforms around the hospital and up to a two-mile radius beyond the hospital. Outside of which it was strictly scarlet coats everywhere else and for all formal invites to public functions. That dress code is essentially still in force, to maintain a public image as well as standards of dress. In recent years, there has been the added the alternative of wearing a good standard of neat civilian clothing, both on-site and off-site. Blue uniform must be worn at all meals in the grand hall, which can mean that you are jumping in and out of 'civvies' to go to the meals, depending upon what any individual's daily activities are.

In all other respects, pensioners were free to come and go as they pleased; of course, you had to inform the admin office if you planned to be off-site for more than 48 hours. On the healthcare question we have an on-site doctor, who under NHS rules is our GP, and he is supported by one or two locums. All except minor ailments are referred to the local hospitals for treatment and any consultation. At his point I should diverge from my story, to set my own health scene on entry to the RHC, as a pensioner.

My date of entry was November, 2011, and prior to that date, in early October, I attended a club reunion weekend in Cumbria, during which time I contracted a bout of flu to return home with. After a few days of fighting off my flu symptoms, I finally succumbed and made an appointment to see my own doctor. Although I was over most of the flu symptoms, my lungs were still full of fluid, which prompted my doctor to prescribe a diuretic, and after a couple of days I was clear. It was during my appointment with my doctor, he noted the fact that my prescription of medication for an existing heart condition had not been reviewed for many years. He therefore made an appointment for me with a cardiac consultant at the local hospital. At that appointment, after checking my pulse and blood pressure and maximum of four minutes discussion with me, the consultant prescribed a whole list of medications, which included a vascular dilator, a beta blocker, a diuretic and a statin.

Within two days of taking the medication on the new prescription, I began to have breathing problems, particularly when lying down. A condition that continually disturbed my sleep, forcing me to sit up, or stand up until my breathing normalised. Eventually, the breathing difficulty on the occasion of an attack was so bad, I passed out momentarily and had to dial 999. The answering paramedics decided I was suffering an angina attack and transported me to the local A&E. There after testing the indicator enzyme for heart muscle damage, they discharged me in the early hours of the morning, expressing the opinion that it was a minor attack and that there was no heart muscle damage. They suggested I contact my own doctor as there was some suggestion that I might be suffering some adverse reaction to one of my new medications.

At the time of my new medicines prescription, I had been referred for regular monitoring by a cardiac support clinic, based at the local hospital. So, I did not go to my doctor, but reported the incident to the clinic. At the support clinic, I passed on the message that there had been a mention of an adverse reaction to one or more of my medications. After reviewing the medications, they eliminated the statin and reduced the diuretic to half the original dose. So, with a month's supply of the modified list of medications, I travelled down to London and became a Chelsea pensioner. Those early weeks were put to good use getting a berth organised, to suit one's individuality, a 9 x 9 berth space does not leave much scope. One could only look forward to moving into updated accommodation with en suite facilities. A weekly bulletin, posted on all ward noticeboards, lists invites for a number of pensioners to attend a variety of public and social events. These are allocated on a first 'get your name on the list' basis, and the top names on the list get to go.

Over the ensuing weeks, months and years everyone builds up his own compendium of hobbies, off-site visits, holidays, day-to-day routines, depending on individual likes and dislikes. Of course, all of this can be and is modified by health factors, plus declining mobility. Most of the old pensioners, who had been resident for over 10 years, regale newcomers with the stories of how the old hospital used to be run for the benefit of the pensioners living there. The first change, that had greatly impinged on their lives, was the changing in organisation of the pensioners' club. Originally conceived by the past RSM Ives as a place where the pensioner could entertain and be entertained, pensioners ran the club themselves. The club was staffed by pensioners and operated at a level to cover all costs, with profit not the primary factor. The more recent approach, approved by the board of commissioners, was to reorganise the club and convert the operation into a commercial one, with paid staff and management. If they had but read the old books, about the days of the club under RSM Ives, they would realise that the new club was doomed to failure. Under the new organisation, no pensioner relates to it as his club and that he was part of it. The result is the club is now simply seen as an on-site commercial enterprise competing with the local area pubs.

A further change the old pensioners mention is the little on-site shop where they could get the little extras. Such as milk, soft drinks, cigarettes, bottled beer, all of the little things they now have to go off-site for; it has been closed now for many years. Yet another change the old pensioners deplore is the fact that the grand hall is always portrayed to the public as the place where all the pensioners have their meals. In fact, the evening meal has to be taken in an under-sized space in the pensioners' club, one third the area of the Grand Hall. The reason for this change of practice was to allow the board of commissioners to approve the renting out of the grand hall in the evenings for private VIP functions. So, the Royal Hospital I entered was not the one of the past or that Charles II envisaged.

Over my past five years here, there had been orchestrated moves to transform the Royal Hospital Chelsea into a theme park for tourists, with the pensioners in their tricorne hats and scarlet coats filling in as performing monkeys. During my early weeks I had to take in and digest all this information about changes past and changes to come. As a new man on the block, I had no yardstick against which to measure the validity of it all. However, with the passing of time, the old saying 'that there is no smoke without fire' still seems a reliable guide.

My early weeks at the hospital were made the more memorable by my original supply of medications running out, which should pose no problem. After all, my medical records will have been transferred to the Royal Hospital and the doctor here could sign a refill prescription. What I did not know was that the changes made to my original prescription by the cardiac support clinic was not updated on to my medical records. It was the original consultant's prescription (overdose and reaction source) that had been transferred to the Royal Hospital Chelsea. Within days of starting on the refill prescription, I started to have breathing difficulties, ending with my being transferred into the infirmary, usually ending up in hospital. The result of each hospital admission was always the same, admitted as suffering an angina attack and tests showing no damage to the heart muscle.

To explain it, the cardiac consultants said I was suffering from attacks of 'alternative angina', which did not behave like a standard angina. During this 'alternative angina' experience I was in and out of so many London hospitals that the rest of pensioners who knew me said, "Jim Fellows is writing the Michelin Guide to London hospitals." Whether or not my prescription was eventually updated and I moved on to the amended one I shall never know, but the angina episodes came to an end.

After that life became more normal, and I indulged myself in my hobbies of wood-carving and painting. Life here has satisfied my needs and those of many others who have come and will come from a background of life in the British army, to await the coming of their last posting. I have indulged in the many invites to off-site functions in the past, as well as visiting friends and relatives, but it seems the time has arrived when I have to reduce my activities. My legs do not carry me as far as they used to, and a feeling of fatigue overtakes me before the day is through. I spend a lot of time writing *The Story of Jim*, the editing of which prompts me to recall in detail the events of my life. I also spend hours reading all sorts, ranging from novels to scientific papers on religion, philosophy, physics, neuroscience, biology and computing. Even to reading some of the old history of the Royal Hospital Chelsea as well as the story detailing the ruin of the Royal Hospital at Greenwich (the home for ex-navy personnel). The main theme seems to be a record of the fraudulent use of land and money, intended to have been for the welfare and accommodation of the pensioners of old.

Most pensioners are satisfied with their life here and feel it was the best option offered to them and eliminated the one problem facing us all when we get old 'loneliness'. Some pensioners have opted to leave and become an out-pensioner. Their reasons for leaving were varied, and in many cases were relative to that individual and did not really reflect on the life they could have enjoyed as an in-pensioner. Many of the older pensioners feel 'short-changed' with the slow disappearance of the level of military ethos. I think most old people who function well on their own do so because they live to a daily routine and for ex-military people those routines are well-established. The newer entries to Royal Hospital Chelsea seem to have accepted the new conditions and the organisation as they find them and readily believe they will enjoy life here. For myself, I expect the changes in health will dictate the path for the remainder of my life as a pensioner. In the meantime, I have friends from around Chelsea, who I see regularly for lunch and coffee and manage to fill the rest of my day with my hobbies, until the time comes for me to proceed on my final posting.